G000320364

PARTY POLITICS IN JAPAN

PARTY POLITICS IN JAPAN

HANS BAERWALD

Professor of Political Science,
University of California, Los Angeles

Boston
ALLEN & UNWIN
London Sydney

Allen & Unwin, Inc.,
8 Winchester Place, Winchester, Mass 01890, USA

Allen & Unwin (Publishers) Ltd,
40 Museum Street, London WC1A 1LU, UK

Allen & Unwin (Publishers) Ltd,
Park Lane, Hemel Hempstead, Herts HP2 4TE, UK

Allen & Unwin (Australia) Ltd,
8 Napier Street, North Sydney, NSW 2060, Australia

First published in 1986
Reprinted in 1987

Library of Congress Cataloging in Publication Data

Baerwald, Hans H.
Party politics in Japan
Bibliography: P.
Includes index.
1. Political parties – Japan.
2. Japan. Kokkai – elections.
I. Title.
JQ1698.A1B34 1986 324.252'009 86-8040
ISBN 0-04-320183-0 (Alk. paper)
ISBN 0-04-320184-9 (Pbk.: alk. paper)

British Library Cataloguing in Publication Data

Baerwald, Hans
Party politics in Japan.
1. Japan – Politics and government – 1945–
I. Title
320.952 JQ1681
ISBN 0-04-320183-0
ISBN 0-04-320184-9 Pbk

Set in 10 on 11 point Goudy by Columns, Reading, Berkshire
and printed in Great Britain by Billings and Sons, London and Worcester

CONTENTS

ACKNOWLEDGEMENTS

Many individuals in Japan have helped me in my studies of Japanese politics over the past three decades. Countless members of the Diet (National Assembly) and their administrative assistants (*hishokan*) allowed me to interview them. Officials in the secretariats (*jimukyoku*) of the House of Representatives and House of Councillors provided me with detailed data. Government officials (*yakunin*) in various ministries and agencies of the Japanese government assisted me in gaining an understanding of their perspective, particularly during the course of my assignment to prepare the background report for the OECD's *Social Sciences Policy: Japan* (1977). Journalists, whose assignment included covering the political parties, the Prime Minister's Official Residence (*Sōri Kantei*) and the National Assembly (Diet) were enormously helpful in disentangling the surface from the sub-surface of Japanese politics. Academic colleagues in Japanese universities did their best to help me avoid making too many errors. Without their unstinting assistance and encouragement, I could not have written this book. Only lack of space has precluded my listing all of them, but my debt to them is immense.

None of them should be held responsible for my interpretation of party politics in Japan. It is more than just possible that they will disagree with parts of my perspective. That outcome is inevitable. First, the Japanese themselves disagree about their country's politics, as is true of any system that permits dissent. Secondly, the perceptions of a foreigner (*gaijin*) tend to be biased despite all efforts to overcome ethnocentric cultural values.

I am compelled, however, to mention by name a small number of specific individuals because of their extraordinary contributions to my understanding of Japanese politics. Former Prime Minister Ōhira Masayoshi, whose sudden death in June 1980 was a personal as well as national tragedy, was always immensely kind and patient as *Sensei* (teacher). My indebtedness to him, his family and his close political associates is profound. Mr Sasagawa Takeo of the *Sankei Shinbun* (newspaper) began the process, in the summer of 1963, of introducing me into the special world of political journalism. Mr Watanabe Tsuneo of the *Yomiuri Shinbun* did more than anyone else in sharpening my appreciation of the importance of factions, and much else about the intricacies of party politics.

Among my academic colleagues, there are several who have done far more than friendship and the sharing of common interests would have required. Over the years, they often did so under circumstances that must have tried their goodwill and patience to the utmost. They include Professors Hashimoto Akira (Chairman of the Department of Political Science at Meiji University), Kobayashi Katsumi (formerly of the National Defense College), Tomita Nobuo (Dean of Academic Affairs at Meiji University), Uchida Mitsuru (of the Faculty of Political Science at Waseda University), and Watanabe Yasuo (President of International Christian University). Mr Sam Jameson, Tokyo Bureau Chief of the *Los Angeles Times* and the best foreign correspondent in Japan, has been a true friend, a generous host, and a marvelously perceptive critic of my writing, both in style and in substance.

I would also like to express my appreciation to Professor Arthur Stockwin, Director of Oxford University's Nissan Institute of Japanese Studies. He and the Institute's faculty, staff and graduate fellows provided an invigorating and supportive environment while I was a Senior Associate Member in the autumn of 1985.

My late colleague James S. Coleman, who was the founding director of UCLA's Office of International Studies and Overseas Programs, and Vice Chancellor Elwin Svenson were exceptionally helpful. They made it possible for me to have the benefit of both a special leave and a succeeding sabbatical leave from my regular duties at UCLA in order that I might have time to write. Mr Yasuo Sakata and Mrs Mariko Kitamura Bird, my associates in UCLA's Japan Exchange Program, have done yeoman service during my extended absence, and in translating my drafts into acceptable typescripts. Steve Clemons, my most recent teaching assistant, made numerous helpful suggestions.

My sister, Ann Lenway, has been a source of encouragement and support throughout. My wife Jennifer, new to the world of Japanese politics, asked challenging and penetrating questions. She also encouraged me to keep writing, even when it was difficult to do so. It is to them that this book is dedicated.

Oxford
December, 1985

FOREWORD

This brief book is an introduction to Japanese national party politics: political parties and factionalism (Chapter 1), national elections (Chapter 2), the Diet or National Assembly (Chapter 3), the changing relationship between the governing and opposition parties (Chapter 4), and a recapitulation with speculations for the future (Chapter 5). My principal purpose has been to provide a broad survey that would assist anyone who wishes to enter into the bamboo thicket of domestic politics in Japan.

At the national level of Japanese politics, it is the Diet that remains the focal point. What is the Diet? It is, as it has been since its inception in 1890, Japan's National Assembly. In fact, "National Assembly" would be a more accurate, certainly a more literal translation of either *Teikoku Gikai* (Imperial Assembly) which was the name of this institution under the Meiji Constitution of 1890, or *Kokkai* (National Assembly), the current name of this body under the 1947 Constitution. In *Gikai*, the first Chinese–Japanese character can be translated as "discussion," "proposal," or "to discuss," "to propose," "to consult with," and the second character (*kai*) can be translated as "assemblage," "meeting" or "to assemble," "to meet"; and in *Kokkai*, the first character (*koku*) means "country" or "nation." Permit me to hasten to add that this book is not about the proper translation of political terminology. To do so thoroughly would be to raise a host of problems, and would require a separate essay, at the least.

Nomenclature is often a problem in discussing politics in a language that is different from the one used in its native habitat. For example, in an earlier book that I had written about Japanese politics, I used "Parliament" in the title. One critic noted in his review that my book was about an institution that did not exist – at least by that name – in Japan. Yet, in earlier consultations with my editor, he had raised strong objections to my using "Diet" in the title of the book for fear that it might be shelved alongside weighty tomes on the finer points of eating habits.

Quigley, in his *Japanese Government and Politics* (1932), the standard reference on this subject prior to the Second World War, solved the problem as follows: "Japanese call their parliament [*sic*] the *gikai*. From its inauguration, they have translated *gikai* as 'Diet,' revealing thereby the German pattern used by the framers of the constitution. The prototype of the *gikai* was the Prussian Diet, which was a deliberative body of two houses" (p. 160). Furthermore, in the official translation of the 1890 Constitution, the heading for Chapter III was "The Imperial Diet" (Quigley, p. 338), and the "Law of the Houses of the Diet" was the official translation of the rules and regulations governing that institution (Quigley, pp. 364–77).

When the framers of the Meiji Constitution were searching for a model of a national assembly that they might adapt to their needs, the Prussian Diet seemed particularly appropriate. Marriott and Robertson in *The Evolution of Prussia* (1937) described that institution in the following paragraphs:

> The legislature (*Landtag*) consists of two Houses. The House of Lords (*Herrenhaus*) contains some 365 members. Of these, 115 are hereditary . . . ; nearly 200 are official and ecclesiastical members; the rest are nominated for life by the Crown . . . The Lower House of Representatives (*Abgeordnetenhaus*) contains 433 members elected, by a process of double election, on the ultimate basis of universal manhood suffrage. But the suffrage, though universal, is "neither equal nor direct" . . . [because] property secures representation as well as mere numbers.
>
> The legislative powers of the *Landtag* (Diet), though ample on paper, are in practice confined to the consideration and amendment of projects submitted by the Crown. Still less conclusive is its control over the executive. It can interrogate ministers, but they need not answer. It can appeal to the King, but he may heed it or not as he wills. (pp. 320–1)

Under the Meiji Constitution, the Imperial Diet was severely circumscribed in the degree to which it represented the people (universal male suffrage did not come into force until 1925), and in the role that it could play in the legislative process. The institution (as in Prussia) was subordinate to the royal power. "The Emperor exercises the legislative power with the consent of the Imperial Diet" (The Meiji Constitution, Chapter I, Article V). Translating *Gikai* as "Diet" underlined this constitutional imperative. If, on the other hand, *Gikai* had been translated as "Parliament," it might have been interpreted as having a significant share of power as in the British model. That was precisely what the fathers of the Meiji Constitution wished to avoid.

Fifty-five years later, when officials in General MacArthur's Headquarters in Tokyo began thinking about a new constitution for Japan, they had very different objectives in mind. Their goal was to elevate the position of the national legislature. It was to be achieved on the basis of a set of premises that were elaborated in the following terms:

> A truly representative legislative body, based upon universal adult suffrage, responsible to the electorate, free of domination by the executive, and having full legislative powers, including control over the raising and spending of all public moneys, is a primary requisite of any blueprint for democracy under a representative form of government. The Japanese Imperial Diet . . . failed in every respect to meet these specifications. (Government Section, 1949, Vol. 1, p. 145)

Despite these lofty aspirations, the English name of the legislative institution remained "Diet." In fact, the above sentences from the official report of MacArthur's Headquarters' Government Section in which the new constitution had been drafted were quoted from the chapter entitled "The National Diet." Furthermore, in the same volume's extensive and candid commentary on the origins of the new constitution, the national legislature was consistently referred to as "Diet." What makes it even more incomprehensible is that the name of the institution had been changed from *Teikoku Gikai* (Imperial Diet) to *Kokkai* (National Assembly).

There is no satisfactory explanation for the continued use of "Diet," an anachronistic and out-dated term, in English. As a former member of Government Section, I cannot remember any of us questioning the continuing use of "Diet." It had, by then, been in common usage, at least in Japan, for over half a century. That alone should not have been sufficient, however, to justify its being used as the translation for *Kokkai*.

It seems to me that the time has come to reconsider this issue. No one, except for a few specialists, immediately understands what "Diet" means. There is, therefore, no good reason not to translate *Kokkai* into English correctly: "National Assembly." I have begun to use this term in this book, but not consistently because "Diet" is still commonly used in the English-language literature about Japanese politics. In its implications, however, "Diet" is misleading and archaic. Only the Japanese themselves, of course, have the power to alter the official translation of *Kokkai*. It is my hope that they might wish to consider this modest proposal to translate the name of their legislature as "National Assembly."

Japanese names have been written in the traditional Japanese style throughout the text with the surname first.

CHAPTER 1

The Political Party System, 1955–1985

During the first decade after the end of the Second World War in August 1945, Japan's political party system was extraordinarily fluid. Two major "conservative" parties organized themselves almost as soon as the war ended. By the end of 1945, two "progressive" groups had organized themselves into the Socialist Party and the Communist Party. In addition, however, there was a bewildering array of minor political groupings that made their appearance prior to one or another election, only to have disbanded by the next.

By the time the Allied (largely American) Occupation of Japan officially ended in the spring of 1952, the political landscape still included two "conservative" parties (with a number of sub-groups) and, on the "progressive" side of the political spectrum, two Socialist parties as well as a minor, largely underground, Communist Party. References to these initial years of the postwar period will be made in this chapter only to the extent that they have a bearing on the party system as it currently exists. Instead, the focus will be on what the Japanese refer to as "the political system of 1955 (*gojūgo-nen taisei*)" and how it has changed over the last three decades.

In the autumn of 1955, observers of Japanese politics anticipated the emergence of a two-party system. Most of the "progressive (*kakushin-kei*)" members of the Diet joined with each other in a reunified Japan Socialist Party (JSP) at its Convention on 13 October. One month later their "conservative (*hoshu-kei*)" counterparts coalesced in the Liberal Democratic Party (LDP) as the climax of its Convention on 14 November. A new era of party politics presumably had begun and a modern party system – one that was suited to Japan's desire to project an image of having completed the process of political development – ostensibly had been established. These surface (*omote*) manifestations, however, tended to obscure rather than illuminate the sub-surface (*ura*) – or "sub-text" – of what was transpiring.

On one level of analysis, the observable bifurcation of nearly all national Diet members into two groups was valid; only a handful of them refused to participate. Furthermore, both sides had powerful incentives. The "progressives" believed that they could challenge their opponents only by uniting into one political coalition, the JSP; and the "conservatives" believed that this challenge could be overcome only if they marched under one banner, that of the LDP. Their respective strengths, however, were fundamentally different with the JSP facing the task of trying to increase its control over more than one-third, and the LDP wishing to govern with the support of two-thirds, of the Diet's membership. In effect, as Scalapino and Masumi (1962) noted in their ground-breaking assessment, what had emerged was not a two-party, but a one-and-a-half-party system.

Moreover, both political parties were internally disunited. The JSP included several warring factions that were endlessly disputatious over basic ideological issues. Its "right" and "left" wings were still nursing the self-inflicted wounds that they had suffered by having been separate entities during the first half of the 1950s. Simultaneously, the LDP initially contained at least eight separate groups whose members often were more loyal to their own leaders than to the political party to which they had presumably pledged their fealty. It was a coalition that was united by the desire to remain in power, by some sense of trepidation of what the reunified JSP might be able to accomplish, and by dedication to forego disputes over basic ideological issues. Indeed, one of the most noteworthy features of Japan's political landscape over the past thirty years has been the LDP's ability to hang together, despite periodic centrifugal tendencies. By contrast, the JSP split again in the fall of 1959, and did so permanently when the Democratic Socialist Party (DSP) formally came into existence in January of the following year, thereby exacerbating the difficulties of the "progressives" to challenge the "conservatives" in governing Japan.

In 1955, a deep and wide attitude and policy chasm separated the two unequal groupings. On issues affecting Japan's foreign relations, the LDP and its conservative antecedents had cast their lot with the United States and the western camp, whereas the JSP wished Japan to be neutral in the first Cold War between the eastern and western bloc of nations. In domestic affairs, the LDP wished to blunt many of the immediate postwar Occupation-sponsored reforms that were symbolized by the 1947 "MacArthur" Constitution, or, to use the then popular terminology, to pursue a "reverse-course." By contrast, the JSP pledged itself to preserve and uphold the new Constitution and to obstruct the dismantling of MacArthur's revolution.

If symbols are meaningful, then the JSP and its allies have been successful on one major issue thus far: the Constitution still remains pristine. Formally speaking, it has not been amended even if Article IX (the "no-war" clause) has been legally interpreted to the point that its original intent has become a dead letter (Stockwin, 1982, pp. 196–218).

Table 1.1 Liberal Democratic Party Vote: Popular Vote in House of Representatives Elections 1958–83 (*percentages*)

	1958	1960	1963	1967	1969	1972	1976	1979	1980	1983
LDP	57.8	57.6	54.7	48.8	47.6	46.9	41.8	44.6	47.9	45.8
NLC	—	—	—	—	—	—	4.2	3.0	3.0	2.7
Total	—	—	—	—	—	—	46.0	47.6	50.9	48.5

Source: Kokkai Binran [Diet Handbook], for relevant years.
Notes: LDP = Liberal Democratic Party; NLC = New Liberal Club.
This table excludes the percentage of votes cast for "Unaffiliated (*mushozoku*)" conservative candidates who later, upon election, joined the LDP. As these statistics indicate, the LDP by itself has not been able to obtain over half of the popular votes cast since the 1963 election. Nevertheless, it has been able to retain a majority of the seats in the House of Representatives (see Chapter 2).

By any other conceivable yardstick, however, the three decades between the mid-1950s and the mid-1980s have been years of LDP dominance. Indeed, not until the Second Nakasone Cabinet came into power in December 1983 did the LDP find it necessary to invite a coalition partner – the New Liberal Club (NLC) – into the Japanese government's executive organ, the Cabinet. Moreover, NLC members had been Liberal Democrats until the summer of 1976 when they bolted because of their despair regarding the issue of financial corruption exemplified by the Lockheed scandal (Baerwald, 1976).

For a single political party to have remained dominant for thirty years is a formidable achievement. This is especially the case if recognition is given to its having done so within a multiple-party system, as well as its having managed to do so in the midst of staggering socio-economic changes. After all, Japan moved from an economic system in which roughly half its population was initially engaged in agriculture and fishing (in the immediate postwar period), through a period of extraordinarily high commercial and industrial growth (in the 1960s), to its current status as a post-industrial, information-age, high technology society with over 50 percent of its working population engaged in the service sector (Stockwin, 1982; Tsurutani, 1977; Benjamin and Ori, 1981). Japan in the mid-1980s is definitely not the same as it was in the mid-1950s. Yet, the LDP has continued to dominate the political system despite this massive change, and despite periodic prognostications that in the next election it is bound to be toppled from its accustomed perch.

To be sure, it has come perilously close to proving its doomsayers as being correct. During the latter half of the 1970s, the LDP governed with the narrowest of majorities in both the House of Representatives and the House of Councillors. Furthermore, with the results of the 1980 "double election" (Baerwald, 1980b) – that is, the simultaneous polling for the entire membership of the House of Representatives and half of the membership of the House of Councillors – as a notable exception, the LDP has been governing under the constraints imposed by "near parity (*hakuchū*)" since the mid-1970s. Nonetheless, the party remains in power. How has it managed to do so? As is so often the case, posing the question is considerably easier than suggesting – much less, determining – possible answers.

The Opposition Parties

One conceivable response is that the LDP has been fortunate in the character of its Opposition. Thirty years ago, it was faced with a reunited and, many observers predicted, a re-invigorated Socialist Party. Had the Socialists been able to live up to their own expectations and had they been able not only to remain united but to appeal to all of the various segments of the electorate that were not LDP supporters, Japan's electoral map would have developed very differently. The Opposition did not meet either condition. By January of 1960, the Democratic Socialist Party's establishment as an independent political organization had shattered Socialist unity. By the mid-1960s, the neo-Buddhist Kōmeitō had begun its mercurial rise. By the end of the 1960s, the Japan Communist Party (JCP) had re-emerged as a major force in left-wing politics, after two decades of almost total impotence. By the end of the next decade, the *Shaminren* (Social Democratic Federation) had split off from the JSP. Furthermore, the JSP itself was so dis-united that its critics derisively referred to it as the *Ni-hon* (two-volumed) *Shakaitō* (Socialist Party) – a play on words made possible by substituting the character "two (*ni*)" for "sun" (also pronounced ni) which is the first character in "Japan (*Nihon*)."

One consequence of this noteworthy fragmentation is that Japan's "progressive" parties have devoted much of their energy to competing with each other, instead of their presumptive major antagonist, the LDP. (This factor will appear even more significant when it is linked with the strategic requirements imposed by the electoral systems for the two Houses of the Diet in Chapter 2.) Of course, the Opposition has tried on numerous occasions to establish a united front. Thus far, all of these efforts have failed, more often than not because there is basic disagreement over the issue of including or excluding the Communists.

Moreover, there have been disagreements among the others as well. Subsequent to Prime Minister Nakasone's invitation to the NLC to become a coalition partner in the Cabinet in 1983, the leaders of both the DSP and Kōmeitō hinted (some would say pleaded) that they too would be delighted with a ministerial appointment. Both parties, therefore, seem to have lessened their commitment to being members of a coalition that opposes the LDP. Instead, they would appear to be more interested in joining

Table 1.2 Opposition Parties' Popular Vote: House of Representatives Elections 1958–83 (*percentages*)

	1958	1960	1963	1967	1969	1972	1976	1979	1980	1983
JSP	32.9	27.6	29.0	27.9	21.4	21.9	20.7	19.7	19.3	19.5
Kōmeitō	—	—	—	5.4	10.9	8.5	10.9	9.8	9.0	10.1
DSP	—	8.8	7.4	7.4	7.7	7.0	6.3	6.8	6.6	7.3
JCP	2.6	2.9	4.0	4.6	6.8	10.5	10.4	10.4	9.8	9.3
Total	35.5	39.3	40.4	45.3	46.8	47.9	48.3	46.7	44.7	46.2

Source: *Kokkai Binran* [Diet Handbook], for relevant years.

Notes: JSP = Japan Socialist Party; DSP = Democratic Socialist Party; JCP = Japan Communist Party.

This table excludes the New Liberal Club (because its role as an opposition party is ambiguous), the Social Democratic Federation (because it is still minuscule) and the "unaffiliated (*mushozoku*)" (because they are often LDP-affiliated).

an LDP-dominated coalition. Whether that will come to pass is as dependent on the LDP as it is on the DSP's and Kōmeitō's continued commitment to "progressive" policies on such issues as defense and the security relationship between Japan and the United States.

One additional element has affected the calculations of each of the parties that styles itself – to a greater or lesser degree – as being opposed to the continuation of LDP dominance. As is made clear in Table 1.2, each of these opposition parties reached a plateau in the last decade as far as public support is concerned. The halcyon days of their ability to make substantial electoral gains, especially in the percentage of nation-wide aggregate vote totals, reached a peak in the 1976 House of Representatives election, a contest that, for the governing LDP at least, was conducted under the darkest clouds of the Lockheed scandal.

The Socialists

As is evident, the JSP has been the principal loser, declining from nearly one-third of the voting public's support to roughly one-fifth. Of course, it still remains the largest of the opposition parties, but it has suffered badly. One of the reasons for its decline has been the growth of support for the DSP and Kōmeitō (the "centrist" parties) and for the JCP (at the radical end of Japanese politics). A second reason is the stagnation of its principal base of support, the "General Council of Japanese Trade Unions (*Sōhyō*)" which largely consists of public sector trade unions such as the Japan Teachers, the Communication Workers, and the Transportation Workers. *Sōhyō*'s membership has remained at the four and a half million level since the mid-1970s (Tsuneta Yano Memorial Society). Without its support, the JSP would have almost no organizational base. With its support, the JSP has been unable to broaden its appeal to other sectors of Japan's society since it cannot afford to offend the union leaders who remain committed to the ultimate victory of the urban industrial proletariat in its struggle with Japanese "monopoly capitalism," as exemplified by the LDP.

The JSP's dilemma is, in its essentials, not different from that faced by similar parties in other advanced industrialized countries that are closely tied to the apron strings of trade unions which espouse the interests of organized labor. Well over half of the JSP's candidates for the Diet now come from the ranks of trade union officials. By contrast, in its early years the party's leaders tended to be ideological activists, including academicians and intellectuals and some middle-class professionals. The decline of the influence of these groups has had a deleterious influence on the party's public image. As Gerald Curtis (1979) has noted, the JSP "is disparagingly referred to as the 'political affairs section of Sōhyō'."

Nothing better exemplifies the JSP's internal strains and stresses, and its inability to resolve them, than the separation of what became the Democratic Socialist Party (DSP) from the parent body in 1960. Members of the DSP had belonged to the most moderate right-wing faction while in the JSP. Their debates with their more militantly ideological comrades among the Socialists had deep roots and ranged across a broad spectrum of issues.

These disagreements became irreconcilable at the Socialist Party's 1959 Convention. In summary, the militants argued that the party should be primarily interested in upholding the interests of the working class as exemplified by the trade union movement, that it should be prepared to engage in violence in defense of its interests, and that it should oppose the security treaty with the United States. By contrast, the moderates (who ultimately joined the DSP) argued that appeals for electoral support should be made to diverse social strata, that pledges to non-violent change and a commitment to parliamentarism should be upheld, and that Japan should work towards broadening its international relationships within the framework of an acceptable security treaty with the United States (Cole, Totten and Uyehara, 1966, pp. 69–82).

Inevitably, these arguments over the basic character of the Socialist Party, the tactical and theoretical issues concerning parliamentarism, the most burning foreign policy problem of that period, as well as many other disputes, were exacerbated by personality clashes. Nishio Suehiro, the leader of the dissidents, had long been a burr under the saddle as far as many "mainstream" Socialists were concerned. His lack of popularity had occasioned a motion of expulsion even prior to his and his supporters' formal exit from the JSP. Regardless of the rights and wrongs of these disputes, however, what ultimately took place as their consequence was the weakening of the Socialist movement. That result might have been inevitable given Japan's astonishing economic growth in the decade of the 1960s, but the Socialists (whether in the JSP or the DSP) certainly promoted the process of their own decline by their lack of unity.

The Democratic Socialist Party remains to this day the smallest of the organized opposition parties. It has become increasingly dependent on *Dōmei*, the second largest trade union federation –

which is made up principally of private sector unions in such fields as the automobile, textile, private railroad and electrical industries – both for financial and organizational support, as well as for its candidates. (*Dōmei* also has not grown beyond the 2,200,000 members that it had in 1976.) Together with the Kōmeitō, the DSP considers itself as being in the center of the spectrum of Japanese politics and is the most likely potential coalition partner for the LDP, should the latter find it necessary to invite its participation.

The Kōmeitō

In certain respects, the Kōmeitō's emergence and growth reflect the greatest failure of vision on the part of the JSP in particular, but a failure that must be shared by the DSP and JCP as well. The Kōmeitō is the only genuinely new political party in post-World War II Japanese politics. Virtually its entire support is drawn from the membership of the "Value Creation Society (*Sōka Gakkai*)," a neo-Buddhist lay organization. Its basic strength is in the heavily urbanized regions of Japan into which a massive migration took place during the decades of high economic growth, from the early 1950s until the early 1970s (White, 1970).

These newly urbanized voters – many of whom were workers in small commercial and industrial establishments, or in low-skilled occupations such as taxi drivers (admittedly, considerable skill is required to navigate the streets of Tokyo or Osaka), bar hostesses (they, too, require a modicum of conversational skills) and similar employment at the bottom rung of Japan's status-conscious society – were disoriented by their unfamiliar surroundings. The *Sōka Gakkai* came to their assistance by activities that were not too dissimilar from those engaged in by American urban political machines during the high tide of American immigration at the turn of this century. It provided such services as guidance in finding a place to live, in job placement, and in medical assistance. Above all, the *Gakkai* provided its members with a sense of self and the kind of group support that these newcomers to the strains and stresses of urban life so desperately needed.

None of the established trade unions made much of an effort to recruit these people into their ranks. It is one of the many ironies of Japanese left-wing politics that the organized labor movement did not see in this segment, which might legitimately be termed the new urban lower class, political supporters who could be added to its ranks. This failure on the part of the JSP and DSP spawned what was, for Japan at least, an unusual national political organization, the Kōmeitō. It is the only religion-based party and thus stands in sharp contrast to all of the others which have memberships whose religious affiliation is basically irrelevant to their behavior as voters.

After recording phenomenal growth rates in the decade from 1965 to 1975, the Kōmeitō apparently has peaked at about 10 percent of Japan's voting population. Its parent *Sōka Gakkai* claims a membership of ten million households, but the more generally accepted statistic is about seven million. While the Kōmeitō's goals have remained vague – anti-militarist and pro-expanded social welfare programs – it has tended to move towards an ideologically centrist position, especially on such issues as the legitimacy of the Self-Defense Forces and the alliance with the United States.

The Kōmeitō's parent organization has also become far less militant in its proselytizing techniques that had contributed to its earlier image of being, potentially at least, proto-fascist. More than anything else, however, it is probable that its growth slowed with the decline in urban in-migration after the 1973 "oil shock" ended the era of high economic growth. It is also entirely conceivable that the *Gakkai*'s hold on its members will become less awesome as greater affluence spreads throughout Japanese society and, as members drift away, that they will express their innate conservatism by becoming supporters of the LDP. This prospect is all the more likely if a Kōmeitō leader actually joins an LDP-led Cabinet.

The Japan Communist Party

Communism has not been a popular political doctrine in Japan. None the less, the JCP consistently has outpolled the moderate "non-Communist Left" DSP since the 1972 House of Representatives election. From the high-water marks it posted in the 1972 and the 1976 elections (polling slightly over 10 percent of the popular vote), the JCP's fortunes have declined somewhat, although aggregate electoral support remains above 9 percent.

In contrast to nearly everyone else in Japan, Communist activists had opposed the militarist government and its wartime policies in the 1930s and the first half of the 1940s. Many of these leaders had spent those years in exile (mostly, in Yenan with the Chinese Communists) or in jail from which the Allied Occupation authorities released them by the issuance of the "Civil Liberties" directive of 4 October 1946 (Government Section, 1949, pp. 463–5). For most of the Occupation period, the party projected itself as being "lovable" and was rewarded, in 1949, by winning 36 seats in the House of Representatives with very close to 10 percent of the popular vote.

Over twenty years were to elapse before the JCP regained this level of support (Scalapino, 1967; Langer, 1972). The party had suffered two terrible blows in the first half of 1950. First came the Cominform criticism which challenged the party to become more radical in its policies and tactics. (Whether this attack was launched against the party in anticipation of the outbreak of the Korean War on 25 June remains an unanswered question.) Secondly, as the party dutifully responded by having its Diet members engage in virulent diatribes against the Occupation authorities and by taking part in acts of violence in the street, the Supreme Command for the Allied Powers (SCAP) ordered the political purge of the party's leadership (Baerwald, 1959, pp. 18–19). As a consequence, during the 1950s and first half of the 1960s, the party never polled more than 5 percent of the popular vote nor won more than 5 seats in the House of Representatives.

By the mid-1960s, however, the JCP had begun to regain some semblance of respectability. Its senior leaders were graduates of the University of Tokyo. Its strategy emphasized constituency services. Its Youth League (*Minsei*) was disciplined – if purposeful – in its behavior during the years of "university struggles (*Daigaku Funsō*)," in sharp contrast to the non-Communist, albeit stridently radical student leaders many of whom were affiliated with the JSP, especially its pro-Marxist wing that wanted to introduce China's Great Proletarian Cultural Revolution into Japan. Hence, the wilder student activists criticized both the JCP and its Youth League as having succumbed to "bureaucratism" and "establishmentarianism."

The party's years of growth, however, lasted little more than a decade. Chairman Miyamoto Kenji, who had been the architect of success, never fully recovered from the (probably correct) allegation that he had participated in the lynching of a police informant some four decades earlier. Sales of the "Red Flag (*Akahata*)," the party's newspaper, as well as its many other publications declined, as anything with "Communist" in its label lost some of its appeal. By contrast, during the decade between 1965 and 1975, the popularity of JCP-sponsored publications had been such that the party officially was the wealthiest political organization, and was derisively referred to as being nothing more than the "Yoyogi Publishing Company." (Yoyogi is the Tokyo district in which the party's headquarters is located.) These factors, as well as popular perceptions that the Soviet Union was being increasingly unfriendly towards Japan, and that the JCP, despite its "autonomously independent line (*jishu dokuritsu rosen*)", was still linked with Moscow, contributed to the end of its real growth. Nevertheless, the party does remain a haven for those voters who believe that the JCP may well be the sole real alternative to the LDP on the assumption that all of the other parties are either inept or have had their independence (from the LDP) compromised, or maybe both.

Opposition Party Demographics

Tables 1.3 to 1.6 summarize certain basic data about the opposition parties. Only the Socialists have national support (see Table 1.3). Each of the other parties, the DSP, Kōmeitō, JCP, and Social Democratic Federation, has its strength concentrated in the central regions of Honshu (Kantō, Chūbu and Kinki) in which Japan's major metropolitan cities are located. It is these parties that vie for the support of Japan's urban voters. By contrast, the JSP has managed to win its share of seats in the less urbanized electoral districts, especially on the islands of Hokkaido in the north and Kyūshū in the south.

There is not as much difference among the opposition parties in the age distribution of their Diet members. In the 1960s, when the Kōmeitō burst upon the national scene, the average age of its members was weighted much more heavily in the "under forty" age groups. It, too, is now dominated by members in their fifties and sixties, as has been true for the JSP and JCP, both of which have suffered from a paucity of younger members.

As far as formal education is concerned (Table 1.5) the opposition party representatives tend to have been educated at universities that are generally not considered to be among the most prestigious institutions of higher education in Japan. Only a small percentage, for example, are graduates of the University of Tokyo, with the significant exception of the JCP. It and the miniscule Social Democratic Federation are the only opposition parties that compare favorably with the LDP (see Table 1.13) in this particular respect. Nonetheless, it is noteworthy that well over half of all opposition party members have college degrees. From that

Table 1.3 Opposition Parties, 1985: Regional Distribution, Members of House of Representatives and House of Councillors (Local Constituencies) (*percentages*)

			Region															
			Hokkaido		Tōhoku		Kantō		Chūbu		Kinki		Chūgoku		Shikoku		Kyūshū/ Okinawa	
Party		No. of seats	HR	HC	HR	HC	HR	HC	HR	HC	HR	HC	HR	HC	HR	HC	HR	HC
JSP																		
	HR	113	7		11		25		18		12		7		5		15	
	HC	26		11		8		30		19		5		11		0		15
DSP																		
	HR	39	2		5		25		23		29		2		0		14	
	HC	6		0		0		0		33		50		17		0		0
Kōmeitō																		
	HR	57	2		2		38		7		28		8		4		10	
	HC	10		0		0		30		20		30		0		0		20
JCP																		
	HR	27	0		7		26		11		38		3		3		11	
	HC	6		17		0		33		0		50		0		0		0
SDF																		
	HR	3	0		33		33		0		0		33		0		0	
	HC	0																

Source: The information in Tables 1.3 to 1.6 and 1.9 to 1.14 is based on data in *Kokkai Binran* [Diet Handbook] February 1984 edn. I would like to express my gratitude to Mrs Mariko Kitamura Bird for her unstinting assistance in the preparation of these tables.

Notes: HR = House of Representatives; HC = House of Councillors.

JSP = Japan Socialist Party; DSP = Democratic Socialist Party;

JCP = Japan Communist Party; SDF = Social Democratic Federation.

Tōhoku includes Aomori, Iwate, Akita, Miyagi, Fukushima Prefectures. Kantō includes Ibaragi, Tochigi, Gunma, Saitama, Chiba, Tokyo, Kanagawa Prefectures.

Chūbu includes Niigata, Toyama, Ishikawa, Fukui, Nagano, Yamanashi, Shizuoka, Aichi, Gifu Prefectures.

Kinki includes Kyoto, Osaka, Hyōgo, Mie, Shiga, Nara, Wakayama Prefectures.

Chūgoku includes Okayama, Hiroshima, Tottori, Shimane, Yamaguchi Prefectures.

Shikoku includes Tokushima, Kagawa, Ehime, Kōchi Prefectures.

Kyūshū includes Fukuoka, Saga, Nagasaki, Kumamoto, Ōita, Miyazaki, Kagoshima Prefectures.

perspective, there is not much to distinguish them as a group from their counterparts in the LDP.

In terms of career background (Table 1.6), however, one major difference with the LDP (see Table 1.14) becomes immediately apparent. There are virtually no former government bureaucrats,

Table 1.4 Opposition Parties, 1985: Distribution by Age of Members, House of Representatives and House of Councillors (National and Local Districts) (*percentages*)

			Age											
		No. of	25–40		41–50		51–60		61–70		71–80		80+	
Party		seats	HR	HC	HR	HC	HR	HC	HR	HC	HR	HC	HR	HC
JSP														
	HR	113	2		9		55		28		6		—	
	HC	43		—		2		53		35		10		—
DSP														
	HR	39	2		33		33		23		5		2	
	HC	13		—		8		54		30		8		—
Kōmeitō														
	HR	57	5		34		58		3		—		—	
	HC	27		—		11		65		18		7		—
JCP														
	HR	27	4		4		70		11		11		—	
	HC	14		—		14		64		14		7		—
SDF														
	HR	3	—		33		66		—		—		—	
	HC	1		—		—		—		100		—		—

whether national or local, who are Diet members belonging to the opposition parties. It is this lack of former career bureaucrats in their ranks of Diet members that most sharply differentiates the composition of the opposition parties from that of the LDP. It is also this absence of ex-bureaucrats that tends to put the opposition Diet members at a disadvantage in knowing how to utilize the sinews of government in a manner that is favorable to their constituents.

Among the opposition parties' members, it is also noteworthy that many of the Socialists, Democratic Socialists and Communists began their careers as trade union officials. One of the categories that stands out is the relatively large percentage of former "administrative assistants (*hishokan*)" of Diet members who have used that experience as a springboard to being elected themselves. Finally, in sharp contrast to the dominant career background of American Congressmen, is the very small group of lawyers that is to be found among Diet members – once again, with the sole exception of the Communists.

Table 1.5 Opposition Parties in House of Representatives and House of Councillors: Education (*percentages*)

			Education																					
			Highest level achieved												University graduates as a group									
			Elementary school		Kōtō Shogakko[a]		Middle school		Higher school		Military academy and special schools		University		University of Tokyo		University of Kyoto		Waseda		Keio		Other universities	
Party		No. of seats	HR	HC	HR	HC	HR	HC	HR	HC	HR	HC	HR	HC	HR	HC	HR	HC	HR	HC	HR	HC	HR	HC
JSP	HR	112	0		3		4		11		31		50		8		6		17		2		65	
	HC	41		0		5		7		10		20		57		18		0		0		7		75
DSP	HR	38	0		8		2		2		9		79		20		12		12		10		46	
	HC	13		0		7		7		7		0		79		10		10		0		0		80
Kōmeitō	HR	58	0		0		3		8		22		67		4		2		13		7		74	
	HC	27		0		3		4		15		4		74		9		9		9		6		67
JCP	HR	26	0		4		0		15		0		81		42		5		5		0		48	
	HC	14		0		0		0		22		0		78		17		17		9		0		67
SDF	HR	3	0		0		0		0		0		100		33		0		0		0		67	
	HC	1		0		0		0		0		0		100		100		0		0		0		0

Note: [a]Higher elementary school, under the prewar system of education, was roughly the equivalent of junior high school.

Table 1.6 Opposition Parties in House of Representatives and House of Councillors: Career Background (*percentages*)

Party	No. of seats		National government bureaucrat		Local government bureaucrat		Local notable		Members' administrative assistant		Business-man		Journalist		Lawyer		Labor union		Other	
			HR	HC	HR	HC	HR	HC	HR	HC	HR	HC	HR	HC	HR	HC	HR	HC	HR	HC
JSP	HR	112	0		3		30		28		0		2		5		28		4	
	HC	41		0		5		25		27		2		2		2		25		12
DSP	HR	38	3		0		24		29		5		0		0		18		21	
	HC	13		0		0		0		23		0		15		8		39		15
Kōmeitō	HR	58	0		5		29		41		1		1		10		0		13	
	HC	27		0		0		22		48		0		7		0		22		0
JCP	HR	26	0		4		8		27		0		0		30		4		27	
	HC	14		0		0		7		50		0		0		14		29		0
SDF	HR	3	0		0		63		33		0		0		0		0		0	
	HC	1		0		0		0		0		0		100		0		0		0

Factionalism

If the increasing fragmentation among the ranks of the opposition parties has been of assistance to the LDP in retaining its ability to be Japan's governing party, a second factor has been the LDP's flexibility. As has been said, its partisans have not been noteworthy for their commitment to ideological posturing and debates over basic issues of policy, both of which contributed so heavily to the JSP's difficulties. Instead, LDPers have been dedicated to remaining in power. In doing so, their party's internal structure has been immensely helpful. For the LDP, from its establishment to the present, has been a coalition of factions.

No other set of issues has provided as much controversy in the study of Japanese politics as factions and factionalism (Watanabe, 1964a; Fukui, 1978; Uchida, 1983). Almost no one now denies that both are at the core of that country's political process. Disagreement arises over evaluation. Critics assert that factions make it virtually impossible for the political decision-making system to function "rationally" because of the interplay of faction leaders and their followers; secondly, that they weaken the authority and power of political leaders, especially the Prime Minister; thirdly, that they contribute to the excessive infusion of "money politics (*kinken seiji*)," thus perpetuating what is frequently referred to as "structural corruption"; and fourthly, they obscure the differences between the governing and the opposition parties by allowing the factional shifts in the former to provide the appearance, but not the substance, of changes in leadership that reflects the acceptance of responsibility (Fukui, 1978, pp. 43–72; Thayer, 1969, pp. 15–57). Frequently, these separate points are brought together with the assertion that as long as factions continue to exist, it will not be possible for the Japanese political system to be classified as either "modern" or "democratic."

Let me hasten to make my own bias clear. I support the continued existence of factions, at least for the foreseeable future. First, they provide a barrier against the dictatorial exercise of power. To be sure, the Japanese have never engaged in a "cult of personality," and the group basis of their society – even though it does allow for individual initiative and self-expression as, for example, in the bizarre behavior of famed novelist Mishima Yukio – provides a protective shield against any political megalomaniacs. Nonetheless, I keep wondering, for example, what might have happened in the case of former Prime Minister Tanaka

Kakuei (July 1972–November 1974), had it not been for the countervailing power of his intra-party opponents who prevented his becoming the unchallenged leader in the late 1970s and early 1980s, not only of the LDP, but of Japan itself. After all, Tanaka had remained the most powerful single individual in the LDP even after having been found guilty of accepting a $1.8 million bribe from Lockheed, until he was felled by a cerebral infarction in late February 1985.

Secondly, factions and their leaders provide for alternative policies and policy options to be heard in the highest councils of the LDP. If a high rate of economic growth becomes dominant under one coalition, there will be another which will take up the cudgels on behalf of protecting the environment – not necessarily out of conviction, but because doing so provides an opportunity to lay claim to the succession. Of course, these kinds of struggles take place in most governing parties. In the case of the LDP, it is the factions that have provided the institutional framework for these disputes to be constructively channeled into the process of leadership changes, and, thereby, to enable the party to respond flexibly to changing circumstances.

Thirdly, and possibly most important of all, factions and sub-factions have been components of Japan's society for a very long time, much longer than the period since the Meiji Restoration in 1868, which is generally considered to be the beginning of contemporary Japan. There have been the "clan oligarchs (*hanbatsu*)," the "militarists (*gunbatsu*)," "family lineages (*iegara*)," "higher school and university ties (*gakubatsu*)" *ad infinitum*; and each faction also had and has its sub-factions. Hence, to anticipate or wish that factionalism could or should be eliminated from the LDP, as its critics so ardently desire, is to expect this political party to become something other than a Japanese organization. Only if Japan changes in some fundamental fashion – and the Allied (American) Occupation certainly tried, at least initially, to bring about some basic reforms – to the degree that factionalism no longer is endemic, could one realistically expect the LDP, and all other political organizations as well, no longer to be blessed or cursed (depending on one's preferences) with factions. In the meantime, all of the fulminations against factionalism would seem to be based on criteria drawn from other (than Japan's) political cultures about how political parties might be organized internally.

Despite the foregoing, it is always possible that the LDP will be forced to abjure some quotient of factional infighting if it were to be faced with a united opposition capable of mounting an effective challenge. Evidence is lacking on behalf of such a prospect. If anything, the infighting became fiercer during the latter half of the 1970s when the party was teetering on the brink of losing its majority in the Diet. (This theme will be elaborated in Chapter 4.) Furthermore, the agony suffered by the LDP's principal opposition party, the JSP, also provides evidence that an erosion of popular support would not necessarily increase party unity. If anything, the JSP's history, since the onset of its decline in the early 1960s, suggests that substantial losses of either aggregate vote totals or seats in the Diet tend to bring about even greater degrees of disharmony.

It can also be argued that if Japan actually did have a two-party system instead of a system in which one dominant party includes different factional coalitions that alternate with each other in the exercise of power, its politics would be more comprehensible to those – especially foreigners – who try to study it. Or, that Japanese politics would thereby be in greater conformity with systems that exist in other "advanced" countries. Both sets of expectations, while understandable from a non-Japanese perspective, reflect the most egregious kinds of ethno-centricism and assumptions based on culture-bound criteria that area studies in the social sciences should have laid to rest long ago.

What is even more troubling is that so many Japanese intellectuals seem to have accepted these judgments of "western" social science all too uncritically. Their views would seem to reflect one remnant of late nineteenth-century attitudes: Japan must learn from and catch up with the West; advanced Western nations (especially England and the United States) have two-party systems; hence Japan, to be on an equal footing politically, must also have the presumed benefits of two large, aggregating organizations that alternate with each other in governing. No one, among the many Japanese with whom I have discussed this issue, has put it quite so bluntly or simply but these assertions reflect the litany that underlies the endless criticism of factionalism in Japan.

LDP Factions

Let us proceed, then, into the LDP's labyrinth of factions. As has been noted, factionalism has been an endemic fact of life in Japanese society. There were, however, some very specific circumstances that helped to generate factions among the ranks of the "conservatives" when they united in the LDP. The first was that two major conservative political parties – "Liberal" and "Democratic" – joined with each other in creating the LDP. Both could trace their genealogy back to the 1880s, and both also included their own factions. These earlier associations lived on within the new organization.

A second factor was another legacy of the past, albeit one that was more recent in origin. During the early reformist years of the postwar Occupation of Japan, the political purge had cut a wide swath through the ranks of prewar politicians (Baerwald, 1959). Gradually, those who had been barred or removed from public office began to re-enter the national political arena. This process had begun during the waning years of the Occupation (1949–52) and was made complete when the peace treaty did not include any provision specifying that the purgees should remain outside the pale, as the Potsdam Declaration had required: "There must be eliminated *for all time* (italics added) the authority and influence of those who have deceived and misled the people of Japan into embarking on world conquest . . ." (Government Section, 1949, p. 413).

Instead, as the old guard tried to reassert its prerogatives, it came into direct conflict with the newer generation of politicians who had been elected in the interim. Many a battle ensued, the most famous of which was between Yoshida Shigeru, a senior Foreign Ministry diplomat and Prime Minister for much of the Occupation era, and Hatoyama Ichirō, a long-time conservative parliamentarian whom the Occupation authorities had designated as undesirable on the eve of his selection as Prime Minister in the spring of 1946 (Baerwald, 1959, pp. 21–4).

The Yoshida–Hatoyama imbroglio exemplified a third factor that contributed to factionalism: the split among conservatives between "ex-bureaucrats" and "pure politicians." Yoshida was in many ways the quintessential Foreign Ministry bureaucrat who had capped his distinguished career with his appointment as Ambassador to the Court of St James. He also had participated in an unsuccessful plot to negotiate an early surrender by Japan during the spring of 1945, for which effort the Japanese military police authorities had jailed him. Even more to the point, after becoming Prime Minister in 1946, he recruited ex-bureaucrats into the Liberal Party. He did so in part because, from his perspective, they constituted the best talent in Japan. Furthermore, the political purge criteria covered only a small increment of the civilian bureaucracy, in sharp contrast to their requiring the disbarment of the entire Imperial Army's and Navy's officer corps: that is, the military bureaucracy.

Hatoyama, on the other hand, exemplified the elected politicians. Even if he had not himself been an unquestioning ally of the militarists, many of his fellow parliamentarians had actively supported Japan's expansionist policies. For this assistance, the military had officially endorsed their political allies in the 1942 election for the House of Representatives, a controlled electoral contest that had been conducted during the initial year of the Pacific War.

Subsumed under the roiling conflict between the "ex-bureaucrats (*kanryo-ha*)" and "party politicians (*tōjin-ha*)" have been other divisions based on educational credentials, social status and overall attitude. Specifically, it is the civilian bureaucrats who are the best and the brightest because they are the graduates of the most prestigious academic institutions, especially the Law Faculty of the University of Tokyo. (In Japanese universities, a student completes his Law degree as an undergraduate.) By contrast, those who began their electoral careers as members of Prefectural or City assemblies tend to have had less distinguished academic training even if they had graduated from one or another institution of Japan's highly diverse system of tertiary education. Of course, there have been a few who have had extremely successful careers without any formal academic credentials whatsoever. Former Prime Minister Tanaka Kakuei (1972–4) is the incarnation of this group. Not only had he never gone to college, but he had not even gone beyond middle school. Furthermore, his family origins had been modest, and he had come from the wrong (western) side, geographically, of Honshu, the largest of Japan's four principal islands.

Not only is there the general expectation in Japan that "government officials (*yakunin*)" or "bureaucrats (*kanryo*)" (there is the same subtle distinction in Japanese and English between the alternative appellations) will have been better educated and will have come from a better social background – or will have acquired the necessary social graces while in government employment – but there is also the implicit belief that they, alone, know what is in the national interest. Politicians, on the other hand, often have the reputation of being mentally less well-equipped and being more imbued with the protection of local, as opposed to national, interests. These distinctions remain palpable in the factional struggles within the LDP even if they continue to be difficult to define. This is especially so, because it is the bureaucrats (while they are on active service in the government, or after their transfer into the realm of electoral politics) who tend to have been dominant and who, therefore, have been able to exercise control over the character of the debate regarding their prerogatives as the real governors of Japan.

A fourth factor that promoted and assisted in sustaining the proliferation of LDP factions was the "economic combine (*zaibatsu*)" dissolution program that the Occupation had promulgated during the high tide of its varied reforms (Bisson, 1954; Hadley, 1970). Its basic intent had been to reduce the enormous concentrations of economic power and political influence that the zaibatsu had enjoyed in prewar Japan.

One important premise of these economic deconcentration programs had been the conviction (rooted in New Deal doctrine) that these multi-faceted banking–commerce–industry conglomerates had controlled an excessive amount of wealth that they could disburse to their benefit and to the detriment of alternative political groupings. While an over-simplification, it had been widely believed that the two principal prewar political parties, the *Seiyukai* and the *Minseito*, had been respectively the instruments of the Mitsui and Mitsubishi zaibatsu. Once they, and the lesser giants such as Sumitomo and Yasuda, had been sliced into several components, so had the potential sources of political funds been multiplied.

In many respects, this same process of proliferating the sources of political funding was duplicated at the local "rice-roots" level. Occupation authorities had ordered and overseen a major land reform program, generally considered one of the most successful undertakings of the immediate postwar years (Dore, 1959). Under its aegis, tenancy was virtually eliminated and the power of the large landowners was substantially reduced. Both consequences influenced the structure of political power. Erstwhile tenants became independent farmers who were no longer under the obligation to follow the dictates of dominant landlords. Furthermore, the farmers determined that by organizing themselves into a particular candidate's "support organization (*kōenkai*)," they could – and, often did – elect representatives who would respond to their interests. (Many years later, the dependence of LDPers on the rural voters had unintended consequences, of course, as the farm lobby among them resisted liberalization of agricultural commodity imports.)

Each of the foregoing factors, as well as the long tradition of factionalism in Japan's complex society, provided its particular impetus to the creation of factions within the LDP at the time of its establishment in 1955. None of them, however, provides an explanation of why these factions have survived, have become better organized internally and have become the essential building blocs of decision-making in the LDP – and, so long as that party retains its majority status – in the Diet's political process.

The single most important reason for the survival of factions in the LDP is the medium-sized multi-member district system that provides the basic "rules of the game" for electing the members of the House of Representatives. This system will receive extended treatment in Chapter 2. For the moment, suffice it to say that this system requires candidates who have been endorsed by the same political party to run against each other in the same constituency and thereby to compete for the allegiance of the same group of voters. Therefore, it is rare, for example, for a particular faction to support more than one candidate in a given district. (The exceptions tend to reflect the overwhelming influence of a particular faction leader in a specific region.) Inevitably, candidates from the same party who must oppose each other do not necessarily harbor feelings of brotherly love for their presumed brethren.

The second and third factors are so symbiotic that it is only possible to discuss them simultaneously. They involve the interlocking interests of faction leaders and potential LDP candidates for the Diet.

One of the principal functions of a faction is to provide an organized base of support for its leader. In fact, for some analysts of factionalism in the LDP the "greatest stimulus to the growth of the factions in the present conservative party [the LDP] has been the party presidential elections" (Thayer, 1969, pp. 21 ff.). These contests at the party's periodic national conventions impose the requirement on presidential candidates to have the support of as large a number of delegates as possible. Furthermore, inasmuch as the vast majority (90 percent) of delegates are members of the Diet, it is obviously advantageous for a faction leader to have the largest possible group of his own followers attending the convention as voting delegates. The larger the group, the greater the possibility of victory for that faction's leader; or, at the very least, the greater the prospect of providing that faction's leader with bargaining power in having a voice in the selection of the Party President and in the apportionment of patronage.

Given the constraints imposed by group loyalty, a faction leader faces considerable difficulty in wooing members of other groupings to the ranks of his own followers. By the same token, there are risks involved for those LDPers who exhibit restiveness regarding their prospects for advancement and who toy with the blandishments proffered by an alternative faction's leader. Moreover, nearly all who do switch their factional loyalties – there are, inevitably, some exceptions – tend to lose whatever seniority they have accrued and find themselves among the ranks of the lowly in the new group that they have joined.

These impediments are not present at the outset of one's hoped-for career in electoral politics. Assuming that one's aspirations are to be elected as an LDPer to either chamber of the Diet, a question immediately arises as to which faction leader has the most to offer in financial and other assistance. Another question revolves around the factional affiliations of the other LDP candidates in the constituency in which one wants to be a candidate. As noted, it is rare for one faction to support two candidates in the same district. Yet a third question is, what are the future prospects of a faction leader? Is he on the way up or has he reached the pinnacle of his career? Furthermore, how substantial is his ability to assist in obtaining the party's official endorsement? Conversely, from the faction leader's perspective, what are the potential newcomer's chances of electoral success? The answers to each of these questions assists in determining the LDP's roster of new candidates. Ultimately, it is the party's Secretary General who has a major voice in the making of these decisions.

Faction leaders and the number of followers that they have also play a crucial role in the vast array of personnel decisions that must be made. The LDP, at its convention, elects its "President (*Sōsai*)," but that decision is only the beginning of a chain reaction involving the distribution of the party's Diet members in government and party posts. Generally, the process begins with the selection of the senior party leaders: "Secretary General (*Kanjichō*)," "Chairman of the General [Executive] Council (*Sōmu Kaichō*)," "Chairman of the Policy Research Council (*Seichō Kaichō*)," and (intermittently) "Vice President (*Fuku-Sōsai*)."

This group, in which more often than not, the Secretary General is the most influential, assists the party's President, who will have become Prime Minister by virtue of the LDP's majority, to select the members of the Cabinet, the Parliamentary Vice-Ministers, the Diet's Standing and Special Committee Chairmen, the members of the Diet's committees and the entire roster of personnel in the vast array of party posts. All of these personnel decisions have become elements in the adroit balancing of and infighting among the factions, each of which has its preferred candidates – whether it be for a Cabinet portfolio, a senior party executive post, a Diet Committee chairmanship, *ad infinitum.*

Table 1.7 The Second Nakasone Cabinet 27 December 1983

Post, Ministry/Agency	*Name*	*Age*	*District*	*Faction*
Prime Minister	Nakasone Yasuhiro	65	Gumma 3	Nakasone
Justice	Sumi Eisaku	63	Toyama 1	Suzuki
Foreign Ministry	Abe Shintarō	59	Yamaguchi 1	Fukuda
Finance	Takeshita Noboru	59	Shimane	Tanaka
Education	Mori Yoshirō	46	Ishikawa 1	Fukuda
Welfare	Watanabe Kōzō	51	Fukushima 2	Tanaka
Agriculture, Forestry, Fishery	Yamamura Shinjirō	50	Chiba 2	Tanaka
International Trade and Industry	Okonogi Hikosaburō	55	Kanagawa 1	Nakasone
Transportation	Hosoda Kichizō	71	Shimane	Fukuda
Posts and Telecommunications	Okuda Keiwa	56	Ishikawa 1	Tanaka
Labor	Sakamoto Misoji	60	Ishikawa 2	Kōmoto
Construction	Mizuno Kiyoshi	58	Chiba 2	Suzuki
Local Autonomy (Home Affairs)	Tagawa Sei'ichi	65	Kanagawa 2	NLC
Chief Cabinet Secretary	Fujinami Takao	51	Mie 2	Nakasone
Director General, Prime Minister's Office	Nakanishi Ichirō[a]	68	Hyōgo	Fukuda
Director General, Administrative Management Agency	Gotōda Masaharu	69	Tokushima	Tanaka
Director General, Defense Agency	Kurihara Yūkō	63	Shizuoka 2	Suzuki
Director General, Economic Planning Agency	Kōmoto Toshio	72	Hyōgo 4	Kōmoto
Director General, Science and Technology Agency	Isurugi Michiyuki[a]	70	Iwate	Suzuki
Director General, Environment Agency	Ueda Minoru[a]	69	Kyoto	Tanaka
Director General, Land Agency	Inamura Sakonshirō	66	Ishikawa 2	Nakasone
Senior LDP Officers				
President	Nakasone Yasuhiro	65	Gumma 3	Nakasone
Vice President	Nikaidō Susumu	70	Kagoshima 3	Tanaka
Secretary General	Tanaka Rokusuke	60	Fukuoka 4	Suzuki
Chairman, Executive Board	Kanemaru Shin	69	Yamanashi	Tanaka
Chairman, Policy Research Council	Fujio Masayuki	66	Tochigi 2	Fukuda

Notes:

[a]Members of House of Councillors; all others are members of House of Representatives.

Summary of factional distribution: Tanaka 6 plus LDP Vice President, LDP Chairman Executive Board; Suzuki 4 plus LDP Secretary General; Nakasone 4 plus LDP President; Fukuda 4 plus Chairman PRC; Kōmoto 1; NLC 1.

Table 1.8 Parliamentary Vice-Ministers: The Second Nakasone Cabinet 27 December 1983

Post, Ministry/Agency	*Name*	*Age*	*District*	*Faction*
Justice	Sekiguchi Keizō[a]	57	National	Suzuki
Foreign Ministry	Kitakawa Ishimatsu	64	Osaka 7	Kōmoto
Finance	Horinouchi Hisao	59	Miyazaki 2	Nakasone
Finance	Inoue Yutaka[a]	56	Chiba	Fukuda
Education	Nakamura Yasushi	51	Tokyo 5	Nakasone
Welfare	Yukawa Hiroshi	65	Osaka 1	Nakasone
Agriculture, Forestry and Fishery	Shimamura Yoshinobu	49	Tokyo 10	Nakasone
Agriculture, Forestry and Fishery	Nakagawa Yukio[a]	67	Ehime 2	Tanaka
International Trade and Industry	Satō Shinji	51	Yamaguchi 2	Tanaka
International Trade and Industry	Oki Hiroshi[a]	56	Aichi	Tanaka
Transportation	Tsushima Yūji	53	Aomori 2	Suzuki
Posts and Telecommunications	Sekiya Katsutsugu	45	Ehime 1	Nakasone
Labor	Tsukahara Shunpei	36	Ibaraki 2	Fukuda
Construction	Itoyama Eitarō	41	Saitama 3	no faction
Local Autonomy (Home Affairs)	Itō Kōsuke	42	Tokyo 11	NLC
Administrative Management Agency	Hatoyama Kunio	35	Tokyo 8	Tanaka
Hokkaido Development Agency	Takagi Masaaki[a]	54	Hokkaido	Ishihara
Defense Agency	Nakamura Kishirō	34	Ibaraki 3	Tanaka
Economic Planning Agency	Yamazaki Takesaburō	51	Kagoshima 1	Tanaka
Science and Technology Agency	Okabe Saburō[a]	57	National	no faction
Environmental Agency	Kakizawa Kōji	50	Tokyo 6	Nakasone
Okinawa Development Agency	Ōshiro Shinjun[a]	56	Okinawa	Tanaka
Land Agency	Nakagawa Hidenao	39	Hiroshima 2	Fukuda

Notes:
[a]Members of House of Councillors.
Summary of factional distribution: LDP – Tanaka 7; Nakasone 6; Fukuda 3; Suzuki 2; Kōmoto 1; Ishihara 1; and Unaffiliated 2. NLC – 1.

When viewed in its entirety, the process reflects the triumph of factionalism over all conceivable alternatives to explain why Mr "A" is the LDP's Secretary General or Mr "B" is Foreign Minister.

The factions have not remained constant in their thirty years of existence. Some have split into sub-factions after the death or

Table 1.9 House of Representatives Committee Chairmen 1983

Committee	Name	Age	Party	District	Faction
Standing Committees					
Cabinet	Kataoka Seiichi	72	LDP	Toyama 2	Nakasone
Local Administration	Ōishi Senpachi	48	LDP	Shizuoka 1	Nakasone
Justice	Miyazaki Moichi	66	LDP	Kagoshima 1	Suzuki
Foreign Affairs	Nakajima Gentaro	54	LDP	Gumma 2	Fukuda
Finance	Kawara Tsutomu	46	LDP	Ishikawa 2	Suzuki
Education	Aino Kōichirō	55	LDP	Saga	Tanaka
Social and Labor	Arima Motoharu	63	LDP	Kagoshima 2	Tanaka
Agriculture, Forestry and Fishery	Abe Fumio	61	LDP	Hokkaido 3	Suzuki
Commerce and Industry	Kajiyama Seiroku	57	LDP	Ibaraki 2	Tanaka
Transportation	Fuke Toshiichi	71	LDP	Kagawa 1	Fukuda
Posts and Communications	Shiga Setsu	50	LDP	Iwate 2	Kōmoto
Construction	Hamada Kōichi	55	LDP	Chiba 3	no faction
Science and Technology	Ōno Kiyoshi	53	Kōmeitō	Tokyo 7	—
Environment	Takeuchi Reiichi	57	LDP	Aomori 2	Tanaka
Budget	Kuranari Tadashi	65	LDP	Nagasaki 1	Nakasone
Audit	Yokoyama Toshiaki	66	JSP	Aichi 1	—
House Management	Ozawa Ichirō	41	LDP	Iwate 2	Tanaka
Discipline	Kasuga Ikkō	73	DSP	Aichi 1	—
Special Committees					
Disaster	Satō Kanju	41	JSP	Aichi 3	—
Election System	Nakayama Masaaki	51	LDP	Osaka 2	Nakasone
Coal	Kōsaka Noboru	65	JSP	Fukushima 3	—
Prices	Kaneko Mitsu	69	JSP	Tokyo 4	—
Traffic Safety	Sakai Hiroichi	54	Kōmeitō	Wakayama 1	—
Okinawa and Northern Territories	Watanabe Rō	58	DSP	Shizuoka 2	—
Security	Shiokawa Masajūrō	62	LDP	Osaka 4	Fukuda

Summary: Standing Committees – LDP 15 (Tanaka 5, Nakasone 3, Suzuki 3, Fukuda 2, Kōmoto 1 and Unaffiliated 1); JSP 1; Kōmeitō 1; and DSP 1.
Special Committees – LDP 2 (Nakasone 1 and Fukuda 1); JSP 3; Kōmeitō 1; and DSP 1.

retirement of a major faction's leader. Former Prime Minister Kishi Nobusuke's, for example, separated into three: loyalists (many of whom were ex-bureaucrats) who coalesced around Fukuda Takeo (Prime Minister 1976–8), "party-men (*tōjin*)" who joined Kawashima Shōjirō (LDP Vice President for much of the 1960s) and a third group that assembled around Fujiyama Aiichirō, who failed to achieve his cherished dream of the prime ministership and wasted much of his fortune in the elusive quest. Also noteworthy is the fact that after such a fissure, the erstwhile factional comrades – in this instance, Fukuda and Kawashima – exhibited an even greater degree of antagonism towards each other than the kind of normal rivalry that factionalism might be expected to engender.

Some factions disappear altogether, as was the case with Ōno Banboku's, after his death. Ōno had been LDP Vice President under Prime Minister Kishi (1957–60) and had been one of his party's most colorful and shrewd leaders who could easily have risen to prominence in either Tammany Hall or Mayor Richard Daley's Cook County Machine during its heyday if "Ban-chan" (as he was universally known) could have spoken English, which he – as a prototypical nationalist – did not.

Some six major factions existed at the LDP's founding; but, there were many minor groupings during the early years, an era of high fluidity in internal alignments. Their number swelled to at least eleven in the mid-1960s, especially as a consequence of the deaths of Ōno Banboku and the redoubtable Kōno Ichirō, the

Table 1.10 LDP Factions 1965–85: Genealogy and Numerical Strength

1965				1975				1985				
Faction	*HR*	*HC*	*Total*	*Faction*	*HR*	*HC*	*Total*	*Faction*	*HR*	*HC*	*Total*	*%*
Satō	44	52	96	Tanaka	43	41	84	Tanaka	62	51	113	28
Maeo	47	15	62	Ōhira	38	20	58	Suzuki	50	27	77	19
Fukuda	20	1	21	Fukuda	54	23	77	Fukuda	42	25	67	17
Kawashima	18	—	18	Shiina	10	2	12					
Fujiyama	18	11	29									
Kōno	46	14	60	Nakasone	40	6	46	Nakasone	50	17	67	17
Miki	37	10	47	Miki	32	10	42	Kōmoto	26	7	33	8
Ishii	14	10	24	Ishii	4	—	4					
Murakami (Ōno)	11	9	20	Mizuta	—	2	2					
Funada	12	—	12	Funada	8	3	11					
								Ishihara[a]	6	1	7	2
No faction	16	16	32	No faction	21	20	41	No faction	24	13	37	9
								NLC	8	3	11	

Notes: [a]This group had been founded by the late Nakagawa Ichirō. All members are reported to have joined the Fukuda faction.
Totals may not add up to 100 percent because of rounding.

Japanese Peter Ueberroth of the 1964 International Olympic Games that were held during the late summer in Tokyo. By the beginning of the 1980s, the LDP's internal structure had stabilized into five major factions. Their respective power is not equal, however.

LDP Demographics

Not only are these factions unequal in numerical strength, ranging from Tanaka's with over one hundred members to Kōmoto's with less than forty, but they exhibit some differences with respect to certain variables: (a) regional distribution, (b) age of members, (c) educational achievement, and (d) career background.

(a) Regional distribution. Former Prime Minister Tanaka's group provides a model of maximizing nation-wide penetration, especially among those who are Representatives. Among the Councillors, well over 50 percent come from the Chūbu region (west central) and Kinki region (centering around Osaka). Tanaka (prior to his illness in February 1985) was reported to have a slate of his own candidates whom he was grooming to challenge incumbent LDPers in districts in which none of his faction was represented, as well as to challenge those of his own followers who might be tempted to toy with deviationist tendencies. All of the other major factions (Suzuki, Fukuda, Nakasone, and Kōmoto) had the greater part of their strength in the Tōhoku region (northeastern Honshu), and Kantō region (Tokyo and its surrounding prefectures), as well as vying with Tanaka's forces for their share in Chūbu. With the notable exception of Fukuda's, all had their share of followers from the southern-most main island of Kyūshū. Despite these variations in regional strength – more noticeable among locally elected Councillors than Representatives – these statistics underline the degree to which factions are nation-wide in their reach.

(b) The distribution of factional memberships by major age categories (see Table 1.12) does reflect some differences, most clearly in the case of the Kōmoto group which has not been effective in recruiting younger candidates or, if it has done so, in not having been successful as far as electing them to the Diet. Seventy percent of them (combining both chambers) are in their sixties and older. By contrast all of the other factions have about a quarter of their followers in the "under fifty" categories, with Tanaka and Nakasone having been particularly successful in recruiting younger members in the House of Councillors. It must

Table 1.11 LDP Factions in House of Representatives and House of Councillors[a], 1985: Geographic Origins of Members (*percentages*)

	Region															
	Hokkaido		Tōhoku		Kantō		Chūbu		Kinki		Chūgoku		Shikoku		Kyūshū/ Okinawa	
Faction	HR	HC	HR	HC	HR	HC	HR	HC	HR	HC	HR	HC	HR	HC	HR	HC
Tanaka	3	—	16	9	11	3	22	34	14	22	11	13	3	6	18	12
Suzuki	4	9	19	22	17	9	25	17	4	4	8	9	6	9	17	22
Fukuda	5	—	11	10	32	37	19	10	5	16	16	12	5	5	8	10
Nakasone	—	—	3	—	24	42	24	—	16	—	3	14	8	14	22	28
Kōmoto	—	12	22	—	18	25	15	—	15	12	7	12	7	12	11	25
No faction (including Ishihara)	8	10	8	20	25	10	16	20	11	10	8	—	8	10	14	20
NLC	—	—	12	—	75	—	12	—	—	—	—	—	—	—	—	—

Notes: [a]Only local constituencies 1980, 1983 are included.
Tōhoku includes Aomori, Iwate, Akita, Miyagi, Fukushima Prefectures.
Kantō includes Ibaragi, Tochigi, Gumma, Saitama, Chiba, Tokyo, Kanagawa Prefectures.
Chūbu includes Niigata, Toyama, Ishikawa, Fukui, Nagano, Yamanashi, Shizuoka, Aichi, Gifu Prefectures.
Kinki includes Kyoto, Osaka, Hyōgo, Mie, Shiga, Nara, Wakayama Prefectures.
Chūgoku includes Okayama, Hiroshima, Tottori, Shimane, Yamaguchi Prefectures.
Shikoku includes Tokushima, Kagawa, Ehime, Kōchi Prefectures.
Kyūshū includes Fukuoka, Saga, Nagasaki, Kumamoto, Ōita, Miyazaki, Kagoshima Prefectures.

Table 1.12 LDP Factions in House of Representatives and House of Councillors, 1985: Youth and Gerontocracy (*percentages*)

	Age											
	25–40		41–50		51–60		61–70		71–80		80+	
Faction	HR	HC	HR	HC	HR	HC	HR	HC	HR	HC	HR	HC
Tanaka	3	2	21	16	35	33	30	45	11	4	—	—
Suzuki	8	—	15	4	35	35	30	50	12	11	—	—
Fukuda	4	—	20	4	20	32	27	50	27	14	2	—
Nakasone	—	—	27	12	37	13	18	75	18	—	—	—
Kōmoto	—	—	10	—	22	38	48	38	20	24	—	—
No faction	2	—	14	—	15	44	27	22	22	27	10	7
NLC	12	—	75	—	—	—	12	—	—	—	—	—

also be added that there are reportedly a large number (about 25) of the formally "no faction" LDPers who have been members of Tanaka's group in all but name. Hence, a key variable for the LDP's future internal structure is whether the "Thursday Club

(*Mokuyōkai*)" (the actual name of the Tanaka faction) will manage to remain united after the leader's retirement. Conversely, the exceptionally gerontocratic character of Kōmoto's followers bodes ill for his faction's long-term survival.

(c) A university degree clearly is one of the major prerequisites to becoming an LDPer in either chamber of the Diet (see Table 1.13). In the aggregate, more than 85 percent have been credentialed by a college or university. Furthermore, the well-known dominance of graduates from the University of Tokyo, the crown jewel of Japan's highly developed system of tertiary education, is underlined, especially in the ranks of the Suzuki and Fukuda factions.

There are exceptions, however. Three of Japan's Prime Ministers in the 1970s and 1980s were not *bona fide* members of Japan's educational elite: Tanaka's formal education, as noted, ended very early; Miki Takeo (1974–6) was a graduate of Meiji University and had spent some time at the University of Southern California; and Suzuki Zenkō (1980–2) was a graduate of a Fisheries Polytechnic. Japan may well be the prototypical credential society, but a college degree is not absolutely essential for reaching the top rung of the political ladder. Nonetheless, access within the LDP to major positions of leadership clearly has been facilitated by having obtained an undergraduate degree from a distinguished university.

(d) A prior career in the national government's bureaucracy has been the principal preparation for LDP politicians (see Table 1.14). Former Prime Minister Yoshida Shigeru, as already noted, played *the* consequential role in promoting this pattern of candidate recruitment. Ex-bureaucrats form the largest single group in all of the LDP's factions, regardless of whether the faction leader himself is an ex-bureaucrat. Former Prime Ministers Kishi Nobusuke (1957–60, ex-Ministry of Commerce), Ikeda Hayato (1960–4, ex-Finance Ministry), Satō Eisaku (1964–72, ex-Ministry of Transportation), Fukuda Takeo (1976–8, ex-Finance Ministry) and Ōhira Masayoshi (1978–80, ex-Finance Ministry) all had had this career background in common.

The others have come from different walks of life. Former Prime Minister Tanaka Kakuei (1974–6) had combined business and electoral politics to an unexcelled degree; Miki Takeo (1976–8) was one of the few genuine "party-men [*tōjin*]" to have reached the pinnacle; and Suzuki Zenkō (1980–2) after a brief stint as an official in a Fisheries Co-operative – and who initially was elected as a Socialist – had devoted nearly 40 years to being a Member of the House of Representatives, a span of time that nearly everyone

Table 1.13 LDP Factions in House of Representatives and House of Councillors, 1985: Education (*percentages*)

Faction	Education										University graduates									
	Elementary school		Middle school		Higher school		Military academy and special schools		University		University of Tokyo		University of Kyoto		Waseda		Keio		Other universities	
	HR	HC	HR	HC	HR	HC	HR	HC	HR	HC	HR	HC	HR	HC	HR	HC	HR	HC	HR	HC
Tanaka	1	—	1	—	7	10	6	—	85	90	26	39	3	13	14	11	16	5	41	42
Suzuki	—	—	5	5	1	9	1	—	93	86	50	45	—	5	11	5	11	—	28	45
Fukuda	—	—	2	9	9	5	4	—	85	86	40	45	5	5	11	5	17	5	27	40
Nakasone	—	—	—	—	12	22	8	—	80	78	25	29	2	29	30	6	8	6	35	29
Kōmoto	—	—	—	10	3	20	—	—	97	70	32	43	3	—	14	—	7	—	43	57
No faction	—	—	9	—	3	—	—	—	88	100	26	80	3	10	20	10	8	—	43	—
NLC	—	—	—	—	—	—	—	—	100	—	25	—	—	—	12	—	38	—	25	—

Table 1.14 LDP Factions in House of Representatives and House of Councillors: Career Background (*percentages*)

Faction	National government bureaucrat HR	National government bureaucrat HC	Local government bureaucrat HR	Local government bureaucrat HC	Local notable HR	Local notable HC	Career politician HR	Career politician HC	Members' administrative assistant HR	Members' administrative assistant HC	Business-man HR	Business-man HC	Journalist HR	Journalist HC	Lawyer HR	Lawyer HC	Other HR	Other HC
Tanaka	55	36	3	6	18	30	6	—	5	4	3	8	2	—	3	—	5	16
Suzuki	41	53	8	3	15	23	8	—	8	—	3	—	5	—	3	—	8	20
Fukuda	48	33	4	4	30	33	2	—	2	4	2	—	6	—	2	—	4	25
Nakasone	48	50	—	—	31	38	9	—	6	—	—	—	—	—	4	—	2	12
Kōmoto	41	38	7	12	24	50	14	—	3	—	3	—	—	—	7	—	—	—
No faction	64	41	2	—	14	18	9	—	2	—	2	5	2	—	—	—	4	36
NLC	—	—	—	—	12	—	38	—	25	—	12	—	12	—	—	—	—	—

would consider sufficient to designate him as a career politician. Prime Minister Nakasone Yasuhiro (1982–) also fits into the *tōjin* category even though he had spent a few years as an official in the old Ministry of Home Affairs (*Naimushō*) before winning his first electoral contest in 1947. He is currently in his fifteenth consecutive term as a member of the House of Representatives.

Local notables – that is, city councilmen and prefectural assemblymen as well as others who have been active in sub-national politics – constitute the second largest group, again with very little variation among the factions, whether in the House of Representatives or in the House of Councillors. Indeed, the lack of differences in the overall make-up of all the groups is what strikes one most forcefully. It is, of course, not unusual for the members of national assemblies to be predominantly of a particular background, e.g. the preponderance of lawyers in the American Congress; however, it must also be remembered that similarity of background is no guarantee for unanimity of outlook.

Changes are looming for each of the factions. Former Prime Minister Tanaka's illness, and the uncertainties of his being able to return to an active political career, have hung like an ominous cloud over that nearly 30 percent of the LDP's Diet members who are his presumed loyal followers. Finance Minister Takeshita Noboru is the heir apparent, but it is by no means certain that he will be able to inherit all of that faction's members. Former Prime Minister Suzuki Zenkō in late 1982 relinquished day-to-day control over his group to potential Prime Minister Miyazawa Kiichi. Former Prime Minister Fukuda Takeo permitted Foreign Minister Abe Shintarō to be that faction's candidate for Party President in the LDP's 1982 Primary Election, thus giving his approval to the long-anticipated succession. None the less, questions have been raised whether this grouping too can remain united. Kaifu Toshiki would appear to be the crown prince of the Kōmoto faction, but that is not absolutely certain, nor is the faction's survival assured.

An entire generation of LDP leaders stands on the threshold of retirement – that generation which had emerged during the first postwar decade. Its departure will bring about changes in the LDP's internal structure. However, displacement among the ranks of its leaders will not, in all likelihood, bring an end to factionalism in the LDP. Factions and factionalism will endure and, in so doing, will provide that essential ingredient of flexibility that has played so crucial a role in the LDP's ability to survive as the party that governs Japan – whether by itself, or in a coalition with the increasingly moderate DSP, or the Kōmeitō.

Summary

In 1955, the Japanese seemed to have established a two-party system, with nearly all "conservative" members of the Diet in the Liberal Democratic Party (LDP), and most of their opponents in the Japan Socialist Party (JSP). The conservatives have remained united in the intervening thirty years, but their opponents have become fragmented. This development has benefitted the LDP, and has contributed to its long tenure as the party that governs Japan.

Factionalism in the LDP has also proved to be beneficial to the party's capacity to survive primarily because it has enabled the party to be flexible in responding to the vast socio-economic changes that Japan has undergone during the last three decades of its history. On the other hand, factional disputes in the LDP have brought the party perilously close to splitting, especially during the latter half of the 1970s. Furthermore, those were also the years when the LDP's decline in popular support brought its strength in the Diet to "near parity (*hakuchū*)" with its opponents. Succeeding chapters will examine the implications of these developments in relation to the electoral systems for members of the House of Representatives and House of Councillors, as well as the functioning of the Diet itself.

CHAPTER 2

The Electoral Systems of the Diet

Electoral systems have not been as important a topic among political analysts in recent years as have studies of voting behavior. This is especially true for those who write in the United States and England. Nonetheless, "the rules of the game" for electing members of the Diet have a profound influence on the outcome of the periodic electoral contests that have been conducted in Japan. This assertion is the underlying hypothesis of this chapter.

Other variables do intervene, of course. Endless surveys of prevailing political attitudes among Japanese voters do reflect some shifts in priorities. Furthermore, the particular set of circumstances prevailing at the time of a specific election also can sway voter attitudes. Neither of these factors can be ignored. An appreciation of the electoral systems of the Diet is, however, of singular significance in gaining an understanding of the outcomes of elections in Japan. Unfortunately, the systems tend to be confusing to those whose experience has been restricted to national assemblies, the members of which have been elected in single-member districts as is the case for the United States House of Representatives and the British House of Commons.

The Japanese people like to think that elections are a kind of festival (*omatsuri*). Voter turnout is high by American standards, normally above 70 percent, and in the increasingly less rural hinterland is often well above 90 percent. Substantial sums of money are spent and even greater quantities of food and drink are dispensed. Political party strategists dream up inspiring slogans (often with the help of highly-skilled public relations specialists) that are reproduced on brightly colored placards which dot the cities and the landscape.

The candidates themselves have equally colorful posters that are displayed on special billboards, where each candidate in a given constituency has been allocated a numbered space, so that the voters can become familiar with the faces and names of all of the contestants on an equal basis. The Japan Broadcasting System's Television Network (NHK Channel 1) provides two and a half minute slots for each of the candidates – free – to allow each of them to set forth their views briefly on issues of the moment. Some candidates have become highly skilled in using this medium of communication; others give every appearance of being desperately uncomfortable and read their carefully prepared scripts in a dull monotone.

These official campaigns are short – no more than forty days, officially. The Public Office Election Law and the Political Funds Control Law include many restrictions on political activities prior to and during the official portion of the campaign. Nevertheless, many "runners-up (*jiten*)" have been known to begin their next election campaigns on the day after their near loss. Many elected members of the Diet devote themselves (as part of their re-election campaigns) to the needs of their constituents when they come to the nation's capital or, conversely, when members return to their electoral districts on weekends, national holidays and other occasions when the Diet is not in session. In many respects, therefore, electoral campaigns have become continuous even if that portion of them which is legally sanctioned is extremely short. This is especially true in comparison with campaigns as they are conducted in the United States where presidential and congressional contests begin long before the first party caucus or primary election.

None of the foregoing description of political campaigning in Japan is to imply that illegal activities are rampant. They are not. Instead, it is intended to indicate that there are some disparities between that which is legally permissible and that which creative campaign managers practice, a distinction that is considered useful in discussing electoral campaigns that are conducted in political systems which can be labeled as being free. The Japanese have struck a nice balance between legal restrictions and permissible practices that fits neatly into the widely accepted dichotomy: "form (*tatemae*)" and "substance (*honne*)."

Underneath all of the surface festival-like manifestations of political campaigning in Japan – the splashes of color, the unconscionably loud and blaring loudspeakers that are mounted on cars or small trucks and proclaim the name of a candidate (and little else), the *sake* and noodles, the to-ing and fro-ing of personages who travel to the constituencies and participate in "speech meetings (*tachiai enzetsu*)" in order to lend their support to a particular candidate, and the Central Election Administration

Committee's supervisory efforts to keep all of these activities under some semblance of control – the serious business of electing the members of the Diet does take place. Furthermore, these elections have been conducted with virtually no violence and very little overt ill-will. That much having been said, it is still necessary to describe the specific features of the electoral systems and how each of the political parties has tried to adjust to their imperatives because these respective efforts have not been equally successful.

The Japanese Diet is bicameral, with the members of the House of Representatives – the far more powerful of the two chambers – elected to four-year terms and those of the House of Councillors for six years. However, the Constitution empowers the Prime Minister to dissolve the House of Representatives, and thereby to create the need for the holding of a General Election, so that there were four contests for that chamber for instance between December 1976 and December 1983. On the other hand, the House of Councillors is a continuing body with half of its members facing an election every three years, a system comparable to that for the United States Senate which served as a partial model. House of Councillors elections are held in the latter half of June or early July, whereas those for the House of Representatives must be conducted within forty days of a dissolution that can be proclaimed at any time that the House of Representatives is in session.

While 44 new seats were added during the 1966–76 decade, since the December 1976 General Election the number of Representatives has remained constant at 511. In the December 1983 election, slightly over 57 million Japanese voters (about 68 percent of the roughly 84 million eligible) cast their ballots. If these votes had been cast exclusively for the winners – an assumption that is, of course, not valid – then each Representative could be expected to have been elected by about 110,000 votes. However, some winners have been elected with as few as 40,000 votes, whereas some losers have been defeated despite obtaining over 130,000 votes. There is, of course, no known system of apportionment that insures absolute numerical equality in the weight of one vote.

The situation in Japan has become an increasingly serious problem (as Table 2.1 reflects) despite periodic, albeit limited, reapportionment. In Hyōgo's 5th District, for example, some 200,000 voters elected three Representatives, for a ratio of one to about 67,000 voters. By contrast, in Chiba's 4th District, nearly 640,000 voters also elected three Representatives, for a ratio of one to about 210,000. Similar disparities have resulted in efforts to

Table 2.1 Population per Seat in the House of Representatives

Most underrepresented				Most overrepresented			
District	No. of seats	Population	Population per seat	District	No. of seats	Population	Population per seat
Chiba 4	3	1,499,290	499,763	Hyōgo 5	3	330,152	110,051
Kanagawa 3	3	1,405,950	468,650	Kagoshima 3	3	348,927	116,309
Saitama 2	3	1,359,986	453,329	Ishikawa 2	3	365,344	121,781
Tokyo 11	4	1,718,221	429,555	Ehime 3	3	373,830	124,610
Chiba 1	4	1,684,098	421,025	Akita 2	4	510,479	127,620
Saitama 4	3	1,249,206	416,402	Yamagata 2	4	549,041	137,260
Osaka 3	4	1,643,449	410,862	Niigata 4	3	412,420	137,473
Hokkaido 1	5	2,013,111	402,622	Niigata 2	4	552,599	138,150
Osaka 5	4	1,590,684	397,671	Nagano 3	4	557,795	139,449
Kanagawa 4	4	1,583,116	395,779	Ōita 2	3	421,232	140,411

Source: PHP Kenkyūjo [PHP Research Institute] (1984), *The Data File 1984*, p. 26.

reduce the most egregious imbalances through judicial proceedings and the Supreme Court, in November 1983, actually declared the existing districting contrary to the Constitution. Nonetheless, any action that might resolve this issue is painfully slow.

The Nakasone Cabinet introduced limited reapportionment draft legislation in the Diet in the spring of 1985. Under its terms six districts would gain one seat (Saitama 2 and 4, Chiba 1 and 4, Tokyo 11, and Kanagawa 3), while six districts would lose one seat (Akita 2, Yamagata 2, Ishikawa 2, Hyōgo 5, Aichi 3, Kagoshima 3). One problem with the draft is that, if adopted, it would result in the last mentioned four districts reducing their number of representatives to two seats, thus creating a new category. Another is that, in all likelihood, some of the new seats would result in gains for one or another of the opposition parties. In any case, observers believe that this "six – six" reapportionment plan (as it is popularly known) has practically no chance of being adopted. They also believe that the Cabinet introduced the draft legislation in the hope that by so doing it would prove its sincerity to the voters, as well as the Supreme Court; and that it had recognized the problem and really was trying to do something about it. (The International Bureau of the Liberal Democratic Party in June 1985 kindly made available to me a photocopy of the draft legislation "*Kōshoku Senkyo Hō no Ichibu o Kaisei Suru Hōritsuan Yōkō* [Summary of amendments to one section of the Public Office Election Law]".)

Reapportionment tends to touch some of the most sensitive nerves of elected politicians, as well as of the political parties to which they belong. Numerically underrepresented voters may fulminate and judges (including those of the Supreme Court) may hand down decisions, but it is the members of the Diet themselves who must make the final decisions regarding whose ox is to be gored. That is the dilemma, and few anticipate that the governing Liberal Democratic Party will allow itself to be stampeded into the adoption of any plan that would do major damage to itself or to some of its members. Simultaneously, the opposition parties can be expected to continue to raise the issue of fairness in the numerical allocation of seats, whenever it is to their political advantage to do so.

The House of Representatives Electoral System

The 511 members are elected from only 130 districts all but one of which are multiple-member constituencies, with 47 districts that elect three Representatives, 41 that elect four and another 41 that elect five. There is one single-member constituency, that of the Amami Islands off the southern coast of Kyūshū – an anomaly resulting from their return to Japanese administrative jurisdiction shortly after the end of the Occupation era, but some twenty years prior to the reversion of Okinawa in 1972.

In all of the districts, a voter casts his ballot for only one candidate, with the top three, four or five (depending on how many are to be elected in a particular constituency) being declared the winners. Over the years, various proposals have been put forth to simplify the system, even though most Japanese do not find it to be particularly perplexing. For example, while Tanaka Kakuei was Prime Minister (1972–4) he introduced a plan that would have combined a single-member district system with proportional representation. His proposal proved to be extremely controversial and politically damaging to his standing as an individual who presumably understood better than anyone else the art of the possible in the world of Japanese politics. (This particular episode has been overshadowed in recent years by his apparent lack of judgment in accepting tainted funds from agents of the Lockheed Corporation in their efforts to insure the sale of Tristar L1011s to All Nippon Airways.)

One additional factor needs to be considered at the outset in assessing the electoral system of the House of Representatives. It is that this chamber has the final voice in formally electing Japan's chief political executive, the Prime Minister. "The Prime Minister shall be designated from among the members of the Diet . . . If the House of Representatives and the House of Councillors disagree . . . the decision of the House of Representatives shall be the decision of the Diet (Constitution, Chapter V, Article 67)." This individual, as in any parliamentary system, should have the support of a majority of the members, preferably belonging to a single political party or, alternatively, to a coalition of parties. Hence, if one political party wishes to elect its leader as the new Prime Minister, it follows that it must have won at least 256 seats out of the total of 511. There are, however, as has been noted, only 130 districts.

To capture the ultimate prize in Japanese politics, therefore, a political party must win an average of two seats in each of the districts, or compensate for losses in some by winning extra seats in some of the others. In turn, achieving this objective absolutely requires that candidates belonging to the same party compete with each other in the same electoral district. It is this circumstance that has contributed to the perpetuation of factionalism, particularly in the Liberal Democratic Party. Only the Japan Socialist Party, of the opposition parties, has had to face a similar dilemma; but, as its fortunes have declined, there are fewer and fewer districts in which it has supported more than one candidate. In the 1983 House of Representatives election, for example, the JSP was able to elect two members in three districts and three members in one district. There were, in fact, only seventeen districts in which the Socialists ran more than one candidate.

The other opposition parties – the Kōmeitō, the Democratic Socialist Party, the Japan Communist Party and the very small Social Democratic Federation – only endorse one candidate in each constituency. (The JCP has supported two candidates in Kyoto's First and Second District, on occasion successfully. However, the party's insistence on running its own candidates in most districts has had deleterious consequences, especially for the Socialists.) This means that none of the opposition parties can hope to elect its leader as Prime Minister, unless it is as head of a coalition. For the time being, that is so unlikely a prospect that it can be dismissed.

Tables 2.2 and 2.3 provide an overview of the respective strengths of the governing LDP and its Opposition in the House of Representatives since the 27 May 1958 General Election. The LDP, until the 1976 election, had controlled between 58 percent and 64 percent of the seats in the House of Representatives. Since 1976, however, it has been barely able to retain control over a majority of seats in that chamber, with the notable exception of the results it achieved in the contest of 22 June 1980 which was exceptional for at least two reasons. First, incumbent Prime Minister Ōhira Masayoshi had died in office ten days prior to the polling date. His death brought out an outpouring of "sympathy votes (*dōjōhyō*)." Secondly, it was the only election in the entire postwar period, when both the entire membership of the House of Representatives and half of the House of Councillors were simultaneously elected, thus bringing out an exceptionally high 74.6 percent of the eligible voters to the polls (Baerwald, 1980b). In 1979 and 1983, by contrast, only 68 percent of those eligible voted. It is generally accepted that the LDP benefits by a higher turnout of voters. Certainly, the 1980 results would support that conclusion.

With the 18 December 1983 General Election, the LDP's number of seats fell back to where it had been in the latter half of the 1970s. Only by inviting the Unaffiliated conservatives to its

Table 2.2 LDP Seats in the House of Representatives 1958–85 (endorsed LDP candidates, Unaffiliated candidates who joined LDP, and NLCers after creation of LDP–NLC Coalition Cabinet in December 1983)

Election date	LDP endorsed	Unaffiliated[a]	NLC	Total LDP	Total seats	% LDP
27 May 1958	287	11	—	298	467	64
20 November 1960	296	4	—	300	467	64
21 November 1963	283	12	—	295	467	63
29 January 1967	277	5	—	282	486	58
27 December 1969	288	12	—	300	486	62
10 December 1972	271	12	—	283	491	58
5 December 1976	249	11	[17]	260[b]	511	51
7 October 1979	248	9	[4]	257[b]	511	50
22 June 1980	284	5	[12]	289[b]	511	57
18 December 1983	250	8	8	266[c]	511	52

Source: *Kokkai Binran* [Diet Handbook], for relevant years.

Notes:

[a] In nearly all of the English language literature on Japanese politics, the Unaffiliated candidates have been listed as Independents. A few actually are; however, most of them are candidates who belong to a political party, but who either could not obtain that party's endorsement or who decided to run with the support of two or more parties which, for tactical reasons, decided jointly to back one candidate.

[b] LDP (Liberal Democratic Party) strength without New Liberal Club (NLC).

[c] LDP strength with New Liberal Club members added.

In the 1976 election, and thereafter, the LDP could also count on the support of the so-called Lockheed LDPers: Tanaka Kakuei (1976–83), Hashimoto Tomisaburo (1976–80), Satō Takayuki (1980–3); and Matsuno Raizo (1980 election only) who was not linked directly to the Lockheed scandal, but was tainted by financial peculations.

ranks could the LDP retain a minimal majority (258 seats), and only by adding the eight members of the New Liberal Club into the coalition could the majority retain control over the major standing committees in the House of Representatives. (This point will be developed further in Chapter 3.) In effect, with the 1983 election, former Prime Minister Ōhira Masayoshi's trenchant insight, "We have entered into the era of a 'close balance of power (*hakuchū*)' between ourselves and the Opposition" (Ōhira, 1979) would seem to be unassailable.

Inevitably, as the LDP's fortunes have declined, those of the

Table 2.3 Opposition Party Seats in the House of Representatives 1958–85 (endorsed Opposition Party candidates, and Unaffiliated candidates who joined one of the Opposition Parties after being elected)

Election date	DSP	Kōmeitō	SDF	JSP	JCP	Unaffiliated[a]	Total opposition	Total seats	% opposition
27 May 1958	—	—	—	166	1	2	169	467	36
20 November 1960	17	—	—	145	3	2	167	467	35
21 November 1963	23	—	—	144	5	—	172	467	37
29 January 1967	30	25	—	140	5	4	204	486	42
27 December 1969	31	47	—	90	14	4	186	486	38
10 December 1972	19	29	—	118	38	2			
				1[b]	1[b]		208	491	42
5 December 1976	29	55	—	123	17	7			
					2[b]		234	511	46
7 October 1979	35	57	2	107	39	6			
	1[b]	1[b]			2[b]		250	511	49
22 June 1980	32	33	3	107	29	4			
	1[b]	1[b]					210	511	41
18 December 1983	38	58	3	112	26	4			
	1[b]	1[b]		1[b]	1[b]		245	511	48

Source: *Kokkai Binran* [Diet Handbook], for relevant years.

Notes:

[a]See note regarding Unaffiliated candidates in Table 2.2.

[b]Unaffiliated candidates backed by a particular party.

DSP = Democratic Socialist Party; SDF = Social Democratic Federation; JSP = Japan Socialist Party; JCP = Japan Communist Party.

NLC has not been included because of its close affiliation with the LDP. Total number of seats will not add up to 511, and percent will not add up to 100 for the 1976, 1979, and 1980 elections unless NLC seats (in brackets in Table 2.2) are included.

opposition parties have prospered, so that they controlled between 46 percent and 49 percent of the seats in the House of Representatives after the 1976, 1979 and 1983 General Elections. However, these parties, as noted in Chapter 1, do not appear to be any closer to being able to elect a Prime Minister by themselves than they were thirty years ago, when the LDP's opposition was much weaker. The LDP has managed to strengthen its position by inviting the New Liberal Club to be its partner and the Democratic Socialist Party and Kōmeitō have leaders who can barely restrain themselves from pleading to allow one of their own to join in a coalition Cabinet with the LDP. To reiterate a point made earlier: as the ranks of the Opposition have swelled, they also have splintered. Nonetheless, the weight of their numbers has influenced proceedings in the Diet, a generalization that will be addressed much more fully in succeeding chapters.

This overview of election outcomes for the House of Representatives is factually correct. What is lacking, thus far, are possible answers to the question: how were these electoral results achieved? Once again, the question is easier to ask than to answer. Few purposes would be served by re-analyzing elections that have been covered previously (Blaker, 1979). Hence, the discussion will focus on the last four elections, those of 1976, 1979, 1980 and 1983, with the relevant data summarized in Table 2.4.

Most analyses of Japanese national elections for the House of Representatives have emphasized the different types of electoral districts (Category A being metropolitan, Category B being urban, Category C being semi-urban and Category D being rural). There are variations on this theme, such as the one used by Nisihira and Passin (1979). In it, the basic variable for distinguishing between differing types of districts is the percentage of the labor force in the primary industrial sector (agriculture, forestry and fishery). Under this scheme, there are five categories of districts (Metropolitan, Urban, Intermediate, Semi-rural and Rural) (Nisihira, 1979). Both of these classifications, especially when combined with the electoral results in the three-, four- and five-member districts, are extremely useful in obtaining an overview of which party is likely to do well, or poorly, in which category of districts. Thus, the LDP does well in rural and semi-urban districts, but has trouble in the densely populated metropolitan constituencies. Conversely, the opposition parties – especially the Kōmeitō, DSP, JCP, NLC and Social Democratic Federation – tend to perform well in the urban districts, and poorly in the countryside. The JSP's support is scattered, as will be indicated.

These kinds of distinctions among types of districts have been helpful in analyses of voting behavior trends and in attempts to predict election results. Japan's major print and electronic media have used these indices to project outcomes and so have foreigners, myself included. My own predictions have tended to be dismally inaccurate, and so have been nearly everyone else's. Our failure, it seems to me, has stemmed from being far too concerned with aggregate vote totals (nation-wide or by category of districts) instead of focusing on the districts themselves, and then attempting to undertake the aggregating.

Admittedly, the Japanese media do try to provide district by district analyses before elections, but it is difficult to determine whether they should be taken literally. One problem with them is that tremendous attention is paid to analyzing who among the candidates will win, rather than the number of seats that the LDP or the opposition parties may be able to control in the House of Representatives. In this connection, it must be emphasized that Table 2.4 does not differentiate among individual Liberal Democrats or Socialists (should there be more than one in a given district) who are elected. Its sole purpose is to indicate the party affiliation of those who have been victorious.

The three-part categorization in Table 2.4 of "Stable" (no change in party affiliation of those elected), "Minimally Unstable" (one seat changed in party affiliation), and "Unstable" (two or more seats changed in party affiliation) over the past four elections emphasizes election results: who won, who lost? Furthermore, this scheme provides a single overview of stability and change in the preferences of voters in specific election districts. Using it should allow us to gain a simple overview of meaningful changes in voter preferences in a given election and to assess the effectiveness of each party's strategy in coping with the imperatives of the multiple-member medium-sized constituency system that provides the most significant variable in elections for the House of Representatives in Japan.

One generalization is immediately apparent. Over the past four elections, 374 of the 511 seats (or 73 percent) have not changed party affiliation. This datum is particularly noteworthy in that over these four contests, a shift of 36 seats among endorsed LDP candidates who were elected was recorded (see Table 2.2). Very few of these shifts could have been anticipated by elaborate analyses of slowly changing socio-economic variables characterizing Japanese voters. Instead, the specific situations in each district – for example, the number of endorsed LDP candidates as opposed to the number of opposition party candidates that ran, and how the popular vote was distributed among them – tended to be considerably more important in determining electoral outcomes. These generalizations will be tested by analyzing what transpired in six districts.

The "Stable" Category of Districts

Among the stable districts the vast majority have a pattern of two Liberal Democrats and one Socialist (thirteen, including Hokkaido's third district) or three Liberal Democrats and one Socialist (twelve) for a total of 25 out of the 34 constituencies in

Table 2.4 House of Representatives Elections 1976, 1979, 1980, 1983: Seats by Party and Type of Districts

	No. of districts	Type of district	No. of seats	Stable seats: LDP and allies	Stable seats: Opposition parties	Stable seats: Total	Unstable seats: LDP and allies	Unstable seats: Opposition parties	Unstable seats: Total
Stable		3A		74L	33S		—	—	—
districts		6*B*		1U	5K		—	—	—
(no seats		17C			5C		—	—	—
changed)		8*D*			1D		—	—	—
					1F		—	—	—
Sub-total	34		120	75	45	120			
Minimally		16A		103L	36S		72L	74S	
unstable		13*B*		1N	19K		13N	21K	
districts		19C		1U	5C		13U	30C	
(one seat		12*D*			16D			16D	
changed)								1F	
									(240)
Sub-total	60		241	105	76	181	98	142	60

Unstable districts (two or more seats changed)		14*A* 9*B* 10*C* 3*D*		45L 1N	11S 8K 1C 7D		86L 16N 21U	62S 59K 37C 23D 4F	(308)
Sub-total	36		150	46	27	73	123	185	77
Totals		33*A* 28*B* 46*C* 23*D*		222L 2N 2U	80S 32K 11C 24D 1F		158L 29N 34U	136S 80K 67C 39D 5F	(548)
	130		511	226	148	374	221	327	137

Notes:
Type of district: *A* = metropolitan; *B* = urban; *C* = semi-urban; *D* = rural.
Parties: L = Liberal Democratic Party; N = New Liberal Club; U = Unaffiliated; S = Japan Socialist Party;
K = Kōmeitō; C = Japan Communist Party; D = Democratic Socialist Party; F = Social Democratic Federation.
Numbers in parentheses are the total of unstable seats contested over 4 elections.
For detailed data, see Table 2.26 at the end of this chapter.

Table 2.5 Gumma Third District (4 members)

Candidate	Votes received in elections of 1976	1979	1980	1983
Fukuda Takeo (L. Fukuda)	148,736+	122,542+	128,542+	129,100+
Nakasone Yasuhiro (L. Nakasone)	56,454+	95,961+	96,930+	117,970+
Yamaguchi Tsuruo (Socialist)	65,061+	62,148+	64,971+	77,301+
Obuchi Keizo (L. Tanaka)	76,012+	62,375+	59,647+	49,028+
Kōmeitō candidate	45,048*	43,537*	41,641*	—
Communist candidate	18,485*	18,079*	15,643*	18,643*

Source: *Kokkai Binran* [Diet Handbook], for relevant years.
Notes: + = winner; * = loser.
(L. . . .) = Liberal Democratic Party and the faction affiliation.

this category, or 71.4 percent of the total. A typical district in this grouping would be Gumma's Third District, which is also famous in the annals of Japanese politics because of having been the personal battleground of two of Japan's Prime Ministers, Fukuda Takeo (1976–8) and Nakasone Yasuhiro (1982–).

This district has been a model of regularity in electing three Liberal Democrats, two of whom are world-famous, and one Socialist. Results are predictable as soon as the official list of candidates has been determined. The only excitement – and it can be fierce – is generated by the question of which of the two top contenders will come in first. It is this aspect of the contest that brings out the campaign workers and the voters, and accounts for the enormous energy that is expended.

I toured this constituency again three days prior to the 1983 election and was once more impressed by the extraordinary effort that the surrogates for the principals (who are above campaigning for themselves) were putting forth, especially for Nakasone who, as the incumbent Prime Minister, should – by all that was presumed to be proper – come in first. Nonetheless, his old rival, former Prime Minister Fukuda, won with more votes, probably with help from Kōmeitō adherents whom the Fukuda forces assiduously wooed and who (in 1983) did not have a candidate of their own to support.

That both Fukuda and Nakasone, as well as Liberal Democrat Obuchi and Socialist Yamaguchi had been assured of victory all along (the fifth candidate in the four-member district was a Communist who had minimal support) was of less moment than that a former Prime Minister ultimately won with a larger number of votes than the incumbent. Just because a district is in the "stable" category does not mean, therefore, that all is quiet on the campaign front. Quite the contrary can be (and often is) the case.

The "Minimally Unstable" Category of Districts

The category of districts in which one seat has changed over the last four elections includes a limited variety of patterns. Kagawa's Second District is tucked away into the north central region of Shikoku (the smallest of Japan's main islands) and is "rural" (Category D) instead of "semi-rural" (Category C) as in the case of Gumma, Third District.

Until 1983, this district too had been returning two Liberal Democrats – one of whom, Ōhira Masayoshi, became Prime Minister of Japan in late 1978 for an all-too-brief one and a half

Table 2.6 Kagawa Second District (3 members)

Candidate	Votes received in elections of 1976	1979	1980	1983
Ōhira Masayoshi (L. Ōhira)	98,412⁺	126,890⁺	—	—
Morita Hajime (L. Suzuki)	—	—	151,546⁺	81,078⁺
Kato Tsunetaro (L. Miki–Kōmoto)	56,050⁺	52,636⁺	35,435⁺	53,734⁺
Kubo Hiroshi (Socialist)	55,778⁺	48,369⁺	44,027⁺	53,425*
Tsukihara Shigemasa (L. Fukuda)	—	—	—	54,082⁺
Communist candidate	16,927*	12,484*	9,829*	6,033*
Unaffiliated candidate	—	3,345*	3,016*	906*

Source: *Kokkai Binran* [Diet Handbook], for relevant years.
Notes: + = winner; * = loser.
(L. . . .) = Liberal Democratic Party and the faction affiliation.

years – and one Socialist. Ōhira died just ten days prior to the 1980 election and his son-in-law Morita Hajime stepped in at the last moment as the deceased Prime Minister's replacement. The results reflect an enormous outpouring of "sympathy votes (*dōjōhyō*)" for Morita; so many, in fact, that had the configuration of LDP and non-LDP votes been different, the results might have allowed another opposition party candidate to defeat Kato who managed to win with an exceedingly small share (14.5 percent) of the votes cast. Had the over 200,000 votes cast for LDP candidates been distributed among three Liberal Democrats, all of them could have been elected.

This insight allowed a third LDPer, Tsukihara (Fukuda adherent), to seek and receive the party's endorsement for the 1983 election, and by winning to lead to the defeat of Socialist Kubo who had been in office for four consecutive terms. It is also noteworthy that this change in the party affiliation of one of the elected representatives would not have been noticed on the basis of aggregate vote totals for the LDP candidates alone. To all intents and purposes, the total LDP vote (186,981 in 1980 and 188,894 in 1983) remained constant between the two elections.

Inevitably, there are also districts in this group of constituencies in which only one seat changed where Liberal Democratic Party Headquarters allows a secure seat to be squandered by endorsement decisions that are lax or excessively optimistic. Osaka's Fifth District illustrates what can happen.

As Table 2.7 indicates, the voters had returned a Liberal Democrat, Democratic Socialist, Kōmeitō and Communist combination of candidates during each of the 1976, 1979 and 1980 elections, with the Socialist, Wada Sadao, coming in as the losing "runner-up (*jiten*)." In each of these contests, the Liberal Democratic Party had endorsed one candidate, Kino Haruo (Ōhira-Suzuki faction). He was popular and had come in as the first-place winner twice, in 1980 by a comfortable 30,000 plus vote margin. Yet, in 1983, the LDP endorsed four candidates. As might have been predicted with complete certainty, all four went down to defeat by splitting up the available "conservative" votes among themselves; thus Wada, the Socialist, was allowed to win his second term. He had been elected once before in the 1972 contest.

Far more frequent, however, is the tendency for the opposition parties to permit an extra Liberal Democrat to be elected. In Osaka's Fifth District, the LDP had made an error, but it is the kind of mistake that Headquarters can control if the party's leadership is willing to enforce discipline over various faction chiefs

Table 2.7 Osaka Fifth District (4 members)

Candidate	Votes received in election of 1976	1979	1980	1983
Kino Haruo (L. Ōhira–Suzuki)	136,176+	122,565+	176,649+	59,039*
Nishimura Shozo (Democratic Socialist)	133,590+	111,445+	142,196+	109,497+
Masaki Yoshiaki (Kōmeitō)	125,672+	136,399+	132,246+	143,532+
Araki Hiroshi (Communist)	109,352+	—	—	—
Fujita Sumi (Communist)	—	132,150+	134,646+	122,200+
Wada Sadao (Socialist)	103,891*	99,983*	110,495*	100,734+
	U.30,951*	N. 33,079*	—	—
Ikejiri Hisakazu (L.)	—	—	—	58,527*
Harada Takashi (L.)	—	—	—	49,062*
Yamanaka Akiyoshi (L.)	—	—	—	29,490*

Source: *Kokkai Binran* [Diet Handbook], for relevant years.
Notes: + = winner; * = loser.
(L. . . .) = Liberal Democratic Party and the faction affiliation;
U. = Unaffiliated; N. = New Liberal Club.

who are pleading for their followers to be among those potential candidates who are officially endorsed. By contrast, the opposition parties each have their own claimants. Furthermore, their rivalries are between and among separate political parties rather than factions within one (admittedly loose) organization. This generalization is illustrated by Tokushima's Prefecture-wide District which elects five members.

The voters of this constituency consistently had returned three Liberal Democrats and one Socialist, with the fifth seat going twice each to either a fourth Liberal Democrat or a Kōmeitō candidate. As a semi-rural (Category C) district, it is a traditional stronghold of the conservatives and the home base of former Prime Minister Miki Takeo (1974–6) who celebrated his eighteenth re-election in 1983, thus making him the most senior parliamentarian in the Diet. It is also unusual in that two Liberal Democrats (Morishita and Gotōda) belong to the same faction (Tanaka). However, in

Table 2.8 Tokushima Prefecturewide District (5 members)

Candidates	Votes received in elections of 1976	1979	1980	1983
Miki Takeo (L. Miki)	102,519+	72,566+	90,544+	63,891+
Gotōda Masaharu (L. Tanaka)	68,990+	66,948+	85,710+	81,975+
Morishita Motoharu (L. Tanaka)	61,464+	71,935+	67,409+	56,855+
Hirosawa Naoki (Kōmeitō)	58,623+	58,230*	—	—
Endō Kazuyoshi (Kōmeitō)	—	—	54,425*	70,032+
Inoue Hironori (Socialist)	54,136+	74,187+	67,127+	54,262+
Maeda Sadaichi (Socialist)	—	—	—	48,339*
Akita Daisuke (L. Fukuda)	53,965*	87,719+	70,090+	47,666*
Bandō Kazuo	38,786*	—	—	—
(Democratic Socialist) Shimizu Ryōji			—	11,900*
Abe Fumiaki	29,798*	20,208*	—	—
(Communist) Fukui Takao			13,588*	
Zinno Yoshiaki				13,315*

Source: *Kokkai Binran* [Diet Handbook], for relevant years.
Notes: + = winner; * = loser.
(L. . . .) = Liberal Democratic Party and the faction affiliation.

the 1979 election, one of the Liberal Democrats could have been defeated by the Kōmeitō's Hirosawa if the Communist Abe, who had no chance of election, had not entered the lists. The same lack of mutual support allowed the fourth LDPer to win in 1980. In 1983, the second Socialist (Maeda) would have been an easy winner if the Democratic Socialist Shimizu and the Communist Zinno had not syphoned off 25,000 meaningless votes – again.

The "Unstable" Category of Districts

It is, as might have been anticipated, those districts in which two or more seats changed in the party affiliation of those elected that one can observe the full flowering of the multiple-member district system. Two-thirds of them are in the highly congested metropolitan (A) and urban (B) categories: Tokyo and its surrounding Prefectures (Saitama, Chiba and Kanagawa) to which so many Tokyo-ites return to sleep; the Chūbu (centering on the city of Nagoya in Aichi Prefecture) and the Kansai (Osaka and its environs, especially Hyōgo Prefecture) regions; the belt that extends along the Inland Sea coast of Honshū (Okayama, Hiroshima and Yamaguchi Prefectures); and finally, the increasingly congested northeastern region of Kyūshū, centering around Fukuoka, Ōita and Kumamoto Prefectures. These are the geographic areas in which the greatest volatility of voter attitudes and preferences are reflected. It is here, also, that Japan's future politics are being shaped. Each of these districts is worthy of extensive analysis, but the two examples that will be discussed are drawn from Japan's pre-modern and ancient capitals: Kyoto and Nara. Both are located in the Kansai region.

Kyoto has been a stronghold of the Communist Party for many years, despite its reputation as a tourist attraction for its temple gardens and as a museum of traditional Japanese arts. Nonetheless, over these four elections, its citizens have shown their three favorite candidates to be one Liberal Democrat, one Democratic Socialist and one Kōmeitō member. The other two seats have fluctuated among a second Liberal Democrat twice, and a Socialist and Communist three times each. In the 1979 election, Maeo Shigesaburō, who had been Speaker of the House of Representatives, lost by an agonizing 174 votes to Socialist Yamada whom he in turn displaced by an enormous margin of nearly 100,000 votes eight months later. It was Maeo's last triumph as he died in July 1981.

In 1983, the Communist Teramae lost for the simple reason that his presumed comrade Arita picked up (in comparison with 1980) an additional 8,500 votes, thus insuring the defeat of both. (Kyoto, as was noted, is the only Prefecture in which the Communist Party has supported two candidates simultaneously.) In neighboring Kyoto's First District, it did manage to have both elected in 1972 and 1979. Clearly, however, in Kyoto's Second District the JCP had badly miscalculated the level of voter support available for its candidates in 1983. One other point: the factional affiliation of the two Liberal Democrats changed. Both Tanigaki Sen'ichi and his son Tanigaki Sadakazu were Ōhira-Suzuki faction loyalists; Maeo (also of the Ōhira-Suzuki faction), however, was replaced by Nonaka who belongs to the Tanaka group. It is this

Table 2.9 Kyoto Second District (5 members)

Candidate	Votes received in elections of 1976	1979	1980	1983
Teramae Iwao (Communist)	136,103⁺	136,730⁺	104,122⁺	92,666*
Nishinaka Kiyoshi (Kōmeitō)	126,331⁺	106,917⁺	94,105⁺	108,665⁺
Maeo Shigesaburō (L. Ōhira)	119,984⁺	103,005*	182,922⁺	—
Nonaka Hiromu (L. Tanaka)	—	—	—	136,357⁺
Yamada Yoshiharu (Socialist)	118,684⁺	103,179⁺	94,053*	—
Yamanaka Sueharu (Socialist)	—	—	—	98,516⁺
Tamaki Kazuya (Democratic Socialist)	108,223⁺	121,344⁺	113,649⁺	104,515⁺
Tanigaki Sen'ichi (L. Ōhira)	100,785*	112,719⁺	119,631⁺	—
Tanigaki Sadakazu (L. Suzuki)	—	—	—	125,446⁺
Unaffiliated candidate	2,195*	3,633*	—	—
Arita Mitsuo (Communist)	—	—	49,431*	58,023*

Source: *Kokkai Binran* [Diet Handbook], for relevant years.
Notes: ⁺ = winner; * = loser.
(L. . . .) = Liberal Democratic Party and the faction affiliation.

kind of shift in the factional allegiance of elected Liberal Democrats which adds that extra element of spice to elections; and if multiplied throughout the 129 multi-member districts, results in the ever-changing balance of power among the factions in the governing party. Nara's Prefecture-wide Constituency illustrates the foregoing point as well as other imponderables in the workings of the multiple-member district system.

Nara is, with Kyoto, one of the two most ancient capitals of Japan's recorded history. It remains as a marvelous repository of traditional arts and architecture. Nara's contemporary citizens, however, are as politically divided and inconstant in their preferences as their counterparts in the major metropolitan centers of Tokyo, Nagoya, Osaka and Kita-Kyushu in Fukuoka. Over the last four elections, they have returned two Liberal Democrats (one

Table 2.10 Nara Prefecturewide District (5 members)

Candidate	Votes received in elections of 1976	1979	1980	1983
Okuno Seisuke (L. no faction)	100,550⁺	115,285⁺	128,654⁺	85,927⁺
Yoshida Yukihisa (Democratic Socialist)	97,309⁺	89,858⁺	85,303⁺	86,423⁺
Kawamoto Toshimi (Socialist)	81,546⁺	65,186•	89,152⁺	76,378•
Hayashi Takanori (Kōmeitō)	77,912⁺	85,318⁺	77,188•	—
Morimoto Koji (Kōmeitō)	—	—	—	95,923⁺
Hattori Yasuji (L. Ōhira)	75,265⁺	104,119⁺	—	77,213•
Maeda Masao (L. Ishii)	69,186•	—	—	—
Maeda Takeshi (L. Tanaka)	—	—	116,530⁺	58,228•
Tsuji Daiichi (Communist)	60,351•	92,150⁺	91,265⁺	80,307⁺
Kagita Chōzaburo (U., joined L. Nakasone)	—	—	—	83,523⁺

Source: *Kokkai Binran* [Diet Handbook], for relevant years.
Notes: ⁺ = winner; • = loser.
(L. . . .) = Liberal Democratic Party and the faction affiliation; U. = Unaffiliated.

of whom ran as an Unaffiliated candidate), Socialist Kawamoto twice, Kōmeitō candidates Hayashi twice and Morimoto once, Democratic Socialist Yoshida four times, and Communist Tsuji three times.

Put differently, in 1976 Democratic Socialist Yoshida replaced then incumbent Liberal Democrat Maeda Masao (of the old Ishii faction that has since disappeared from the scene); in 1979 Communist Tsuji replaced Socialist Kawamoto; in 1980 Kawamoto made a come-back and displaced the Kōmeitō's Hayashi; in turn in 1983, the new Kōmeitō candidate Morimoto replaced the Socialist, and simultaneously new Liberal Democrat Kagita (who ran as an Unaffiliated candidate but joined the governing party's Nakasone faction after being elected) defeated the by now Tanaka faction's Maeda Takeshi (Masao's son), resulting in a Nakasone adherent being victorious over a potential Tanaka follower.

Only Okuno (LDP with no factional affiliation) and Yoshida (DSP) have been consistent winners over the entire span of four elections covered in this analysis. The second LDP seat has moved from Hattori (Ōhira faction) to Maeda (Ishii, and later, Tanaka faction), to Kagita (Nakasone faction), and the fourth and fifth seats have been the battlegrounds of the Socialist, Kōmeitō and Communist candidates. By way of summary, two-fifths of Nara's voters support Liberal Democrats and three-fifths prefer their opponents, in various combinations.

Each of these districts – Gumma Third, Kagawa Second, Osaka Fifth, Tokushima, Kyoto Second and Nara – reflects certain variations on basic themes that can be replicated in each of the remaining multi-member constituencies. For the Liberal Democrats, the essence of the tactical problem is three-fold: (1) to endorse the correct number of candidates, (2) to balance the votes that each candidate obtains, and (3) to search for methods that might limit the number of Unaffiliated candidates whose goal (if they are conservatives, and most are) is to unseat one of the officially endorsed Liberal Democrats.

For the opposition parties, the essence of coping with the requirements imposed by the electoral system is basically the same, but is complicated by their pursuit of separate strategies: the Socialists wish to continue to be the major Opposition Party and, therefore, endorse more candidates than their shrinking level of voter support would prudently dictate; the Kōmeitō and the DSP tend to run exactly that number of candidates that have a realistic chance of being elected in targeted districts (this is far more difficult than might immediately be apparent, if for no other reason than that the percentage of voter turnout is not easily predictable); and the JCP tends to run one candidate in nearly every district, even in those in which its candidates have extremely limited support, have no chance of success and who, therefore, syphon off votes from other opposition party candidates who do have a chance of being elected. For both the governing and opposition parties, this electoral system is a species of Russian roulette in which one's presumed political allies often turn out to be one's most severe rivals.

"Joint Candidate" Strategy among Opposition Parties

In recent elections, the opposition parties have tried to experiment with joint candidacies as one method of coping with their lack of unity. They began to do so, on a limited basis, in the 1972 election when the Kōmeitō and Democratic Socialist Party jointly endorsed thirteen candidates (seven Kōmeitō and six Democratic Socialists). Two of them, one from each party, were successful. In 1976, these two parties again joined in supporting ten candidates (five from each), six of whom were successful (three from each party). That same year, the Socialists in one instance backed a Kōmeitō candidate (who won) and there were three Socialist candidates who received the Kōmeitō's support, of whom two won. Table 2.11 summarizes the performance of these joint candidates in the 1979, 1980 and 1983 elections.

These joint candidacies have helped some of the opposition parties, especially the centrist Kōmeitō and Democratic Socialist Party. However, the Socialists have hardly benefitted at all; probably for one major reason. One opposition party is notable by

Table 2.11 Joint Opposition Party Candidacies: House of Representatives

		Elections of	
Parties	1979	1980	1983
S-D-K	—	1K^{+}	—
S-K-F	—	—	1K^{+}
S-K	1S^{+},1K^{+}	3S^{+}	4S(3^{+},1$^{\bullet}$), 1K^{+}
S-F	—	—	3S(2^{+}, 1$^{\bullet}$)
K-D-N-F	2U^{+},2K(1^{+},1$^{\bullet}$), 2D^{+}, 2N$^{\bullet}$, 2F^{+}	5K$^{\bullet}$, 6D(2^{+},4$^{\bullet}$), 2N^{+}, 1F^{+},1U^{+}	2K^{+}, 4D(3^{+},1$^{\bullet}$), 1N^{+}, 1F^{+}
K-D-N	—	1K^{+}	—
K-D-F	—	5K(2^{+}, 3$^{\bullet}$), 4D(3^{+}, 1$^{\bullet}$)	2K^{+}, 3D(2^{+}, 1$^{\bullet}$), 1U^{+}
K-D	12K(10^{+}, 2$^{\bullet}$), 10D(4^{+}, 6$^{\bullet}$)	7K(2^{+}, 5$^{\bullet}$), 4D(2^{+}, 2$^{\bullet}$)	11K(10^{+}, 1$^{\bullet}$), 5D^{+}
K-N	—	—	1K^{+}
K-F	—	—	2K^{+}
D-N-F	—	1N$^{\bullet}$, 1F^{+}	4D(2^{+}, 2$^{\bullet}$), 2F(1^{+}, 1$^{\bullet}$)
D-N	—	—	2D^{+}, 1N$^{\bullet}$
D-F	—	—	5D(4^{+}, 1$^{\bullet}$)
N-F	—	1F^{+}	3N$^{\bullet}$
Summary	34(23^{+}, 11$^{\bullet}$)	43(22^{+}, 21$^{\bullet}$)	59(46^{+}, 13$^{\bullet}$)

Source: *Yomiuri Shimbun*, 20 December 1983, p.7.

Notes: $^{+}$ = winner; $^{\bullet}$ = loser.

S = Socialist; K = Kōmeitō; D = Democratic Socialist; N = New Liberal Club; F = Social Democratic Federation.

its absence: the JCP. Yet, it is the Communist candidates who frequently are the spoilers, as will be indicated shortly.

Before discussing this issue, it is necessary to stop for a moment, and to explore the implications of using the designation "going down together (*tomodaore*)" in connection with the lack of cooperation between the Socialists and Communists. *Tomodaore* has been used thus far exclusively in connection with too many Liberal Democrats (including some who pose as Unaffiliated candidates) running in the same district and splitting up the available "conservative" voters among themselves (each voter being only allowed to write the name of *one* candidate on the ballot) and, therefore, having all of them "go down together" in defeat.

Thus, in the examples of *tomodaore* that follow, customary usage is being violated. Furthermore, the situation that Socialist supporters and Communist partisans face is fundamentally different from that of their "conservative" counterparts who all tend to be LDP supporters. The JSP and JCP are separate political parties, however, with each having its distinctive ideology and policy agenda.

Hence, it can (and, undoubtedly will be) argued that *tomodaore* should not be used in assessing the consequences of a lack of cooperation among, primarily, the Socialists and Communists. After all, there is absolutely no guarantee that Communist voters would support a Socialist candidate, or vice versa. Using the concept does have meaning, nonetheless, if for no other reason than that it illuminates the adverse consequences for the opposition parties in persisting to split up the potentially available anti-LDP vote between separate candidates who go down to defeat together.

Table 2.12 Opposition Parties "*Tomodaore* (Going down Together)": (House of Representatives, 18 December 1983 Election)

Iwate 2 (4 members)	*Miyagi 1* (5 members)	*Saitama 1* (3 members)	*Saitama 2* (3 members)
D. 67,778[+]	L. 135,259[+]	K. 112,551[+]	N. 181,385[+]
L. 66,734[+]	L. 114,369[+]	L. 107,209[+]	L. 128,152[+]
L. 64,739[+]	K. 107,574[+]	L. 105,660[+]	K. 121,939[+]
L. 63,212[+]	L. 102,785[+]	C. 99,174[a]	S. 83,257[a]
S. 61,141[a]	L. 98,224[+]	S. 55,701[a]	C. 76,503[a]
C. 11,401[a]	C. 88,990[a]		
	S. 81,868[a]		
[b] 72,542	[b] 170,858	[b] 154,871	[b] 159,760

Saitama 4	*Chiba 3*	*Tokyo 7*	*Niigata 3*
(3 members)	(5 members)	(4 members)	(5 members)
K. 131,715+	L. 85,327+	F. 127,700+	U. 220,761+
L. 112,445+	L. 67,008+	K. 110,458+	L. 48,324+
L. 104,722+	L. 58,238+	C. 103,751+	L. 47,118+
L. 96,816•	K. 58,085+	L. 99,110+	S. 44,088+
S. 94,592[a]	L. 50,552+	S. 80,496[a]	L. 40,931+
C. 38,099[a]	S. 45,904[a]	L. 70,908•	U. 28,045•
	U. 45,605•	D. 49,227[a]	S. 27,597[a]
	L. 38,344•		C. 16,321[a]
	C. 18,377[a]		
[b] 133,051	[b] 64,281	[b] 129,723	[b] 43,918

Mie 2	*Kyoto 1*	*Wakayama 2*	*Tottori*
(4 members)	(5 members)	(3 members)	(4 members)
L. 79,584+	L. 58,059+	L. 58,684+	L. 80,046+
L. 61,355+	K. 56,293+	L. 53,611+	S. 67,603+
S. 57,759+	D. 54,913+	U. 47,713+(L.)	L. 67,054+
L. 55,583+	C. 47,135+	L. 36,927•	L. 66,121+
S. 48,654[a]	L. 46,994+	C. 32,241[a]	S. 61,752[a]
C. 11,992[a]	C. 44,662[a]	S. 27,574[a]	C. 8,935[a]
	S. 38,302[a]		
[b] 60,646	[b] 82,964	[b] 59,815	[b] 70,687

Hiroshima 3	*Kagawa 2*	*Fukuoka 1*	*Kagoshima 1*
(5 members)	(3 members)	(5 members)	(4 members)
L. 91,719+	L. 81,078+	K. 146,295+	S. 100,732+
D. 80,503+	L. 54,082+	S. 145,011+	L. 83,092+
K. 76,049+	L. 53,734+	L. 142,419+	L. 70,421+
L. 73,862+	S. 53,425[a]	L. 136,532+	S. 66,962[a]
S. 67,056[a]	C. 6,033[a]	L. 118,039+	C. 10,167[a]
C. 21,572[a]		F. 114,502[a]	
		C. 60,050[a]	
[b] 89,078	[b] 59,458	[b] 174,552	[b] 77,129

Source: *Kokkai Binran* [Diet Handbook], 1984, pp. 293–306.

Notes: + = winners; • = losers, but their party affiliation makes them irrelevant to the outcome.

[a] = Opposition party candidates, one of whom might have become a winner if the other had withdrawn and been willing to support the remaining opposition candidate. In each instance, a Liberal Democrat would have been defeated. This is basically the underlying rationale of "joint candidacies," but the Communists have not participated.

[b] = Total vote cast for the two opposition party candidates. In each instance, this vote total is at the very least higher than the last place winner.

L. = LDP; S. = JSP; K. = Kōmeitō; D. = DSP; C. = JCP; N. = New Liberal Club; F. = Social Democratic Federation; U. = Unaffiliated.

Only the most egregious examples have been selected. What is abundantly clear is that in most instances the Communist candidate interfered with the possibility of a Socialist being elected and thereby replacing that Liberal Democrat who came in last among the winners. Also to be noted is that in many constituencies (for example, in Iwate Second, Saitama Fourth, Chiba Third, Niigata Third – a very special case, because it is former Prime Minister Tanaka's district, Nagano Fourth, Gifu Second, Mie Second, Tottori, Hiroshima Third, Kagawa Second, Fukuoka First, and Kagoshima First), the Communist candidate had absolutely no chance of success. Inevitably, the JCP is going to have to decide whether its opponent is the governing LDP or the JSP. Until then, all the posturing about a "united front" is empty rhetoric.

The LDP also has its problems. Once again, only the most extreme examples, all from the 1983 election, have been included in Table 2.13. In each instance, the LDP quite simply endorsed too many candidates, or an LDP candidate had the misfortune of having the added competition of an Unaffiliated candidate who syphoned off enough votes to insure that both would lose. One can only empathize with the party's strategists in their efforts to determine how many supplicants for official endorsement should be anointed. The multiple member constituency system continues to impose its imponderable imperatives that do affect the outcome of an election.

The House of Councillors Election System

In actuality, of course, the 252 members of the House of Councillors compete in two different systems. One hundred are elected nation-wide. The only comparison that is readily available would be if all Senators in the United States Congress were elected from one national constituency instead of two from each State! The mind truly boggles even if Japan is much smaller geographically (roughly the size of Montana). On the other hand, Japan's population (120 million) is about half that of the population of the United States.

The remaining 152 Councillors are elected from Prefecture-wide constituencies: two elect eight Councillors, four elect six, fifteen elect four, and twenty-six elect two. However, only half the members are elected every three years. Hence, in each House of Councillors election, fifty national constituency seats (plus unfilled

Table 2.13 LDP "*Tomodaore* (Going down Together)": (House of Representatives, 18 December 1983 Election)

Hokkaido 5 (5 members)	*Chiba 1* (4 members)	*Tokyo 2* (5 members)	*Tokyo 6* (4 members)	*Tokyo 11* (4 members)
L. 163,755+	K. 115,920+	L. 96,386+	K. 69,691+	L. 125,892+
S. 71,955+	L. 105,993+	K. 80,013+	L. 65,209+	N. 125,207+
S. 71,643+	C. 101,287+	D. 64,407+	C. 61,129+	K. 124,010+
U. 67,436+ (L.)	S. 96,892+	S. 63,732+	D. 56,266+	S. 123,309+
S. 65,151+	D. 92,235•	C. 58,960+	L. 51,955[a]	C. 110,321•
L. 64,866[a]	L. 86,676[a]	L. 40,393[a]	L. 27,004[a]	L. 76,154[a]
L. 63,340[a]	L. 51,468[a]	N. 36,225[a]		L. 42,046[a]
		L. 18,303[a]		
[b] 128,206	[b] 138,144	[b] 94,921	[b] 78,959	[b] 118,200

Nagano 3 (4 members)	*Gifu 1* (5 members)	*Shizuoka 1* (5 members)	*Shizuoka 3* (4 members)	*Aichi 1* (4 members)
L. 81,147+	L. 108,785+	S. 106,648+	U. 91,613+ (L.)	D. 75,998+
L. 74,967+	K. 95,523+	U. 103,627+	S. 86,581+	K. 74,655+
S. 60,354+	L. 94,117+	L. 103,128+	L. 84,255+	U. 72,782+ (C.)
C. 54,936+	S. 82,729+	L. 101,507+	D. 80,458+	S. 66,445+
L. 48,838[a]	C. 78,898+	K. 99,188+	L. 78,975[a]	L. 63,825[a]
N. 10,639[a]	L. 77,935[a]	L. 85,725[a]	L. 66,680[a]	L. 46,899[a]
	L. 63,113[a]	C. 82,644•		
	L. 37,262[a]	N. 21,231[a]		
[b] 59,477	[b] 178,330	[b] 106,956	[b] 145,655	[b] 112,724

Osaka 5 (4 members)	*Hyogo 3* (3 members)	*Fukuoka 3* (5 members)	*Miyazaki 1* (3 members)
K. 143,532+	S. 86,029+	S. 76,766+	S. 96,133+
C. 122,200+	D. 81,360+	K. 76,328+	L. 84,419+
D. 109,497+	K. 79,435+	L. 72,091+	D. 83,345+
S. 100,734+	L. 77,056[a]	L. 60,293+	L. 75,405[a]
L. 59,039[a]	U. 64,037[a] (L.)	D. 59,518+	L. 51,983[a]
L. 58,527[a]		L. 53,034[a]	
L. 49,062[a]		L. 45,781[a]	
[b] 166,628	[b] 141,093	[b] 98,815	[b] 127,388

Source: *Kokkai Binran* [Diet Handbook], 1984, pp. 293–306.

Notes: + = winners; • = losers, but their party affiliation makes them irrelevant to the outcome.

[a] = LDP candidates, one of whom might have become a winner if the other LDP candidate(s) had withdrawn and lent his (her, or their) support to the remaining LDP candidate. In each instance, an opposition candidate would have been defeated.

[b] = Total vote cast for the losing LDP candidates.

L. = LDP; S. = JSP; K. = Kōmeitō; D. = DSP; C. = JCP; N. = New Liberal Club; U. = Unaffiliated.

vacancies) are contested, and the same is true of the "local" (that is, Prefecture-wide) constituencies: four, three, two, one. It has therefore become customary to refer to the latter as four, three, two and one member districts, and it is this designation that will be used. Voters cast two separate ballots. One for a national constituency candidate (or, since the 1983 election, political party), and one for a Prefectural constituency candidate.

In the House of Councillors elections, the results achieved by each of the parties in terms of the percentage of the popular vote that they received do not differ substantially from those for House of Representatives elections. These statistics are provided in Table 2.14. In effect, the Liberal Democrats' share has gone down by about ten points, and so has that of the Socialists. It is the other opposition parties that have picked up the difference. However, these percentages of aggregate vote totals that each of the parties obtained have not been reflected in the number of seats that each party has won. Much of the remainder of this chapter will be devoted to this anomaly.

Before turning to this issue, however, one other general point needs to be made. Until the 1983 House of Councillors election, candidates in the national constituency ran as individuals, either as those endorsed by political parties or as Unaffiliated. For the 1983 election, however, a proportional representation system was introduced under which voters cast their ballots for political parties: LDP, JSP, etc. Each political party compiled lists of its candidates so that the top twenty, ten or seven, etc., depending on the percentage of the votes cast that the party had obtained, would be declared the winners. Counting of the ballots was by the d'Hondt system, with each party's vote being successively divided by whole numbers (one, two, three, etc.) until the fifty that were to be elected had been determined.

Some commentators worried that many citizens would not vote if they had to write the name of a party – the characters for Liberal Democratic Party (*Jimintō*) or Communist Party (*Kyōsantō*) – on the ballots; a candidate, yes, but a political party, never! This expectation proved itself to have been based on partially invalid assumptions; however, as Table 2.14 indicates, there was a substantial discrepancy between the total vote cast for each of the parties in the National and the Prefecturewide (local district) constituencies.

Table 2.14 House of Councillors Elections 1959–83
(a) Liberal Democratic Party percentage of popular vote

Constituency	1959	1962	1965	1968	1971	1974	1977	1980	1983
National	41.2	46.4	47.2	46.7	44.4	44.3	35.8	42.5	35.2
Local	52.0	47.1	44.2	44.9	43.9	39.5	39.8	43.5	43.2

Note:
There have been some variations in the Liberal Democratic Party's ability to obtain votes between the "National" and "Local" (that is, Prefectural) constituencies over the years. The disparity in the 1983 election has been explained as resulting from the need of the voters to write the name of the party (as opposed to the name of a candidate) on the ballot in the National Constituency Proportional Representation system.

(b) Opposition Parties percentage of popular vote

Party	Constituency	1959	1962	1965	1968	1971	1974	1977	1980	1983
S.	N.	26.5	24.3	24.3	19.8	21.3	15.2	17.4	13.1	16.3
	L.	34.1	32.8	32.8	29.2	31.0	26.0	25.9	22.4	24.3
K.	N.	—	11.5	13.7	15.4	14.1	12.1	14.2	11.9	15.7
	L.	—	2.6	5.1	6.1	3.4	12.6	6.2	5.0	7.8
D.	N.	—	5.3	5.9	6.0	6.1	5.9	6.7	6.0	8.3
	L.	—	7.3	6.1	6.9	4.7	4.4	4.5	5.2	5.7
C.	N.	1.9	3.1	4.4	5.0	8.0	9.4	8.4	7.3	8.9
	L.	3.3	4.8	6.9	8.3	12.0	12.0	9.9	11.7	10.5
F.*	N.	—	—	—	—	—	—	5.6	1.1	2.6
	L.	—	—	—	—	—	—	2.1	1.7	6.9
Total	N.	28.4	44.2	47.4	46.2	49.5	42.6	52.3	39.4	51.8
	L.	37.4	47.5	50.9	50.5	51.1	55.0	48.6	46.0	55.2

Source: *Kokkai Binran* [Diet Handbook] for relevant years provides the election results which were used to calculate the statistics in the tables.

Notes:
S. = Japan Socialist Party; K. = Kōmeitō; D. = Democratic Socialist Party; C. = Japan Communist Party; F.* = Social Democratic Federation and its antecedents, as well as New Liberal Club – Democratic Coalition [*Shin Jiyu Club-Minshu Rengo*] in 1983 only.
N. = National Constituency; L. = Local Constituency.
Total does not add up to 100% if LDP share of popular vote is included because vote for Unaffiliated and minor party candidates has been excluded. That percentage of the popular vote is nearly impossible to divide between potential LDP and opposition party supporters.

The National Constituency

One of the principal stated reasons for the introduction of the proportional representation system for the National Constituency was to reduce the upward spiralling costs of nation-wide campaigning by individual candidates. In fact, the amendments to the House of Councillors Election Law that created the new system specifically prohibited individual candidates from engaging in campaign activities in the National Constituency (Liberal Democratic Party, 1984). It was all to be done by the political parties only, and worked reasonably well for established political party candidates, although there was considerable scrambling for the top positions on each party's list. So much so, in fact, that the costs to individual LDP candidates (reportedly) were as high, or higher, than under the old system. (Party Headquarters – principally the Secretary General – determined a candidate's ranking by a combination of factors. One was how many votes he or she had obtained in the 1977 House of Councillors election. Another was how many new members he or she had encouraged to join the party. The latter, of course, required the payment of party dues.) An LDP candidate would benefit by being among the top fifteen, for example, inasmuch as his (or her) party anticipated obtaining votes sufficient to elect between seventeen and twenty-two. In point of fact, enough votes were cast for the LDP to elect nineteen.

However, the new system placed would-be Unaffiliated candidates, as well as those belonging to the smaller parties at a distinct disadvantage. The Unaffiliated were forced to create a new organization, such as the "Party of the Unaffiliated (*Mutōha Shimin Rengo*)." Others in the smaller parties, were forced to swell the list of candidates to conform to the requirements that each party had to (1) have a list of ten candidates, or (2) have five or more previously elected members of the Diet, or (3) have received more than 4 percent of the popular vote in the previous election – even though everyone understood that the group, at the very best, would have enough voter support to have one, or possibly two, actually elected.

It was out of this new imperative that some new and somewhat novel "parties" were born: the "Salaryman's New Party (*Sarariman Shinto*)," the "Welfare Party (*Fukushitō*)," the "New Liberal Club Democratic Federation (*Shinjiyū Kurabu Minshu Rengō*)," the "Second Chamber Club (*Dai Niin Kurabu*)" which actually had had an amorphous existence among previously elected Unaffiliated Councillors, as well as the Party of the Unaffiliated, and several others that failed completely. One of the most unusual of the latter called itself the "Federation of Convenience to Purge Tanaka Kakuei from the Political World (*Tanaka Kakuei o Seikai kara Tsuihōsuru Katteren*)," which actually obtained a bit over 200,000 votes out of the forty-six and a half million cast. Be that as it may, the new system imposed formidable constraints on potential Unaffiliated candidacies, a not insignificant factor in the governing party's ability to obtain the support of the Socialists (the major opposition party) when the amendments to the existing Election Law were adopted. The new system, in the aggregate seat totals won by each of the existing parties, did not materially affect the outcome of the 1983 House of Councillors election.

Table 2.15 Party Seats in House of Councillors, 1959–83: National Constituency

1959	1962	1965	1968	1971	1974	1977	1980	1983
22L	21L	25L	21L	21L	19L	18L	21L	19L
—	—	—	—	—	—	1N	—	—
17S	15S	12S	12S	11S	10S	10S	9S	9S
—	7K	9K	9K	8K	9K	9K	9K	8K
—	3D	2D	4D	4D	4D	4D	3D	4D
1C	2C	2C	3C	5C	8C	3C	3C	5C
12U	3U	2U	2U	1U	4U	5U	5U	5U

Source: *Kokkai Binran* [Diet Handbook], for relevant years.

Notes:

L = Liberal Democratic Party; S = Japan Socialist Party; K = Kōmeitō; D = Democratic Socialist Party; C = Japan Communist Party; N = New Liberal Club; U = Unaffiliated.

Unaffiliated: 1959, includes "Green Breeze Society," small party and truly Unaffiliated candidates. At least ten were of the conservative persuasion;
1962, all conservatives;
1965, both Unaffiliated;
1968, 1 conservative, 1 progressive;
1971, Unaffiliated;
1974, 1 JSP, 3 Unaffiliated;
1977, 1 LDP, 1 NLC, 2 Unaffiliated;
1980, 5 progressives;
1983, all elected as members of "minor parties": 3 conservatives, 2 progressives.

As is immediately apparent from even a cursory glance at Table 2.15, the Liberal Democrats and Socialists have sustained the same erosion of support in this chamber as in the House of Representatives. In the National Constituency, the extent of the LDP's decline is obscured by the fact that in 1959 twelve Unaffiliated conservatives were elected. Four belonged to the "Green Breeze Society (*Ryokufūkai*)," a loose association of Councillors that consistently supported the LDP, and another six (for a total of 10) were conservatives who aligned themselves with the LDP. Hence, it can be argued that the true strength of the conservatives in 1959 was 32 and not 22. By 1969, that total had declined to 22, and in 1983 to 20 (nineteen LDP plus one Unaffiliated conservative). In sum, a loss of one-third of the seats.

The Socialists have suffered an even worse debacle, going from 17 in 1959, to 12 in 1968, to 9 in 1983 – in effect losing almost half of their seats. Once again, the same splintering of Opposition (to the LDP) votes is the culprit, inasmuch as it reduced the percentage of the popular vote that any one of the opposition parties might obtain. The Kōmeitō, beginning with the 1962 election, has won between 7 and 9 seats, the Democratic Socialist Party 3 or 4, and the Communist Party between 3 and 5 (the 1974 election in which eight Communists were elected was a fluke).

Put another way, the ratio of governing to opposition party adherents elected has gone from 32:18 (1959) to about 22:28 over the last two decades. In the National Constituency, the LDP has not won a majority of seats (with the exception of the 1965 contest in which it picked up exactly half) for the last two decades.

Alternative Analyses of Election Results

What is the explanation for these electoral outcomes? The standard analysis of election results for the House of Councillors has involved the following variables:

(1) Degree of representativeness by size of the Prefecturewide (that is, "Local (*chihō*)") Constituencies;
(2) Seats won by each party in relation to degree of urbanization of the Prefecturewide Constituencies;
(3) Comparison of percentage of popular vote by party and percentage of seats won by party (Passin, 1979, pp. 1–9; Nisihira, 1979, pp. 81–112).

This mode of analysis is useful in illuminating certain basic disparities, especially the lack of equality in the size of the population among the constituencies, as well as the advantage that the LDP enjoys by virtue of its greater appeal among semi-urban and rural voters who have a disproportionate share of the Councillors that they elect.

Yet, as Passin and other analysts admit (Passin, 1979, pp. 6–7), the disparities in degree of representativeness among US Senators is infinitely greater; in 1980, California's 7.5 million voters were represented by two Senators, and so were Nevada's 240,000 voters for a ratio of about 32:1, to the great advantage of Nevada's rural as opposed to California's metropolitan, urban and semi-urban residents. Of course, the United States Senate is supposed to represent states and not people, but the House of Councillors – having had the Senate as a partial model – should not be faulted for its members not representing a more or less equal number of voters, nor that its members reflect agrarian rather than urban interests. Furthermore, the disparities among numbers of voters that elect one Councillor are very much less flagrant than is the case for US Senators.

As a consequence, it would be better to accept the electoral system for the House of Councillors as it is, and to base one's analysis on each of the existing groups of constituencies. That is, to make comparisons among the national, four-, three-, two- and single-member districts, and to analyze the success or failure of the political parties to win seats in relation to each of these categories. Using this approach should produce a better understanding of how the system allows one or another party to have its candidates elected, and thereby to assess the outcomes that have been achieved.

As noted, the governing Liberal Democratic Party has been able to elect close to twenty Councillors in the National Constituency since 1968. This number is five seats less than it should be able to elect if it wished to retain majority status (25 out of the 50 that are contested in each election). Yet, the LDP has managed to retain control over the Second Chamber. Where have the extra seats been won?

The Four-Member Constituencies

The two four-member constituencies (Hokkaido and Tokyo) elect eight members. Yet as Table 2.16 indicates, the LDP has only been able to elect half the seats once (in 1959) in the last seven House

Table 2.16 Party Seats in House of Councillors: Four-Member Constituencies

District	1959	1962	1965	1968	1971	1974	1977	1980	1983
Hokkaido	LLSS	LSSU	LLSS	LLSS	LLSS	SSKC	LLSS	LLSC	LLSS
Tokyo	LLUU	LLCU	SKCU	LSKD	LKDC	LSKC	LKDN	KCUU	LKCU
Summary	4L	3L	2L	3L	3L	1L	3L	2L	3L
	—	—	—	—	—	—	1N	—	—
	2S	2S	3S	3S	2S	3S	2S	1S	2S
	—	—	1K	1K	1K	2K	1K	1K	1K
	—	—	—	1D	1D	—	1D	—	—
	—	1C	1C	—	1C	2C	—	2C	1C
	2U	2U	1U	—	—	—	—	2U	1U

Source: *Kokkai Binran* [Diet Handbook], for relevant years.

Notes: L = Liberal Democratic Party; S = Japan Socialist Party; K = Kōmeitō; D = Democratic Socialist Party; C = Japan Communist Party; N = New Liberal Club; U = Unaffiliated.

Unaffiliated: 1959, 1 Kōmeitō, 1 progressive;
1962, 1 LDP, 1 Kōmeitō;
1965, 1 progressive;
1980, 1 conservative, 1 progessive;
1983, 1 Unaffiliated (ex-NLC).

of Councillors elections, over a span of twenty-one years. In all of the recent elections, it has won two (25 percent) or three (37.5 per cent) of the eight seats.

One of the Unaffiliated candidates who won in 1980, Utsunomiya Tokuma, had been a long-time Liberal Democrat in the House of Representatives. He was always a maverick, however, particularly on foreign policy issues such as Japan's establishing diplomatic relations with the People's Republic of China, having been a proponent of that policy at least a decade before the Japanese government accepted it in 1972. He has also advocated establishing relations with the People's Democratic Republic of (North) Korea, a step that is yet to be taken. Furthermore, in his last two elections for the House of Representatives (from Tokyo's 2nd District), he had run with the support of the New Liberal Club. In any case, it would be difficult to classify Utsunomiya as a rock-ribbed LDP partisan.

On the other hand, the second Unaffiliated conservative elected in 1980, Yasui Ken, did rejoin the LDP (Fukuda faction), his lack of party identification having been a function of his service as "President (*Gichō*)" of the House of Councillors. Nozue Chinpei, the lone Unaffiliated candidate elected in 1983, had been one of the few who had eschewed party affiliation, although he did ally himself with the New Liberal Club for a short period of time.

In contrast to the difficulties that the LDP has faced in this category of districts, the opposition parties have won at least half of the seats. The Communists have supplanted, to all intents and purposes, the Democratic Socialists, with the remaining seats going to the Socialist Party and Kōmeitō candidates. The only exception occurred in 1974 when the LDP was blanked out in Hokkaido. This unusual result had nothing to do with a precipitous drop in LDP support, but illustrates perfectly the point that the multiple-member district system has its unpredictable pitfalls.

This particular instance of "*tomodaore* (going down together)" was simply a function of a dispute between LDP Headquarters and a group of young party dissidents who had organized themselves into the "Blue Storm Society (*Seirankai*)." Among its leaders was Nakagawa Ichirō who had been a rising star in the LDP until his – as yet not fully explained – suicide early in 1983. Nakagawa, who was from Hokkaido, and his allies supported the Unaffiliated conservative candidate who was able to obtain enough votes to insure the defeat of the two officially endorsed Liberal Democrats.

Table 2.17 Hokkaido Prefecture-wide Constituency, 1974

Ogasawara Sadako	(Communist)	416,950^{+}
Yoshida Chūzaburō	(Socialist)	412,746^{+}
Tsushima Takakatsu	(Socialist)	404,136^{+}
Aizawa Takehiko	(Kōmeitō)	375,278^{+}
Kawaguchi Yōichi	(L. Miki)	366,788$^{\bullet}$
Nishida Shin'ichi	(L. Ōhira)	360,438$^{\bullet}$
Takahashi Tatsuo	(U. Seirankai)	313,521$^{\bullet}$

Source: *Kokkai Binran* [Diet Handbook], 1977, p. 314.
Notes: $^{+}$ = winners; $^{\bullet}$ = losers.
(L. . . .) = Liberal Democrat and faction affiliation; U. = Unaffiliated.
The results in this particular House of Councillors local (Prefectural) constituency election is a classic illustration of "*tomodaore* (going down together)." Takahashi ran as an Unaffiliated candidate with the support of the "*Seirankai* (Blue Storm Society)," a group of younger Liberal Democrats who tended to be nationalistic in their outlook and impatient with the moderate conservatism of their party elders. By splitting up the available support among LDP voters in Hokkaido, Takahashi and his supporters helped to bring about the defeat of the two officially endorsed LDP candidates Kawaguchi and Nishida.

The Three-Member Constituencies

In the three-member constituencies too (see Table 2.18), the LDP has suffered a continued erosion. It has not been able to do better than winning one seat in each of the districts, or one-third of the total of twelve. Nor has it been helped by Unaffiliated candidates. In 1980, they were Kōmeitō and Democratic Socialist Party candidates who had run with the joint backing of these parties; and, in 1983, the lone Unaffiliated was Yokoyama Nokku (who is what the Japanese call a "talent" or entertainer) who joined the Democratic Socialist Party after having been an Unaffiliated Councillor during his previous twelve years (while he had run as a candidate and been elected in the National Constituency). If the Communists and Socialists had been willing to co-operate – an admittedly idle speculation – the Liberal Democrats might have been excluded from winning their seats in Osaka and Hyōgo in 1983.

In Osaka, the combined Socialist–Communist vote would have been more than sufficient to defeat the Liberal Democrat; and, the

Table 2.18 Party Seats in House of Councillors: Three-Member Constituencies

District	1959	1962	1965	1968	1971	1974	1977	1980	1983
Aichi	LLS	LLS	LLS	LSK	LLS	LSD	LKD	LDU	LKD
Osaka	LSS	LSU	LSK	LKD	LSK	LKC	LKC	LKU	LKU
Hyōgo	LLS	LLS	LSD	SKD	LSD	LKC	LSK	LSC	LKD
Fukuoka	LLS	LLS	LLS	LLS	LLS	LSK	LSK	LSK	LSK
Summary	7L	7L	6L	4L	6L	4L	4L	4L	4L
	5S	4S	4S	3S	4S	2S	2S	2S	1S
	—	1K	1K	3K	1K	3K	4K	2K	4K
	—	—	1D	2D	1D	—	1D	1D	2D
	—	—	—	—	—	2C	1C	1C	—
	—	*U=K	—	—	—	—	—	2U	1U

Source: Kokkai Binran [Diet Handbook], for relevant years.
Notes:
L = Liberal Democratic Party; S = Japan Socialist Party; K = Kōmeitō;
D = Democratic Socialist Party; C = Japan Communist Party; U = Unaffiliated.
Unaffiliated: 1962, Unaffiliated joined Kōmeitō;
1980, 1 Kōmeitō, 1 Democratic Socialist;
1983, 1 Democratic Socialist.

Table 2.19 Three-Member Constituencies "*Tomodaore* (Going down Together)": 1983 House of Councillors Election

Osaka Prefecture		Hyōgo Prefecture	
Candidate	Vote	Candidate	Vote
Yamada Isamu (U./D.)	867,308⁺	Yahara Hideo (K.)	456,233⁺
Tashiro Fujio (K.)	799,106⁺	Nukiyama Eiko (D.)	383,524⁺
Morishita Tai (L.)	672,409⁺	Ishii Ichiji (L.)	373,339⁺
Kutsunugi Takeko (C.)	636,622*	Oku Mokichi (S.)	313,795*
Makiuchi Masaya (S.)	268,210*	Ōno Emio (L.)	257,555°
		Koga Tetsuo (C.)	215,572*
C. + S.	904,832	S. + C.	529,387

Source: *Kokkai Binran* [Diet Handbook], 1984, p. 309.
Notes:
⁺ = Winner; * = Loser; ° = Loser whose vote is only marginally relevant.
L. = Liberal Democratic Party; D. = Democratic Socialist Party; K. = Kōmeitō; S. = Japan Socialist Party; C. = Japan Communist Party; U. = Unaffiliated.

Explanation. In Osaka, if the Communist and Socialist vote had been combined in support of one candidate, the total vote would have been more than sufficient to defeat the Liberal Democrat in third place.

In Hyōgo, if the Socialist and Communist votes had been combined in support of one candidate, the total vote would have defeated the Liberal Democrat in third place. However, if the Liberal Democrat in fifth place (°) had not been a candidate, then the combined Liberal Democratic vote (631,350) would have been sufficient to insure the Liberal Democrat's victory in first place.

same would have been the case in Hyōgo, unless the LDP had decided to endorse only one candidate. These speculations aside, the governing party can be expected to continue having its difficulties in these metropolitan-urban constituencies.

The Two-Member Constituencies

The same is definitely not the case in the 15 two-member constituencies (see Table 2.20). Until the 1974 election, these constituencies had been the almost exclusive preserve of the Liberal Democrats and Socialists. In all instances, the LDP has been able to pick up at least half (15) of the seats as the Unaffiliated candidates were conservatives. Furthermore if they, as well as the New Liberal Club member (elected in 1977 and 1983)

Table 2.20 Party Seats in House of Councillors: Two-Member Constituencies

District	1959	1962	1965	1968	1971	1974	1977	1980	1983
Fukushima	LS	LS	LS	LL	LS	LS	LS	LS	LS
Ibaragi	LS	LS	LS	LS	LL	SU	LS	LS	LS
Tochigi	LS	LS	LL	LL	LS	SU	LS	LL	LS
Gunma	LS	LS	LS	LL	LS	LS	LS	LS	LL
Saitama	LS	LS	LS	LS	LS	LS	LN	LS	LN
Chiba	LS	LS	LS	LL	LS	LS	LS	LS	LS
Kanagawa	LS	SD	LS	LS	LS	LS	SU	LS	LK
Niigata	LS	LS	SL	SU	LS	LS	LS	LS	LS
Nagano	LS	LS	LS	LS	LS	LS	LS	LS	LS
Shizuoka	LL	LL	LS	LL	LS	LS	LS	LS	LL
Kyoto	LS	LS	LS	LC	LS	LC	LC	LC	LC
Okayama	LS	LS	LS	LS	LS	LS	LS	LS	LS
Hiroshima	LS	LS	LS	LS	LS	LS	LS	LD	LS
Kumamoto	LL	LL	LS	LL	LS	LL	LL	LL	LL
Kagoshima	LL	LS	LL	LL	LS	LS	LU	LL	LS
Summary	18L	16L	17L	21L	16L	14L	15L	18L	18L
	12S	13S	13S	7S	14S	13S	11S	10S	9S
	—	1D	—	—	—	—	—	1D	—
	—	—	—	1C	—	1C	1C	1C	1C
	—	—	—	—	—	—	—	—	1K
	—	—	—	—	—	—	1N	—	1N
	—	—	—	1U[a]	—	2U[a]	2U[a]	—	—

Source: Kokkai Binran [Diet Handbook], for relevant years.
Notes:
L = Liberal Democratic Party; S = Japan Socialist Party; K = Kōmeitō; D = Democratic Socialist Party; C = Japan Communist Party; N = New Liberal Club; U = Unaffiliated.
[a]All Unaffiliated candidates either joined the LDP after their election, or tended to vote with the LDP.

are added to the ranks of the conservatives, then they have been victorious in either 18 or 19 cases over the last three contests, for a margin of either three or four seats above 50 percent, a function of the party's ability to pick up both seats in three Prefectures.

In this category of districts, however, the results might have been different if the Socialists and Communists had not persisted in each running their own candidates. The caveat discussed in connection with the use of "*tomodaore* (going down together)" for

Table 2.21 Two-Member Constituencies "*Tomodaore* (Going down Together)": 1980 and 1983 House of Councillors Elections

1980 Candidate	Vote	1983 Candidate	Vote
Tochigi Prefecture		*Gunma Prefecture*	
Moriyama Mayumi (L.)	288,104^{+}	Yamamoto Tomio (L.)	301,765^{+}
Ōshima Tomoji (L.)	250,769^{+}	Mogami Susumu (L.)	269,477^{+}
Ōtsuka Takashi (S.)	209,448$^{\bullet}$	Tsunoda Giichi (S.)	259,896$^{\bullet}$
Satō Shin (D.)	82,118$^{\bullet}$	Yoshimura Kin'nosuke (C.)	40,707$^{\bullet}$
Eguchi Yoshitoki (C.)	27,235°		
S. + D.	291,566	S. + C.	300,603
Gunma Prefecture		*Saitama Prefecture*	
Fukuda Hiroichi (L.)	456,665^{+}	Tsuchiya Yoshihiko (L.)	605,516^{+}
Yamada Yuzuru (S.)	249,943^{+}	Morita Juro (N.)	563,811^{+}
Mogami Susumu (L.)	241,171$^{\bullet}$	Tadamatsu Yūji (S.)	375,471$^{\bullet}$
Yoshimura Kin'nosuke (C.)	47,829$^{\bullet}$	Fujino Yasuhiro (C.)	214,657$^{\bullet}$
L. + L.	697,836	S. + C.	590,128
1/2:	348,918		
Kagoshima Prefecture		*Shizuoka Prefecture*	
Inoue Kichio (L.)	323,615^{+}	Takeyama Yutaka (L.)	421,038^{+}
Kawahara Shinjiro (L.)	292,275^{+}	Kojima Shizuma (L.)	387,279^{+}
Kubo Wataru (S.)	287,975$^{\bullet}$	Kikuta Akira (S.)	370,662$^{\bullet}$
Kameda Tokuichirō (C.)	35,321$^{\bullet}$	Abe Moto'o (C.)	168,070$^{\bullet}$
S. + C.	323,296	S. + C.	538,732
		Kumamoto Prefecture	
		Sawada Issei (L.)	324,531^{+}
		Urata Masaru (L.)	234,916^{+}
		Uogaeshi Masaomi (S.)	227,333$^{\bullet}$
		Kurita Kazuya (C.)	25,004$^{\bullet}$
		S. + C.	252,337

Source: *Kokkai Binran* [Diet Handbook], 1984, pp. 308–11, 313–16.

Notes:

$^{+}$ = Winner; $^{\bullet}$ = Loser; $^{\circ}$ = Loser, but irrelevant to outcome.

L. = Liberal Democratic Party; D. = Democratic Socialist Party; S. = Japan Socialist Party; C. = Japan Communist Party; D. = Democratic Socialist Party.

opposition party candidates in the House of Representatives is, of course, equally applicable to the House of Councillors.

In the 1980 election one of the Liberal Democrats would have been defeated in Tochigi if the Socialists and Democratic Socialists had not run separate candidates; however, the Liberal Democratic Party could have elected both of its candidates in Gumma if the votes between the two would have been better distributed; while in Kagoshima, the meaningless Communist candidate took away enough votes from the Socialist so that both Liberal Democrats were victorious. In the 1983 election the Communist candidate, who had minimal voter appeal, could have helped the Socialist defeat the second Liberal Democrat; in Saitama, a combined effort between the Socialists and Communists could have defeated the New Liberal Club candidate; in Shizuoka and Kumamoto, a similar effort could have defeated one of the two victorious Liberal Democrats. Competition among the opposition parties, especially between the Socialists and Communists, for the support of anti-conservative voters has provided crucial benefits to the LDP.

The One-Member Constituencies

It is, however, in the one-member constituencies that the LDP still enjoys a virtual monopoly. After all, winning 24 or 25 of a possible 26 seats is a level of success that would be difficult to surpass. Even in these constituencies, however, the outcomes would have been different if the opposition parties did not have a penchant for behavior that could be described as mutually suicidal.

In each of the one-member constituencies in Table 2.23, the Liberal Democrat could have been defeated if the Communists had not insisted on running a candidate who competed with the (ultimately defeated) Socialist. As was indicated previously, the Liberal Democrats do derive advantages from the unwillingness of some of their antagonists to co-operate with each other. Obviously, from the LDP's perspective, may this tendency continue.

If the foregoing disaggregated election results (by type of constituency) are once again aggregated, the following profile of the House of Councillors presents itself (see Table 2.24). As is immediately apparent, the LDP currently enjoys a comfortable majority in this chamber, with a twelve-seat margin above 50 percent of the seats (126). Furthermore, it can count on at least the New Liberal Club members and a few of the Unaffiliated for added support.

The conclusion is inevitable that the LDP wins, not because it has overwhelming public appeal, but because it can marshal its voter support behind its candidates in the two-member constituencies and even more so in the one-member constituencies. It is this

Table 2.22 Party Seats in House of Councillors: One-Member Constituencies

District	1959	1962	1965	1968	1971	1974	1977	1980	1983
Aomori	U	L	L	U	L	L	L	L	L
Iwate	L	S	L	L	L	L	L	L	L
Miyagi	L	L	S	L	S	L	L	L	L
Akita	L	S	L	L	S	L	L	L	L
Yamagata	L	L	L	L	L	L	L	L	L
Toyama	L	L	L	S	L	L	L	L	L
Ishikawa	U	L	L	U	L	L	L	L	L
Fukui	L	L	L	L	S	L	L	L	L
Yamanashi	S	L	L	L	S	L	L	L	L
Gifu	L	L	S	L	S	L	L	L	L
Mie	L	L	L	L	L	L	S	L	L
Shiga	U	L	L	S	L	L	L	U	L
Nara	L	L	L	L	L	L	L	L	L
Wakayama	L	L	L	L	L	L	L	L	L
Tottori	S	L	L	S	L	L	S	L	L
Shimane	L	U	S	L	S	L	L	L	L
Yamaguchi	L	L	L	L	L	L	L	L	L
Tokushima	L	L	L	L	U	U	L	L	L
Kagawa	L	L	S	L	S	L	L	L	L
Ehime	L	L	L	L	L	L	L	L	L
Kōchi	L	L	L	L	L	L	L	L	L
Saga	L	L	L	L	L	L	L	L	L
Nagasaki	L	L	L	L	L	L	L	L	L
Ōita	L	L	L	L	S	L	U	L	S
Miyazaki	L	L	L	L	L	L	L	L	L
Okinawa	—	—	—	—	L	U	L	U	U
Summary	20L	22L	21L	20L	17L	24L	23L	24L	24L
	2S	2S	4S	3S	8S	—	2S	—	15
	3U[a]	1U[a]	—	2U[a]	1U[a]	2U[b]	1U[b]	2U[b]	1U[b]

Source: *Kokkai Binran* [Diet Handbook], for relevant years.

Notes: L = Liberal Democratic Party; S = Japan Socialist Party; U = Unaffiliated.

Unaffiliated: [a] Conservative; [b] Progressive.

Until the 1971 election, the number of one-member constituencies was 25. In anticipation of Okinawa's reversion to Japan in 1972, that Prefecture was added to the list of one-member constituencies, raising it to 26.

Table 2.23 One-Member Constituencies "*Tomodaore* (Going down Together)": 1983 House of Councillors Election

Candidate	Vote	Candidate	Vote
Miyagi Prefecture		*Akita Prefecture*	
Hoshi Chōji (L.)	374,554⁺	Deguchi Hiromitsu (L.)	282,420⁺
Ōta Kōsaku (S.)	270,393•	Ishikawa Renjirō (S.)	247,594•
Oki Naoko (C.)	127,430•	Kodama Kanetomo (C.)	46,374•
S. + C.	397,823	S. + C.	293,968
Tottori Prefecture		*Shimane Prefecture*	
Nishimura Shōji (L.)	160,242⁺	Nariai Zenjū (L.)	212,006⁺
Hirota Kōichi (S.)	152,043•	Ishibashi Daikichi (S.)	190,802•
Ushio Tamotsu (C.)	13,656•	Watanabe Setsuo (C.)	24,700•
S. + C.	165,699	S. + C.	215,502

Source: *Kokkai Binran* [Diet Handbook], 1984, pp. 309–11.
Notes: ⁺ = Winner; • = Loser.
L. = Liberal Democratic Party; S. = Japan Socialist Party; C. = Japan Communist Party.
Explanation: In each instance, the Socialist and Communist votes would have been sufficient to defeat the Liberal Democrat if the opposition vote would have been combined in support of a single candidate.

feature of the electoral system that provides the Liberal Democratic Party with substantial advantages which will not disappear until such time as the opposition parties will be willing to co-operate with each other far more fully than they have been able and willing to do thus far.

To be sure, the opposition parties have recognized the problem that they face. Since 1971, they have co-operated, in varying combinations, jointly to support a single candidate. As Table 2.25 indicates, however, these efforts have not met with a great deal of success, even if there were nine victors in 1980 offset by fifteen losers. Also significant is that there were only two instances of co-operation in the 1983 contest, a far cry from the twenty-four cases in 1980. All in all, the extant record bodes ill for joint candidacies as a meaningful strategy for the opposition parties. It would be far better if these parties concentrated on the "going down together" phenomenon, and not insist on running candidates in districts in which doing so interferes with the electability of one of their fellow oppositionists. Thus far, they have not been willing to do so, even though as the numerous instances of *tomodaore* reflect, they could have picked up several seats.

Table 2.24 Results of 1980 and 1983 House of Councillors Elections: Total Seats, by Party

Type of constituency	No., total seats	%, total seats	Political party affiliation of winners						
			L	N	U[a]	D	K	S	C
1980									
National	50	39.7	21	—	5	3	9	9	3
4-Member	8	6.3	2	—	2	—	1	1	2
3-Member	12	9.5	4	—	2	1	2	2	1
2-Member	30	23.8	18	—	—	1	—	10	1
1-Member	26	20.6	24	—	2	—	—	—	—
Sub-total	126		69	—	11	5	12	22	7
1983									
National	50	39.7	19	—	5	4	8	9	5
4-Member	8	6.3	3	—	1	—	1	2	1
3-Member	12	9.5	4	—	1	2	4	1	—
2-Member	30	23.8	18	1	—	—	1	9	1
1-Member	26	20.6	24	—	1	—	—	1	—
Sub-total	126		68	1	8	6	14	22	7
Total	252		137	1	19	11	26	44	14

Source: *Kokkai Binran* [Diet Handbook], 1984, pp. 307–16.

Notes:

L = LDP; N = New Liberal Club; D = DSP; K = Kōmeitō; S = JSP; C = JCP

U[a] = Unaffiliated and minor parties:

1980 *National Constituency* – Ichikawa Fusae (Unaffiliated progressive); Aoshima Yukio (Unaffiliated); Nakayama Chinatsu (Unaffiliated); Minobe Ryōkichi (Unaffiliated progressive, ex-Socialist); Hata Yutaka (Social Democratic Federation).

4-Member – Yasui Ken (LDP); Utsunomiya Tokuma (Unaffiliated, ex-LDP, ex-NLC).

3-Member – Takagi Kentaro (Kōmeitō); Nakamura Eiichi (DSP).

1-Member – Yamada Chōzaburō (Unaffiliated); Kiyan Shin'ei (Unaffiliated progressive).

1983 *National Constituency* – Den Hideo (Social Democratic Federation); Shimomura Yutaka aka "Columbia Top" (Unaffiliated); Maejima Eizaburo aka "Yashiro Eita" (Welfare Party–LDP); Aoki Shigeru and Kimoto Heihachiro aka "Yagi Daisuke" (Salaryman's New Party).

4-Member – Nozue Chinpei ("Tax (*Zeikin*) Party," ex-NLC).

3-Member – Yamada Isamu aka "Yokoyama Knock" (DSP).

1-Member – Kiyan Shin'ei (Unaffiliated progressive).

Table 2.25 Joint Opposition Party Candidacies: House of Councillors

Parties	Elections				
	1971	1974	1977	1980	1983
S–K	—	Toyama (S)* Tottori (S)* Kumamoto (S)* Wakayama (K)*	Akita (S)* Mie (S)+	—	—
S–K–D	Tochigi (S)+ Shimane (S)+ Ōita (S)+	—	—	—	—
S–K–D–F	—	—	—	Iwate (U)* Yamagata (U)* Shiga (U)+ Tokushima (U)* Kōchi (U)*	—
S–F	—	—	—	Fukushima (S)+ Chiba (S)+ Tokyo (S)* Fukui (S)* Shizuoka (S)+ Aichi (S)* Osaka (S)* Hiroshima (S)* Kagoshima (S)*	—

K–D	—	—	Hokkaido (K)* Fukuoka (K)$^{+}$ Tochigi (D)* Hiroshima (D)*	Hiroshima (D)$^{+}$	—
K–D–P	—	—	Saitama (P)* Kanagawa (U)* Shizuoka (U)*	—	—
K–D–F	—	—	—	Hokkaido (K)* Fukuoka (K)$^{+}$ Kanagawa (D)* Saitama (U)*	—
D–N	—	—	—	Osaka (U)$^{+}$	Aichi (D)$^{+}$
D–F	—	—	—	Gifu (D)* Hyogo (D)*	—
N–F	—	—	—	Tokyo (U)$^{+}$	—
S–K–C–SoMa[a]	—	Okinawa (U)$^{+}$	Okinawa (U)*	Okinawa (U)$^{+}$	Okinawa (U)$^{+}$
S–C[a]	—	Kōchi (C)*	Miyagi (S)*	—	—
Total	3^{+}	$1^{+},5^{*}$	$2^{+},9^{*}$	$9^{+},15^{*}$	2^{+}

Source: Ishigami Yamato, 'Election Co-operation among Opposition Parties [*Yato Senkyo Kyōryoku*]' in "Japan's Political Parties" special issue of *Juristo* [Jurist], Summer 1984, pp. 132–8.

Notes:

$^{+}$ = winner, * = loser.

[a] = only instance of JCP co-operation.

S = JSP; K = Kōmeitō; D = DSP; F = Social Democratic Federation; N = New Liberal Club; C = JCP; P = People's Progressive Federation; SoMa = Social Masses Party (Okinawa only); U = Unaffiliated.

Table 2.26 House of Representatives Elections 1976, 1979, 1980, 1983: Seats by Party and Type of District

1 STABLE DISTRICTS (no change in party affiliation of members)

Type of district[a]	District	(No. of seats)	LDP and allies	Opposition parties
B	Hokkaido 2	(4)	2L	2S
B	Hokkaido 3	(3)	1L, 1U	1S
C	Iwate 1	(4)	3L (1L = U in 1976)	1S
D	Miyagi 2	(4)	3L (1L = U in 1979)	1S
C	Yamagata 1	(4)	3L (1L = U in 1979)	1S
D	Yamagata 2	(4)	2L	1S, 1F (F had been S)
C	Fukushima 3	(3)	2L	1S
C	Tochigi 1	(5)	3L	2S
C	Gunma 1	(3)	2L (1L = U in 1983)	1S
B	Gunma 2	(3)	2L	1S
C	Gunma 3	(4)	3L	1S
C	Saitama 3	(3)	2L	1S
C	Chiba 2	(4)	3L (2L = U in 1979)	1S
A	Tokyo 4	(5)	1L	1S 1K 1D 1C
A	Tokyo 5	(3)	1L	1S 1K
C	Toyama 2	(3)	2L	1S
B	Ishikawa 1	(3)	2L	1S

D	Ishikawa 2	(3)	3L	—
C	Nagano 1	(3)	2L	1S
D	Nagano 2	(3)	2L	1S
C	Gifu 2	(4)	3L	1S
C	Aichi 3	(3)	2L	1S
D	Mie 2	(4)	3L	1S
D	Shiga	(5)	2L	1S 1D 1C
A	Osaka 1	(3)	1L	— 1K 1C
A	Osaka 4	(4)	1L	1S 1K 1C
B	Yamaguchi 1	(4)	3L	1S
C	Kagawa 1	(3)	2L	1S
C	Ehime 1	(3)	2L	1S
C	Ehime 2	(3)	2L	1S
C	Kōchi	(5)	2L	1S 1K 1C
C	Nagasaki 2	(4)	3L	1S
D	Kagoshima 2	(3)	2L	1S
D	Amami Shotō	(1)	1L	—
B	Okinawa	(5)	2L	1S 1K 1C
Total 4*A*, 6*B*, 17C,8*D*	35 districts	(125)	75L, 1U	34S, 6K, 2D, 6C, 1F

continued

2 MINIMALLY UNSTABLE DISTRICTS (one seat changed in party affiliation of members)

Type of district	District	(No. of seats)	Stable: LDP and allies	Stable: Opposition parties	Change
A	Hokkaido 1	(5)	2L	1S 1K	1S(2#), 1C(1#), 1U(1#)
B	Hokkaido 5	(5)	2L	2S	1S(3#), 1L(1#)
C	Aomori 1	(4)	3L	—	1S(3#), 1K(1#)
D	Aomori 2	(3)	2L	—	1C(3#), 1N(1#)
D	Iwate 2	(4)	3L	—	1S(3#), 1D(1#)
B	Miyagi 1	(5)	3L	— 1K	1S(3#), 1C(1#)
C	Akita 1	(4)	2L	1S	1S(2#), 1C(2#)
D	Akita 2	(4)	2L	1S	1L(1#), 1S(3#)
D	Fukushima 2	(5)	3L	1S	1L(3#), 1D(1#)
C	Ibaragi 1	(4)	2L(1L as U twice)	1S	1L(3#), 1D(1#)
C	Ibaragi 2	(3)	1L	1S	1L(2#), 1S(2#)
C	Tochigi 2	(5)	2L	1S 1D	1L(1#), 1K(3#)
B	Saitama 2	(3)	1L 1N	—	1S(1#), 1K(3#)
B	Saitama 4	(3)	1L 1N	—	1L(1#), 1S(1#), 1K(2#)
B	Saitama 5	(3)	1L	1S	1N(1#), 1D(3#)
A	Chiba 4	(3)	1L	1S	1L(2#), 1K(2#)
A	Tokyo 2	(5)	1L	1S 1K 1D	1C(3#), 1U(1#)
A	Tokyo 6	(4)	1L	1K 1C	1L, 1N, 1S, 1D
A	Kanagawa 1	(4)	1L	1S 1K	1D(3#), 1N(1#)
A	Kanagawa 2	(5)	1L, 1N	1S 1K	1D(2#), 1C(2#)

A	Kanagawa 4	(4)	—	1S	1K	1D		1L(3#), 1N(1#)
B	Niigata 1	(3)	1L	1S				1L(3#), 1D(1#)
D	Niigata 2	(4)	2L	1S				1L(3#), 1S(1#)
C	Niigata 3	(5)	2L, 1U	1S				1L(1#), 1U(1#), 1S(2#)
C	Niigata 4	(3)	1L	1S				1L(3#), 1U(1#)
C	Toyama 1	(3)	2L	—				1L(1#), 1S(3#)
C	Yamanashi	(5)	3L	1S				1L(3#), 1S(1#)
B	Shizuoka 2	(5)	2L	1S		1D		1L(3#), 1K(1#)
C	Shizuoka 3	(4)	2L (2L as U once)	—		1D		1U(1#), 1S(3#)
B	Aichi 2	(4)	1L	1K(U)		1D		1L(2#), 1S(2#)
C	Aichi 4	(4)	2L	—		1D		1L(3#), 1S(1#)
B	Aichi 5	(3)	2L	—				1S(1#), 1U(3#)
A	Aichi 6	(4)	1L	—	1K	1D		1C(3#), 1S(1#)
C	Mie 1	(5)	2L	1S		1D		1L(1#), 1K(3#)
A	Kyoto 1	(5)	1L	—	1K	1D	1C	1L, 1N, 1C, 1U
A	Osaka 2	(5)	1L	—	1K	1D	1C	1L(1#), 1S(3#)
A	Osaka 5	(4)	—	—	1K	1D	1C	1L(3#), 1S(1#)
A	Osaka 6	(3)	1L	—	1K			1N(3#), 1C(1#)
A	Osaka 7	(3)	1L	—	1K			1S(2#), 1C(2#)
A	Hyogo 1	(5)	1L	1S	1K		1C	1L(2#), 1D(2#)
B	Hyogo 4	(4)	2L	1S				1L(1#), 1K(3#)
D	Hyogo 5	(3)	1L	—		1D		1L(1#), 1S(3#)
B	Wakayama 1	(3)	1L	—	1K			1L(1#), 1C(3#)
C	Wakayama 2	(3)	2L	—				1L(1#), 1S(2#), 1C(1#)
D	Tottori	(4)	2L	1S				1L(1#), 1S(3#)
C	Shimane	(5)	3L	1S				1S(2#), 1C(2#)
C	Okayama 1	(5)	2L	1S	1K			1L, 1S, 1C, 1F
B	Hiroshima 1	(3)	1L	1S				1L(3#), 1K(1#)

continued

2 Minimally Unstable Districts (cont.)

Type of district	District	(No. of seats)	Stable: LDP and allies	Stable: Opposition parties	Change
B	Hiroshima 2	(4)	2L	1S	1L(2#), 1N(1#), 1U(1#)
C	Tokushima	(5)	3L	1S	1L(2#), 1K(2#)
D	Kagawa 2	(3)	2L	—	1L(1#), 1S(3#)
D	Ehime 3	(3)	2L	—	1L(2#), 1S(2#)
C	Fukuoka 3	(5)	2L	1S 1D	1L(1#), 1K(3#)
C	Saga	(5)	4L	—	1S(3#), 1U(1#)
D	Kumamoto 2	(5)	3L	1S	1L(3#), 1U(1#)
C	Ōita 2	(3)	2L	—	1S(3#), 1U(1#)
C	Miyazaki 1	(3)	1L	— 1D	1L(1#), 1S(2#), 1U(1#)
B	Kagoshima 1	(4)	2L	1S	1L(2#), 1S(2#)
D	Kagoshima 3	(3)	2L	—	1L(3#), 1S(1#)
Total 14A, 14*B* 19C, 12*D*	59 Districts	(241)	102L, 2N, 1U	34S, 17K 15D, 5C	74L, 10N, 14U, 1F 72S, 24K, 15D, 26C

3 UNSTABLE DISTRICTS (two or more seats changed in party affiliation of members)

Type of district	District	(No. of seats)	Stable: LDP and allies	Stable: Opposition parties	Change
B	Hokkaido 4	(5)	1L	1S	2L(2#), 1L(1#), 1S(3#), 1K(1#), 1D(3#)
C	Fukushima 1	(4)	2L	—	1L(2#), 1N(2#), 1U(1#), 1S(2#), 1C(1#)
D	Ibaragi 3	(5)	2L	1S	1L(2#), 2L(1#), 1K(3#), 1U(1#)
A	Saitama 1	(3)	1L	—	1L(2#), 1S(1#), 1K(3#), 1C(2#)
A	Chiba 1	(4)	1L	— 1K	1L(1#), 1U(1#), 1S(3#), 1C(3#)
D	Chiba 3	(5)	3L	—	1L(3#), 1K(3#), 2U(1#)
A	Tokyo 1	(3)	1L	—	1L(3#), 1U(1#), 1S(2#), 1K(2#)
A	Tokyo 3	(4)	1L	1S	1L(2#), 1N(1#), 1K(3#)
A	Tokyo 7	(4)	1L	— 1K	1S(3#), 1C(3#), 1F(2#)
A	Tokyo 8	(3)	1L	—	1L(2#), 1U(1#), 1K(3#), 1C(2#)
A	Tokyo 9	(3)	1L	—	1N(2#), 1K(3#), 1C(3#)
A	Tokyo 10	(5)	1L	— 1K 1C	1L(3#), 1N(2#), 1S(3#)
A	Tokyo 11	(4)	IL	1S	1C(2#), 1N(3#)
A	Kanagawa 3	(3)	—	1S	1L(3#), 1N(3#), 1K(2#)
A	Kanagawa 5	(3)	1N	—	1L(2#), 1S(3#), 1D(3#)
C	Fukui	(4)	2L	—	1L(2#), 1U(1#), 1S(2#), 1D(3#)
C	Nagano 3	(4)	2L	—	1L(1#), 1U(1#), 1S(3#), 1C(3#)
C	Nagano 4	(3)	1L	—	1L(2#), 1S(3#), 1D(3#)
C	Gifu 1	(5)	2L	—	3L(1#), 1L(1#), 1S(3#), 1K(3#), 1C(2#)
B	Shizuoka 1	(5)	2L	— 1K	1L(3#), 1U(1#), 1N(1#), 1S(1#), 1C(2#)
A	Aichi 1	(4)	—	1S 1D	1L(2#), 1U(3#), 1K(3#)
B	Kyoto 2	(5)	1L	— 1K 1D	1L(2#), 1S(3#), 1C(3#)

continued

3 UNSTABLE DISTRICTS (cont.)

Type of district	District	(No. of seats)	Stable: LDP and allies	Stable: Opposition parties	Change
A	Osaka 3	(4)	—	1S 1D	1L(3#), 1K(3#), 1C(2#)
A	Hyogo 2	(5)	1L	1S 1K	1L(2#), 1N(1#), 1S(3#), 1C(2#)
C	Hyogo 3	(3)	—	—	1L(3#), 1N(1#), 1S(2#), 1K(3#), 1D(3#)
B	Nara	(5)	1L	— 1D	1L(3#), 1U(1#), 1S(2#), 1K(3#), 1C(3#)
C	Okayama 2	(5)	3L	—	1S(3#), 1K(3#), 1D(2#)
C	Hiroshima 3	(5)	2L	— 1D	1L(3#), 1S(2#), 1K(3#)
C	Yamaguchi 2	(5)	2L	1S	1L(2#), 1K(3#), 1D(3#)
A	Fukuoka 1	(5)	2L	— 1K	1L(3#), 1S(3#), 1F(2#)
B	Fukuoka 2	(5)	1L	— 1K 1D	1L(2#), 1S(2#), 1C(2#), 25(1#)
B	Fukuoka 4	(4)	1L	1S	1L(2#), 1K(3#), 1C(3#)
B	Nagasaki 1	(5)	1L	1S 1D	1L(2#), 1N(1#), 1U(2#), 1K(3#)
B	Kumamoto 1	(5)	2L	1S	1L(3#), 1U(2#), 1K(3#)
C	Ōita 1	(4)	1L	—	2L(2#), 1U(1#), 2S(1#), 1S(2#), 1D(3#)
D	Miyazaki 2	(3)	1L	—	2L(1#), 1L(2#), 1U(1#), 1S(3#)
Total 15A, 8*B*, 10C, 3*D*	36 districts	(151)	45L, 1N	12S, 8K, 7D, 1C	85L, 18N, 61S, 59K, 23D, 38C, 4F, 20U

Grand Total 33*A*, 28*B*, 46*C*, 23*D* 130 districts	(511)	222L, 3N, 2U[b]	80S, 31K, 24D, 12C, 1F	159L, 28N, 133S, 83K, 38D, 64C, 5F, 34U

Notes: L = Liberal Democrat; S = Socialist; K = Kōmeitō; C = Communist; N = NLC; D = Democratic Socialist; U = Unaffiliated; F = Social Democratic Federationist.

(No. #) = Number of times elected over the four elections.

[a]Type of District: *A* = Metropolitan, *B* = Urban, *C* = Semi-urban, *D* = Rural

[b]Satō Takayuki (Hokkaido 3): Unaffiliated L
Tanaka Kakuei (Niigata 3): Unaffiliated L

Conclusion

This discussion of elections for the House of Representatives and House of Councillors has been based on the premise that it is the multiple-member district systems (in both chambers) which provide a more persuasive explanation of electoral outcomes than, for example, analyses of slowly changing attitudes and policy preferences among Japanese voters. To be sure, public opinion analysts and survey researchers have adduced evidence that the citizens of Japan have not remained fixed in their outlook. As noted, over the last quarter century, the LDP has lost between 10 to 15 percent of its aggregate support and the opposition parties have made comparable gains. However, these aggregate indicators must be linked to the inexorable workings of the electoral system if the outcomes of elections are to be appreciated and understood. Without making that linkage, the data compiled by survey researchers provide interesting insights into changes within Japanese society, but not much else. Furthermore, aggregate vote totals begin to make sense only if their distribution in the multiple-member districts is included. It is, therefore, fair to conclude that in elections for Japan's National Assembly the joys and sorrows of multiple-member constituencies must be appreciated, if the results achieved are to be understood.

CHAPTER 3

The Diet: Internal Governance, External Controls

Among the most difficult issues that must be faced in discussing a national legislature is its degree of autonomy *vis-à-vis* other centers of political power. To what extent, for example, are the members of the Diet their own masters; or, in contrast, are they puppets under the control of party leaders or government officials (bureaucrats) or interest groups scrambling for their particular concerns?

In assaying answers to these questions, one basic feature of Japan's constitutional order must be kept in mind: the Diet operates within a parliamentary system in which the Prime Minister and his (or her) Cabinet control executive power precisely because they have been so installed by majority vote in the Diet. Hence, so long as the majority in the Diet supports the Cabinet, the latter controls most of the legislative agenda that the Diet is asked to consider in a given session. There is, therefore, very little room for any parliamentary body – including the Diet – to act independently. It must be the handmaiden of the Cabinet on matters of nearly all legislation and basic national policies. If it becomes recalcitrant – if the Cabinet loses the confidence of a majority in both chambers of the Diet (but especially in the House of Representatives) – then the Cabinet either resigns or dissolves the House of Representatives and calls for a General Election.

Does all this mean, then, that the Liberal Democratic Party (alone, or with one or more coalition parties) can write its script and expect the Diet to approve all of it? Or, to put it in the vernacular, does the LDP, as the governing (majority) party, get what it wants? Sometimes, yes and sometimes, no. One key variable is whether or not the LDP is fully united in its support of a new piece of legislation or policy. Another variable is whether the LDP has a bare, working, or overwhelming majority with which to enforce its will.

In the 1960s, for example, the LDP could, through its control of about 60 percent of the seats in both chambers, ram any piece of legislation that it really wanted enacted through the Diet's ponderous machinery; and it could do so by willfully ignoring the opposition parties' cries of anguish about "the tyranny of majority rule." From the mid-1970s onward, however, the power relationship between the LDP and the opposition parties was much more evenly balanced (*hakuchū*). Furthermore, it was a period during which – as one commentator bluntly put it – a civil war was raging within the governing party (Itō, 1982). Lack of internal unity and much slimmer majorities (especially in comparison with the 1960s) powerfully influenced the relationship between the LDP and its fragmented Opposition. Both factors forced the LDP's leaders to recognize that they could not force the Diet to function solely in accordance with their own wishes.

Moreover, one feature of Japan's political culture all along had limited the LDP's opportunities to act tyrannically. As is mentioned in nearly all studies of Japan, the Japanese are said to prefer to decide important matters by consensus. A majority, even one that approaches two-thirds, cannot ignore the minority with complete impunity. This is not to assert that the LDP has been unwilling to exercise its prerogatives by using "forced vote (*kyōkō saiketsu*)" tactics, but rather that it will not do so consistently, for to do so would be to court the possibility that the Opposition would boycott Diet proceedings. A boycott of this nature could raise doubts in the minds of the Japanese public concerning the viability of the Diet as a parliamentary institution.

Finally, another very different possibility must be considered in trying to determine why the Diet has been far less conflict-ridden since the mid-1970s than it was in the heyday of the LDP with its overwhelming majority (1955–75). Ellis Krauss (1984, pp. 243–93) has approached this question from the perspective that members of the Diet, especially the "presiding officers (*Gichō*)" of both chambers, have consciously and conscientiously adopted norms of behavior intended to control tension from erupting into near violence.

At the heart of this view is the LDP's abjuring the use of the forced vote, or what Krauss prefers to designate as the "snap vote." Essentially, this device allows the majority to overwhelm procedural constraints that protect the minority's right to participate meaningfully in the parliamentary process. Krauss leaves open the answer to the question whether the accommodationist pattern of recent years is a function of an internalized commitment to peaceful parliamentary processes, or a consequence of the LDP's inability to win a significant majority of seats, with the exception of the 1980 "double election."

The presiding officers of the House of Representatives and House of Councillors (in both instances *Gichō* in Japanese, but for some perverse reason "Speaker" and "President" respectively, in English) formally direct the internal operations of the Diet. "The President of each House shall maintain order in the House, adjust its business, supervise its administration and represent the House" (Diet Law, Chapter III, Article 19). They, in turn, are assisted by one of the major standing committees, the Committee on House Management (*Giin Un'ei Iinkai*, generally referred to as *Giun*). These committees – one in each House – are the focal points for determining procedural questions, such as the next day's agenda or which bill is to be assigned to what committee.

The *Giun* also provide primary links between the Diet Strategy Committees (*Kokkai Taisaku Iinkai*, or *Kokutai* for short) of each political party and the ordering of procedures in each chamber. More often than not, one of the vice-chairmen of each political party's Strategy Committee is also a member of the *Giun*. Inasmuch as a great deal of the give and take between the governing and opposition parties involves procedural rather than substantive issues, the discussions in the respective *Giun* are fraught with significance regarding the ultimate fate of a particular piece of legislation. This is especially true, it is said, of the committees' directors' meetings (*rijikai*) which are held behind closed doors, in contrast to the open deliberations of the full committee.

In addition to these political party and Diet committees consisting of elected Representatives and Councillors, each House has a Secretariat that is headed by a "Director General (*Jimu Sōchō*)." He supervises the large bureaucracy that keeps the Diet's internal machinery functioning and serves as that House's senior parliamentarian. While exercising the latter role, the Director General sits next to the Speaker (or President) on a raised dais, front and center, during plenary sessions. Each chamber's Secretariat also includes a "Standing Committees Research Room (*Jōnin Iinkai Chōsa Shitsu*)" with subdivisions for each committee, and a "Legislative Bureau (*Hōseikyoku*)" to assist the Members. For obvious reasons, most of the work of the research and legal staffs is to provide assistance to members belonging to the opposition parties. After all, members of the governing party can rely on the officials of the government's ministries and agencies for any aid they might require.

One possible method for measuring the Diet's autonomy from external control is to examine the character of the presiding officers. House of Representatives Speaker Sakata Michita is a former Liberal Democrat who, as is customary when the governing party has a relatively slim majority, has designated himself as being "Unaffiliated (*mushozoku*)" (*Kokkai Binran*, February 1985, p. 9). Sakata has had a distinguished career, having served as Minister of Justice, as Director General of the Defense Agency, as Minister of Welfare, as Minister of Education (twice) and as Chairman of the House of Representatives Special Committee on Security. This last was a controversial assignment because this committee took decades to be established by virtue of the prevailing taboo against matters involving military affairs. Currently in his sixteenth term, he had been a member of the old Ishii Mitsujirō faction, which disappeared in the late 1970s after having gradually diminished to a small group of four. For nearly a decade, therefore, he has not been affiliated with any Liberal Democratic Party faction.

Sakata's selection as Speaker, which was an LDP decision (although formal election was by majority vote in the House of Representatives), came after Prime Minister Nakasone had floated a trial balloon on behalf of LDP Vice President Nikaido Susumu, who had no intention of accepting. A bare two months earlier, Nikaido had, at the last possible moment, become Nakasone's rival for President of the Party and, therefore, Prime Minister. Having Nikaido selected as Speaker would have removed him as a competitor because it is an accepted, albeit informal, convention that the Speaker will not run for Party President. Both Nakasone and Nikaido understood this political maneuvering; at least that is what political observers maintained. By contrast, Sakata, although an LDP loyalist of long standing, was not clearly identified with any faction and had not been mentioned as being among the known candidates for the post of supreme party leader. Moreover, he had acquired an enviable reputation for having a judicious temperament, an excellent asset for a Speaker to have in his efforts to maintain order in the midst of occasional outbursts of temper among the members of the House.

Deputy Speaker Katsumata Sei'ichi comes from a very different background altogether. He, too, designated himself "Unaffiliated" following his elevation, but everyone has long known him as one of the leaders of the Japan Socialist Party, which he served as Chairman during the 1970s. His selection as Deputy Speaker and that of his predecessors Miyake Shōichi and Okada Haruo (both senior Socialists), dated back to the onset of the "close balance of power (*hakuchū*)" between the governing and opposition parties after the December 1976 General Election.

Installing a long-tenured leader of the major opposition party (Katsumata is in his fourteenth term) as Deputy Speaker was intended to promote the smooth functioning of the House of Representatives. At any rate, the Socialists thereby would become participants in the governance of the House. There is, however, no hard evidence that this expectation has been fulfilled. Even more important, this idea rests on the assumption that both the Speaker and Deputy Speaker would become autonomous actors simply by shedding their erstwhile party labels. If this assumption proved to be correct – and on this issue as well, no empirical data are available – it would have been an exceptional victory of "substance (*honne*)" over "form (*tatemae*)." Nearly all Representatives, as well as the journalists who cover the Diet with whom I have discussed this issue over the years, assert that the exercise of independent judgment by a Speaker or Deputy Speaker is neither expected nor desirable. Their roles are to preside over plenary sessions and to represent the House at ceremonial functions, not to act independently.

Circumstances in the House of Councillors occasionally have differed to some degree from those in the "Lower" House since the early 1970s, but that is not currently the case. Incumbent President Kimura Mutsuo is in his fifth consecutive term as a Councillor, having been returned in a by-election for the first time in 1964. He had been a Liberal Democrat (initially of the Satō, later of the Tanaka faction) who had declared himself as Unaffiliated upon his election as presiding officer of the "Upper" House. His immediate predecessor, Tokunaga Masatoshi, also became Unaffiliated while in the chair, but returned to full membership in the LDP and the Tanaka faction after being replaced. It can be anticipated that President Kimura will do the same.

Kimura has had a distinguished career as a member of the House of Councillors to which he was elected after having been a senior official in the Transportation Ministry (Director of the Automobile Bureau). He had been Parliamentary Vice-Minister for Post and Telecommunications, Chairman of the Committee on Transportation, Chairman of the LDP's Diet Strategy Committee in the House of Councillors, Minister of Transportation, Chairman of the Committee on House Management, Chairman of the Budget Committee – before being elected President of the House of Councillors in 1983. Evidence is lacking that President Kimura would wish to challenge the LDP's leadership in supervising the conduct of business in the Second Chamber, another appellation of the House of Councillors.

Current Vice President Agune Noboru is also in his fifth term as a Councillor. He, too, has declared himself Unaffiliated even though he once was Vice Chairman of the Socialist Party. His predecessor, Akiyama Chōzō, who served from 1980 until 1983, also had been a Socialist before becoming Vice President, upon which he too announced himself Unaffiliated; he has since rejoined the ranks of the JSP. It is this pattern of *temporary* disaffiliation from partisan ranks that casts doubts on the real motive for declaring oneself as being free from the fetters of party control; doing so appears to be no more than "form (*tatemae*)," instead of "substance (*honne*)."

Nonetheless, Vice President Agune has served in a variety of significant posts. After early service as Chairman of the Social and Labor Committee (a post often accorded a Socialist, and for which he was particularly well suited by virtue of having been General Chairman of the Miike Mineworkers' Union), he later became Chairman of the Special Committee on Pollution Countermeasures and Environmental Protection. Subsequently he rose quickly, becoming his party's Diet Strategy Committee Chairman, "Chairman of the JSP's Councillors (*Tō Sangiin Giin Kaichō*)" and a Vice Chairman of the Party itself. In his case too, however, it is doubtful that he could cut his strong party ties merely by declaring himself Unaffiliated.

There was, however, one relatively short period at the beginning of the 1970s when the President of the House of Councillors displayed considerable independence from party control. Kōno Kenzō was elected President of the chamber in the summer of 1971, and while he had been a Liberal Democrat, most of his career as a Councillor had been spent as a member of the "Green Breeze Society (*Ryokufūkai*)," an association of conservatives who, while generally identified with the LDP, had maintained some degree of autonomy. In this, they had been motivated by the hope that the House of Councillors would become something more than a replica of the political partisanship personified by the – from their perspective – "Lower" House.

Kōno replaced Shigemune Yūzo, who had presided over the House of Councillors for most of the 1960s and who had been known as *the* agent of Prime Minister Satō Eisaku (1964–72). During the era of the Satō cabinets, no effort was made to obscure the party identification or factional affiliation of the presiding officers. Shigemune listed himself as a Liberal Democrat and as a loyal retainer of the Prime Minister's faction. He was initially elected in 1947, the first election for the then newly-established House of Councillors, and had risen to become Vice President before becoming President of that chamber.

Why did Kōno decide to challenge Shigemune? Part of the answer is provided by the LDP's factional politics, Kōno Kenzō's older brother Ichirō had been Satō's principal rival for the LDP Presidency – and Prime Minister, of course – in the autumn of 1964. Hence, by staging a revolt against Shigemune, Satō's close associate, the younger brother Kenzō could avenge the defeat of his older brother Ichirō.

I had accepted this interpretation when I wrote about this episode shortly after it happened (Baerwald, 1974, p. 77). Togawa Isamu, a well-known political commentator and close confidante of Prime Minister Tanaka Kakuei (1972–4), cast Kōno's maneuver in a different light (Togawa Interviews, November 1982). Togawa asserted that Kōno challenged Shigemune because the latter had been much too compliant in accepting the LDP leadership's wishes (especially Prime Minister Satō's). Furthermore, Shigemune had been much too willing to employ "forced vote (*kyōkō saiketsu*)" tactics to ram legislation through the House of Councillors.

Kōno, by contrast, pledged himself not to use this tactic, and to rely instead on established rules of procedure and the process of "mutual consultation (*hanashiai*)." His victory, achieved with the support of the opposition parties, presaged similar changes in the direction of greater accommodation between the LDP and its opponents in the House of Representatives. During his six years as President of the House of Councillors (1971–7), the deliberative process became less confrontational. Furthermore, Kōno orchestrated this accommodationist orientation at a time when the LDP enjoyed a substantial working majority (135 out of 252 seats, or 54 percent of the total) in that chamber; that is to say, before the onset of near parity between the governing and opposition parties.

His case, however, is the only one generally mentioned of a President deliberately seeking to emphasize mutual consultation, before the close balance of power in the latter half of the 1970s. All of this does not mean that his successors have returned to earlier norms which favored using high-handed tactics. They have not, but primarily because the relationship between the governing and opposition parties *had* to become more accommodationist as a consequence of the LDP's extremely slim majorities. Moreover, hard evidence is lacking that the kind of autonomy towards the

LDP's leadership that Kōno Kenzō exhibited has characterized the behavior of his successors.

Committees in the Diet

Among the most important innovations introduced by the Allied (American) Occupation authorities during the high tide of reform (fall 1945 – summer 1948) was the introduction of standing "subject matter" committees into both chambers of the Diet.

> The most significant part of the Diet Law, the chapter dealing with standing committees, parallels in several important respects the United States Legislative Reorganization Act of 1946. The system of standing committees more than anything else differentiates the [US] House of Representatives from the British House of Commons and gives the Diet a strong resemblance to the United States Congress. Whether the Diet becomes "the highest organ of state power and the sole lawmaking body," or continues to pursue its historic role as a mere organ of discussion will depend, in the last analysis, upon the degree to which the standing committees use the power conferred upon them and the skill with which they employ the legislative aids and devices provided in the Diet Law (Government Section, 1949, p. 164).

Some fifteen years ago, I wrote an essay (published in 1979) on the Diet's committee system, for a symposium examining and comparing similar structures in various national legislatures (Baerwald, 1979, pp. 327–60). At that time I concluded that grafting a standing (mostly subject matter) committee system based on the American Congressional model (aided and abetted by the separation of powers doctrine) on to an institution that conformed more closely to the Westminster model that fuses Cabinet (Executive)–Legislative relations, had been the most difficult structural problem which had faced the Diet; and furthermore, that most of a committee's work in deliberating Cabinet (that is, Government) sponsored legislation was "a sham" (Baerwald, 1979, p. 346).

In the intervening years, this assessment of the Diet's committees has engendered considerable controversy (Krauss, 1984; and Mochizuki, 1982, pp. 63–78). Krauss and Mochizuki believe that the standing committees became more important during the 1970s, because both the governing and the opposition parties tended to give precedence to the requirements for accommodation ("conflict management") than they did to the majority's use of "forced vote" tactics in the Diet to have legislative bills approved expeditiously.

Let me hasten to add that this sort of significant change in the operations of the Diet's committees was certainly not unreasonable. After all, the close balance of power between the governing and opposition parties that prevailed between the December 1976 and June 1980 House of Representatives elections, and for a slightly longer period in the House of Councillors, did influence the character of deliberations in the Diet. Nonetheless, questions remain concerning the extent to which these newer norms of management – in committees as well as plenary sessions – have become fully institutionalized, and were not merely a passing phase.

What are the criteria and what is the nature of the evidence that can be adduced to arrive at an assessment? These questions lead into a labyrinth: (1) Who are the committee chairmen and how are they selected? (2) To what extent are they autonomous in supervising the committees that they chair? (3) What is the role of a committee's "board of directors (*riji-kai*)"? (4) What staff assistance is available to committee members to help them discharge their duties effectively? (5) How important is a specific committee assignment to a Representative or a Councillor? Answers to these questions – if available – should assist in an understanding of how the Diet's committees function.

A brief word comparing the overall structure of the Diet's committees as they existed in the prewar Imperial Diet and as they currently exist is necessary to show the basic changes that the 1947 Constitution introduced. Prior to the Second World War, the committee structure was simple: Committee of the Whole House; standing committees for the Budget, for Audit, for Discipline and for Appeals; and special or select committees to examine bills. Members of the House of Representatives in the 1930s tried to establish a significant number of standing committees to take care of the larger load of new legislation, but this effort failed. The Cabinet was responsible to the Emperor, not the Diet, and the Privy Council, the House of Peers – and the military establishment, of course – did not wish to see the powers of the "Lower" House (in fact, as well as in name, at that time) enhanced.

The New Diet Law that came into force with the 1947 Constitution on 3 May of that year, established a full panoply of committees – between twenty and twenty-four, originally. These were regrouped by Law No. 3, 28 January 1955 into sixteen committees, twelve of which had substantive jurisdiction over legislation dealing with specific Cabinet ministries or groups of Cabinet agencies (The National Diet of Japan, 1969, p. 35). Thus, the "Committee on the Cabinet (*Naikaku Iinkai*)" became responsible for most of the policy areas associated with agencies such as Economic Planning, Environment, etc.; whereas the "Committee on Foreign Affairs (*Gaimu Iinkai*)" acquired jursidiction over legislation and policy issues originating from the "Foreign Ministry (*Gaimusho*)." In addition, there are four standing committees, two of which have broad jurisdictions – the "Committee on the Budget (*Yosan Iinkai*)" and the "Committee on Audit (*Kessan Iinkai*)"; and two that concern themselves with that chamber's internal governance – the "Committee on House Management (*Giun*)" and the "Committee on Discipline (*Chōbatsu Iinkai*)."

The committees are not equal in their numerical size, nor are they equal in importance. (For a complete listing of committees, see Tables 3.1, 3.2, 3.3, and 3.4.) In both Houses, the Budget Committee is the largest (50 members in the House of Representatives, 45 in the House of Councillors). This committee has jurisdiction over the single most significant legislation emanating from the Government. Furthermore, it – rather than plenary sessions – is the forum for interpellations (question periods) of Cabinet Ministers on any issue of public policy. While these interpellations are highly ritualized and carefully programmed, they do focus public and media attention on current controversies. As such, they perform a significant educational function as well as allowing for some participation by Representatives and Councillors in public policy debates.

The current Cabinet Committee Chairman, 77 years old Amano Kōsei, is a senior Liberal Democrat belonging to Prime Minister Nakasone's faction, and is in his ninth term; he also has had Cabinet experience as Minister of State and Director General of the "Land Agency (*Kokudo-chō*)." His counterpart in the House of Councillors, Osada Yūji, is also a senior Liberal Democrat (67 years old), belonging to the Tanaka faction and is serving his third six-year term. He, too, has had Cabinet experience as Minister of State and Director General of the Science and Technology Agency, and had been Administrative Vice-Minister (that is, the senior official) of the Ministry for Postal Affairs and Telecommunications before embarking on his career in electoral politics.

Committees on House Management (*Giun* for short) are the second pair that have a higher standing than the others primarily because they are the focal points for supervising the work-load of their respective chambers. Furthermore, as noted, these committees provide the crucial linkage between the Diet Strategy Committees of the political parties and what may, or may not, transpire in the Diet in processing legislative bills.

House of Representatives Committee on House Management Chairman Ozawa Ichirō is young (42 years old), but already in his sixth term, a Liberal Democrat and a Tanaka faction adherent who has aligned himself with Finance Minister Takeshita Noboru's new faction-within-a-faction that calls itself the "*Sōseikai* (Creative Politics Association)." Ozawa does not conform to the career background that presumably would have made one eligible for being selected as *Giun* chairman (Krauss, 1984, p. 272). He has not had prior ministerial experience. On the other hand, his elevation to this important post while still young clearly marks him as one who has a bright future – providing that he is successful in future elections and did not damage his prospects by joining the *Sōseikai*, and thereby antagonizing his elders in the Tanaka faction.

His counterpart in the House of Councillors, Endō Kaname (69 years old), is a senior Liberal Democrat who is also a Tanaka faction loyalist. He is nearing the end of his second term as a Councillor (1986) and had had a prior career in the Miyagi Prefectural Assembly of which he had been Speaker. As a Councillor, he has been a Director of the *Giun*, Chairman of the Committee on the Cabinet, and Vice Chairman of his Party's Diet Strategy Committee. Clearly, he is a prototypical Committee on House Management Chairman with wide experience in the give and take of parliamentary politics.

Each of the other committees has its own role to play, and so does each committee's chairman. Since the advent of the close balance of power in the mid-1970s, some of the chairmen have been members of the opposition parties. This method of allocating chairmanships had an earlier beginning in the House of Councillors. By and large, the governing LDP is willing to allow opposition party members to become chairmen of those committees that are deemed to be less significant. The committees on Audit and on Discipline are in this category and so are those on Science and Technology, and – in the past, at least – on Social and Labor Affairs in the House of Councillors.

There are some special committees over which the LDP jealously guards its prerogatives as the governing party. They include the Special Committee on Research of Amendments to the Public Office Election Law that will be the venue for any reapportionment legislation and the Special Committee on Security, which in the House of Councillors is entitled the Special Committee of Research on Diplomacy and Comprehensive Security in order to lessen the possibility that it might restrict itself to discussions of *military* affairs.

How important is it to the governing party to have control over the standing and special committee chairmanships? On one level of analysis, at least, the answer would appear to be that it is of great significance, in fact, of far greater import than I had considered possible. Prior to December 1983, I had accepted the view that the LDP's primary concern, as the governing party, was to gain control of a majority of seats in the House of Representatives. So long as it could do so, it would be in a position to have its leader formally installed as the Prime Minister, and to have the plenary session in that chamber approve its legislative bills regardless of what happened in the various committees.

Prime Minister Nakasone and his allies in the LDP hierarchy indicated, by their actions, that this interpretation was wrong. What happened was relatively simple. In the initial reports of the 1983 election's outcome, the LDP had won 250 seats, or 6 less than the 256 (out of 511) that it needed to retain its majority status. After these preliminary results became known, initially eight and ultimately nine Unaffiliated victors joined the party's ranks, bringing its total to 259, or three above the absolute minimum.

This number of seats would be sufficient to re-elect Nakasone as Prime Minister, but not enough for the LDP to select the chairmen of all significant House of Representatives committees. Article 46 of the Diet Law specifies that "Membership of Standing Committees and of Special Committees shall be allocated to various political parties in proportion to their numerical strength." Furthermore, the Diet Secretariat uses a mathematical formula to determine each party's number of seats on all committees.

Once the LDP's leadership had determined that its majority of four seats would adversely affect its ability to control various committees, it invited the eight New Liberal Club (NLC) victors to join in establishing a coalition Cabinet, the first coalition since 1948. It can be argued, of course, that the new Cabinet was not a true coalition because most of the new partners had been Liberal Democrats prior to the establishment of the NLC in the summer of 1976. Those who had been Liberal Democrats had left because of their belief that the party would not rid itself of the taint of corruption exemplified by the Lockheed scandal, and because – as relatively younger members – their voices would not be heard by their elders who were in control. On major issues of public policy, however, the eight members of the New Liberal Club held views not divergent from those espoused by various segments of the LDP.

In any case, the NLC's eight seats altered the committee line-ups. Table 3.1 summarizes the changes that were effectuated. To illustrate, if the NLC had not joined in the coalition, the Committee on the Budget (the only fifty-member committee) would have been split between 25 LDP and 25 non-LDP (11 Socialists, 6 Kōmeitō members, 4 Democratic Socialists, 3 Communists and 1 NLC). Furthermore, if the LDP wanted to have one of its own as the chairman of this important committee, the membership would be split 24 LDP and 25 non-LDP. In turn, this would mean that the LDP could be outvoted by its opponents because committee chairmen do not vote except to break a tie. Alternatively, of course, the LDP could opt for according the chairmanship to one of the Oppositionists, whose ranks would thereby be reduced by one seat, with the LDP winning a vote in that committee by 25 to 24. That option would entail the obvious risk of the committee chairman indulging himself in a variety of delaying tactics. From the LDP's perspective, therefore, it would be far better to have a Liberal Democrat as chairman and to have a majority – even if it were by a margin of only one seat.

This same pattern is duplicated in the 4 forty-member committees (Finance; Social and Labor; Agriculture, Forestry and Fisheries; Commerce and Industry) and the 8 thirty-member committees (Cabinet; Local Administration; Justice; Foreign Affairs; Education; Transportation; Communications; Construction). On the forty-member committees, the split, without the NLC as coalition partner, would have been 20 LDP, 20 non-LDP. If the LDP would opt for control of the chairmanship, the vote by committee members would be 19 LDP and 20 non-LDP. On the thirty-member committees, the vote would be 15 LDP, 15 non-LDP, with the final vote being 14 LDP and 15 non-LDP if the chairman were a Liberal Democrat.

On the four odd-numbered committees, those with twenty-five members (Science and Technology; Environment; Audit; House Management) the initial pattern would be 13 LDP and 12 non-LDP, with the governing party in complete control if a Liberal Democrat were chairman and he used his vote to break a tie between the rank-and-file committee members. Finally, on the single twenty-member committee (Discipline), the initial 10:10 split became a 10 LDP, 9 non-LDP division, by virtue of the

Table 3.1 House of Representatives Standing Committees and Distribution of Governing and Opposition Parties' Members after 18 December 1983 Election

Standing Committees	Fixed no.	Chairman[a]	Committee Members L.	N.	S.	K.	D.	C.	F.	U.
Cabinet	30	L.-Nakasone	15	0(1)	7	3	2	2	0	0
Local Administration	30	L.-Nakasone	15	0(1)	7	4(3)	2	1(2)	0	0
Justice	30	L.-Suzuki	15	0(1)	6(7)	3	2	2	1(0)	0
Foreign Affairs	30	L.-Fukuda	15	0(1)	7	3	2	2	0	0
Finance	40	L.-Suzuki	20	0(1)	9	5	3	2	0	0
Education	30	L.-Tanaka	15	0(1)	7	3	2	2	0	0
Social and Labor	40	L.-Tanaka	20	0(1)	9	5	3	2	0	0
Agriculture, Forestry and Fisheries	40	L.-Suzuki	20	0(1)	9	5	3	2	0	0
Commerce and Industry	40	L.-Tanaka	20	0(1)	9	5	3	2	0	0
Transportation	30	L.-Fukuda	15	0(1)	7	3	2	2	0	0
Post and Telecommunications	30	L.-Kōmoto	15	0(1)	7	3	3	1	0	0
Construction	30	L.-no faction	15	0(1)	7	3	2	2	0	0
Science and Technology	25	Kōmeitō	12(13)	0	5(6)	2	3(2)	1	0	1[b]
Environment	25	L.-Tanaka	12(13)	0	5(6)	4(3)	2	1	0	0
Budget	50	L.-Nakasone	25	0(1)	11	6	4	3	0	0
Audit	25	Socialist	12(13)	0	4(6)	3(2)	2	1	1(0)	1[c]
House Management	25	L.-Tanaka	12(13)	0	6	3(2)	2	1	0	0
Discipline	20	Dem. Soc.	10	0	3(5)	2	1(2)	1	1(0)	1[d](0)

Sources: Asahi Shinbun, 20 December 1983, p. 3; Yomiuri Shinbun, 27 December 1983, p. 2.

Notes: L. = LDP; N. = NLC; S. = JSP; K. = Kōmeitō; D. = DSP; C. = JCP; F. = Soc. Dem. Fed.; U. = Unaffiliated.

[a]Chairmen are not included in number of members listed by party. LDP chairmen include factional line-up of Tanaka 5, Nakasone 3, Suzuki 3, Fukuda 2, Kōmoto 1, no faction 1. Numbers in parentheses indicate seats per party on each committee, if committees had been organized on basis of LDP seats alone (that is 259 members in the House of Representatives). By including the 8 New Liberal Club members in the coalition, the LDP gained control over all thirty-, forty- and fifty-member committees, but not of three of the less significant committees. Of course, the New Liberal Club thereby lost separate representation on all committees.

[b]Tsuji Kazuhiko (Opposition).

[c]Tanaka Kakuei (pro-LDP).

[d]Satō Takayuki (pro-LDP).

Table 3.2 House of Representatives Special Committees, December 1983

Committees	Fixed no.	Chairman (party and faction)	Committee members L.	S.	K.	D.	C.
Disaster Policy	40	Socialist	21	8	5	3	2
Research on Amendments to Public Office Election Law	25	L.-Nakasone	12	6	3	2	1
Coal Mining Countermeasures	25	Socialist	13	5	3	2	1
Commodity Prices	25	Socialist	13	5	3	2	1
Transportation Safety	25	Kōmeitō	13	6	2	2	1
Okinawa and Northern Territories	25	Democratic-Socialist	13	6	3	3	1
National Security	25	L.-Fukuda	12	6	3	2	1

Source: *Kokkai Binran* [Diet Handbook], February 1984, pp. 165–7.
Notes: L. = LDP; S. = JSP; K. = Kōmeitō; D. = DSP; C. = JCP. L. . . . = LDP and faction.
Chairmen are not included in number of members listed by party. It is clear that the LDP's priorities are those two committees dealing with the Election Law, and National Security (Defense).

chairmanship going to a Democratic Socialist. In this instance, as well as in the cases of the Science and Technology (Kōmeitō member as Chairman) and Audit (Socialist as Chairman) committees, the vote among committee members would be 12 LDP, 12 non-LDP, except that in the Audit Committee, the LDP in case of dire need could count on former Prime Minister Tanaka or his surrogate to vote with the LDP. Given Tanaka's past difficulties with his financial transactions, it seems particularly ironic that he was selected for membership of the Audit Committee. In any case, with the New Liberal Club as its coalition partner, the LDP retained control of all committee chairmen and voting majorities in all standing committees except for the three that party leaders considered least significant.

Nonetheless, the creation of a coalition Cabinet did have its price, in that one Cabinet post had to be accorded to the New Liberal Club. Tagawa Sei'ichi, therefore, became Minister for Local Autonomy (Home Affairs). His selection could not have been an easy one for Nakasone to make, as Tagawa had been among the Prime Minister's most vituperative critics. In the next Cabinet reshuffle, NLC Secretary General Yamaguchi Toshio became Labor Minister and replaced Tagawa, a much happier

Table 3.3 House of Councillors Standing Committees, December 1983

Committees	Fixed no.	Chairman (party and faction)	Committee members L.	S.	K.	C.	D.	U.	V.
Cabinet	20	L.-Fukuda	10	4	2	1	1	1	0
Local Administration	20	L.-Nakasone	10	4	2	1	1	0	1
Justice	20	Kōmeitō	10	2	1	1	1	3	0
Foreign Affairs	20	L.-Suzuki	10	3	2	1	2	1	0
Finance	25	L.-Tanaka	13	4	3	1	1	2	0
Education	20	L.-Tanaka	10	4	2	1	1	1	0
Social and Labor	21	L.-Fukuda	11	4	2	1	1	1	0
Agriculture, Forestry and Fisheries	25	L.-Fukuda	14	4	3	1	1	1	0
Commerce and Industry	21	L.-Nakasone	11	4	2	1	1	1	0
Transportation	20	Kōmeitō	10	4	1	1	1	2	0
Post and Telecommunications	20	Socialist	10	2	2	1	1	2	0
Construction	20	Socialist	10	2	3	2	1	0	1
Budget	45	L.-Tanaka	24	8	5	2	2	3	0
Audit	30	Socialist	17	4	3	2	2	1	0
House Management	25	L.-Tanaka	14	5	3	1	1	0	0
Discipline	10	L.-no faction	4	2	1	1	1	0	0

Source: *Kokkai Binran* [Diet Handbook], February, 1984, pp. 168–72.

Notes: L. = LDP; S. = JSP; K. = Kōmeitō; C. = JCP; D. = DSP; U. = Unaffiliated and minor parties; V. = Vacancies.
Chairmen are not included in number of members listed by party.

choice from Nakasone's personal perspective. Moreover, the need to give a portfolio to the NLC also provided one less ministerial assignment with which to reward an LDP loyalist. This was especially awkward, inasmuch as the NLC was a miniscule group of 8 Representatives, in contrast to Tanaka's 63 or Suzuki's 50 factional followers in that chamber. Even Kōmoto's group of 28 looms quite large by comparison.

In considering these delicate decisions, it is worth remembering that ministerial assignments are highly prized rewards which are, in large measure, apportioned in accordance with the respective numerical strength of the governing party's factions. Furthermore, the NLC's good fortune in having one of its own appointed as a Cabinet Minister resulted in raised expectations among the leaders of other parties – the Kōmeitō (59 members) and the Democratic Socialist Party (39 members). The question, then, is whether the trade-off – increased control over most committees, versus the difficulties of coping with a coalition partner and raising

Table 3.4 House of Councillors Special Committees, December 1983

Committees	Fixed no.	Chairman (party and faction)	Committee members L.	S.	K.	C.	D.	U.
Research on Diplomacy and Comprehensive Security	30	L.-Suzuki	16	5	3	2	2	1
Research on Citizens' Life and Economics	30	Socialist	17	4	3	2	2	1
Disaster Policy	20	Socialist	11	3	2	1	1	1
Election System	25	L.-Tanaka	13	4	3	2	1	1
Science and Technology	20	Kōmeitō	11	3	1	1	1	2
Okinawa and Northern Territories	20	L.-Suzuki	10	3	2	1	1	2
Pollution	20	Socialist	11	3	2	1	1	1
Energy Policy	20	L.-Tanaka	10	4	2	1	1	1

Source: *Kokkai Binran* [Diet Handbook], February, 1984, pp. 172–4.
Notes: L. = LDP; S. = JSP; K. = Kōmeitō; C. = JCP; D. = DSP; U. = Unaffiliated and minor parties.
Chairmen are not included in number of members listed by party.

expectations among other potential claimants – was worthwhile for the LDP.

From the Prime Minister's perspective, the answer would appear to be a resounding affirmative, for various reasons. First, the maneuver may have paved the way for the return of the NLC members to their erstwhile home in the LDP. This is an obvious plus for the governing party under prevailing "close balance of power (*hakuchū*)" circumstances. Secondly, both the Kōmeitō and the Democratic Socialist Party leaders might become more amenable to the LDP's legislative program due to the expectation that they too could aspire to a post in the Cabinet. Both of these advantages were offset by the fact that there would be one less LDP claimant for a ministerial portfolio who could be rewarded. As to the third factor, that of control over the committees, the answer is also obvious providing that the committees are significant. It is this issue that focuses us on the role that committees play in the Diet.

To begin with, this whole episode makes it abundantly clear that committee chairmen who are members of the governing party *must* act as agents of that party; otherwise, it would not have made any sense for Prime Minister Nakasone to invite the New Liberal Club to be a coalition partner in the Cabinet. For him to have done so with the expectation that the Liberal Democrats who were selected to become committee chairmen would act autonomously, or as defenders of a particular committee's prerogatives, would have meant that Nakasone had wasted precious political capital for no gain whatsoever. Furthermore, if obedience to party directives is expected of a chairman, it would follow that the same is true for rank-and-file members of that committee, including those who are committee directors (*Riji*).

Mochizuki avers, on the other hand, that "[Diet] committees, in particular the directorates, provide convenient settings for negotiations to thrash out cross-partisan compromises" (Mochizuki, 1982, p. 77). Unfortunately, he does not provide any specific instances. Everything is possible, of course, but it would be my position that such negotiations only take place if that is what the party's leadership wants. It is this lack of autonomy that makes the committees so dependent on external control and that reduces the members to mere robots, reflecting decisions made elsewhere (Baerwald, 1979, p. 355). In order for independent decision-making to occur, it would be necessary to allow committee chairmen or committee directors to negotiate in a manner contrary to the wishes of the party leadership. This is a scenario which rests on evidence that no known behavior of Representatives or Councillors would support.

Yet what about the committee "directors (*Riji*)," the eight senior members of committees (with the exception of the Committee on Discipline, which has only five). Each party is allocated its share of the available directorships in rough proportion to its numerical strength within that chamber, in this case, awarded as follows: four Liberal Democrats, two Socialists, one Kōmeitō member and one Democratic Socialist. Again, there is one notable exception: the Committee on House Management (*Giun*) has nine directors (despite its being one of the smaller committees, with only twenty-five members); the Liberal Democrats hold the extra seat (*Kokkai Binran*, February 1985, pp. 158–66). On the *Giun*, the chairman, who also sits as a director, would not have to vote to break a tie. Moreover, the expectation that this committee, which plays a primary role in the functioning of each chamber, would have its special coterie of directors unfortunately is not borne out except in the cases of the two Socialists and one Democratic Socialist. Between 1983 and 1985, all of the other directors changed!

That being the case, it is difficult – in Japanese read impossible – to imagine that the directors would develop a sense of *esprit de corps* or autonomy during their tenure on the Committee on

House Management as a consequence of lengthy service. In his admirable discussion of this committee's role as manager of conflict resolution in the House of Representatives during the "close balance of power (*hakuchū*)" years (December 1976 until June 1980), Krauss unfortunately overstates the case that he makes for the *Giun* (Krauss, 1984, pp. 271–8). I say "unfortunately," because I would personally much prefer that the Committee on House Management be the focal point for resolving pressing procedural questions facing both Houses of the Diet.

The *Giun* has the potential to be the arbiter of disputes, but it must – as yet – conform to external party directives. If the various party leaders want accommodation between the governing and opposition parties, then all is well. If, on the other hand, either or both decide to opt for confrontation, then all efforts at compromise can be expected to fail. Party discipline on issues that the leadership believes to be crucial is simply too strong to challenge. Furthermore, members of the Diet tend to eschew the exercise of individual initiative. Nor does anyone, least of all their party's leadership, expect it. In fact, such behavior is derided as "grandstanding" or currying favor with the public. It is precisely because Nakasone, before becoming Prime Minister, was one of the few who had the temerity (or self-confidence) to do so that his fellow Liberal Democrats viewed him with suspicion and therefore delayed, for as long as they could, his election as Party President.

Another criterion for assessing the effectiveness of Diet committees is the availability of staff support. Each chamber's Secretariat has a "Committee Division (*Iin-bu*)," with nine "sections (*ka*)" in the House of Representatives and eight in the House of Councillors. Furthermore, each chamber has a "Standing Committees Research Room (*Jōnin Iinkai Chōsa Shitsu*)" with two specialists assigned to it in the House of Representatives and one in the House of Councillors. In addition, there is a "Legislative Bureau (*Hōseikyoku*)" with a large group of legal specialists in each House. Furthermore, the National Diet Library (modeled on the Congressional Library) employs many researchers who provide support to the members. Hence, it is not any lack of specialized assistance that can be faulted for members not being independent lawmakers.

The problem, if that is what it is – after all, the exercise of independent initiatives by members of national assemblies is not universally applauded – lies elsewhere. One of its aspects is that most specialist-researchers assigned to a committee are on temporary leave from the ministry which is that committee's domain. Hence, the long arm of government officialdom reaches into the very core of those who are supposed to help the committee oversee the policies or legislative proposals emanating from that ministry. Furthermore, inasmuch as these specialist-researchers are only on temporary assignment, their careers are still controlled by their ministry's Personnel Division. It is an arrangement that is particularly well-suited to thwart any deviationist tendencies by these bureaucrats (Baerwald, 1979, pp. 349–50). Furthermore, it is these same officials' fellow bureaucrats who are the drafters of the bulk of legislative bills that the Cabinet submits to the Diet for consideration.

Finally, most Representatives and Councillors still tend to view their Diet committee assignments as a duty to be filled rather than an opportunity to make a mark. They know, or quickly learn, that most committee deliberations are a kind of charade. They attend unless they can prevail upon one of their "juniors (*kōhai*)" to do so, in case there is an official vote that is to be taken. They participate because doing so is among their duties; but they are also aware that the script for their parts in the legislative drama has been determined beforehand by their party's leaders.

Does all of this mean, then, that the committees are nothing more than "ornaments (*kazarimono*)," as one Councillor – echoing similar if less forceful comments by many others – told me? (Baerwald, 1979, p. 382). If the criterion that is used is based on the hope that committees would exercise some autonomy, the answer would have to be affirmative. On the other hand, the committees do exist; therefore they must serve some purpose. Those who would wish to control Diet deliberations cannot ignore them. Particularly from the governing party's perspective, there is always the possibility that something may go wrong in a particular committee, especially so when the governing party's members and their opponents are separated by one vote. Loyal chairmen can be expected to do the majority party leadership's will, but that is not true of chairmen drawn from the ranks of the opposition parties. When the opposition party members are the majority on a committee, they can amend a Cabinet-sponsored bill; and that piece of mischief would have to be overturned in plenary session. This is always possible, but is considered undesirable because it carries the implication of a lack of control on the part of the governing party. Hence, the committees, by virtue of their existence, if not their labors, have influenced the Diet in its conduct of business. They may not be bulwarks of independence, but Diet strategists neglect them at their peril.

The Diet's Strategists

Who, then, are the masters of the Diet? There are two groups with partially overlapping memberships. The governing party's President, who is also Prime Minister, sits at the summit. As President, he is at the apex of the party's Diet members and the vast structure of boards, bureaux, and committees that constitute LDP Headquarters. As Prime Minister, he is the government's Chief Executive, presiding over the Cabinet in which the Constitution vests executive power (1947 Constitution, Chapter II, Article 65).

Certain senior party officials function as the Party President's inner council: the Secretary General (*Kanjichō*) who is assisted by an Executive Deputy Secretary General and eight Deputy Secretaries General; the "Chairman of the Executive Board (*Sōmu Kaichō*)" and the "Chairman of the Policy Research Council (*Seimu Chōsa Kaichō*, more often than not abbreviated to *Seichō Kaichō*)." (For a complete listing of party officers, see *Kokkai Binran*, 1985, pp. 174–9.) The Prime Minister's principal deputy is the "Chief Cabinet Secretary (*Kanbō Chōkan*)" who is also a "Minister of State (*Kokumu Daijin*)" in the Cabinet. Often referred to as the "wife" of the Prime Minister, the Chief Cabinet Secretary combines the roles of "co-ordinator (*matome-yaku*)" of Cabinet policy, Chief Spokesman (Press Secretary) of the Cabinet, and liaison between the Prime Minister, the governing party, and its leadership in the Diet. Incumbent Chief Cabinet Secretary Fujinami Takao is, as were most of his predecessors, a member of the Prime Minister's own faction. He is assisted, in turn, by two Deputy Chiefs who also are parliamentarians.

The Prime Minister is assisted, in addition, by at least nine "Secretaries (*Hisho-kan*)" who are government officials drawn from the ranks of specific ministries (Foreign Affairs, MITI etc.), and several political "Secretaries" to liaise with the governing party. (For a complete listing of officials in the "Prime Minister's Office (*Sōrifu*)" see *Kokkai Binran*, 1985, p. 196.)

The foregoing are the peaks of the two pyramids which extend into the lower reaches of the Liberal Democratic Party on the one hand and the array of government ministries and agencies on the other. It is through the interaction of these two groups that much of the script for a Cabinet's legislative program is written. Most of what transpires is hidden from public view, and that which the public can witness – for example, interpellation of Cabinet

Ministers in a standing committee hearing – has been carefully prepared and thus is highly formalistic and stylized.

Missing from the foregoing description is another set of actors within the party: the heads of the factions and the factions themselves. Their role in the policy-making process within the governing party is murky, even if they play a crucial role (as was noted in Chapter 1) in the allocation of Cabinet portfolios and senior party posts. This process can have an impact on policy, even if indirectly, in that all of the major officials in the government's bureaucracy can be influenced thereby.

Moreover, in the jockeying for succession to the party presidency, alternative policy emphases are sometimes aired. For example, in the summer of 1972, during the battle between Tanaka Kakuei and Fukuda Takeo to succeed Prime Minister Satō Eisaku, Tanaka took a much more forward-looking attitude regarding the establishment of diplomatic relations with the People's Republic of China than Fukuda, who was more cautious and more closely identified with the "Taiwan Lobby" within the LDP. Tanaka won, but it would be a mistake to attribute his victory solely to the position that he had taken on this particular foreign policy issue. Many other factors were involved.

Currently, LDP Executive Board Chairman Miyazawa Kiichi, representative leader of the Suzuki faction, identifies himself with an expansionist economic policy agenda, to contrast his views with those of Prime Minister Nakasone, who has tried his best to pursue extremely conservative and restrictive fiscal policies under the overall goal of "administrative reform (*gyōsei kaikaku*)" with almost no budget increases except for Defense and Foreign Aid. These kinds of debates over large questions of public policy take place at a level of generalized abstraction, and merely reflect alternative tendencies, rather than being concrete and specific. It is the government officials (bureaucrats) who become involved with and generally control the process of drafting specific policy proposals which might include new legislation that is ultimately submitted to the Diet for approval.

One other set of groups in the LDP has become the object of considerable interest among Japanese journalists and political commentators: the "policy tribes (*seisaku-zoku*)." These are LDP Diet members who have become specialists in the policies of specific ministries. Thus, there are the "Commerce and Industry clan (*shōkō-zoku*)" with expertise in MITI policies, or the "Agriculture and Forestry clan (*nōrin-zoku*)" that pursue matters related to the Ministry of Agriculture, Forestry and Fisheries.

It has been reported that currently there are eleven "policy tribes" comprised of about 200 party members (*Shūkan Yomiuri*, 23 June 1985, pp. 132–42). Basically, it is argued that by virtue of their lengthy careers in the Diet – many have been members for a quarter century or more – these "policy tribesmen" have acquired a level of expertise that rivals that of government officials (bureaucrats) in specific ministries. Especially so, because the Government officials rotate within a ministry as an element of their career advancement and are therefore at a disadvantage in terms of expertise in debating a fine point of policy with a Diet member who has spent many years immersing himself in a specific issue area.

Empirical evidence is simply not available, regrettably, on the interaction between these LDP policy tribesmen and government bureaucrats. My discussions with Japanese colleagues and friends have yielded two contradictory viewpoints. A professor of public administration who also has served as a consultant to the government told me that he was surprised by the level of expert knowledge displayed by some Diet members. He had always believed that government officials (bureaucrats) were the only real policy specialists and that they could outwit any Diet member, but that he no longer believed the relationship to be as one-sided as he had assumed. On the other hand, a senior Foreign Ministry official smiled in response to my question and went on to say that "We (officials) must have expertise which is on an entirely different level of specificity than is available to practicing politicians." (In both instances, I would prefer to protect the anonymity of my respondents.) When I asked an incumbent Cabinet Minister who had been a very senior government official before entering electoral politics, "Do you believe that Japan remains a 'heaven for bureaucrats?'," he was at first nonplussed. After thinking about it for a moment, he said: "Not exactly; some politicians are becoming quite knowledgeable." That may be all that can be asserted with plausibility on this issue for the time being.

Party–government interaction is extensive and intensive, however, in a known setting: the study groups of the LDP's "Policy Research Council (*Seichōkai*)." This party structure currently has "study groups (*bukai*)" roughly replicating the domains of the government's ministries and agencies, with "Diplomatic Affairs (*Gaikō Bukai*)" for Foreign Ministry, "Educational Affairs (*Bunkyō Bukai*)" for Ministry of Education, Science and Culture, etc. LDP Diet members of one of the Policy Research Council's study groups often are now identified with the relevant policy "clan (*zoku*)" on the one hand, and may – but, by no means consistently – be members of the relevant standing committee in the House of Representatives or House of Councillors. Even if they are not members of the standing committee, however, they can always attend as observers if they really wish to do so. By that stage of the legislative or policy-making process, it is likely that most of the problems, either between the Government's bureaucrats and the LDP, or among the contending factions within the party, have been ironed out. Thus, though attending a Diet committee meeting does not loom as being particularly compelling, it is an available option.

By contrast, discussions can be substantive between a ministry's emissaries and the LDP's relevant study group members. (At least, that is what I have been told by participants.) Outsiders are excluded from these meetings which is a pity because they are the focal points for hammering out the agreements over issues of policy or new pieces of legislation between the government and the governing party. By comparison, that which occurs later at an open hearing of a Diet committee tends to be ritualistic. In effect, it is all this prior consultation between a Ministry's officials and the party's relevant policy groups that robs much of the Diet's proceedings of their possible impact. On the other hand, it can be argued that if the bureaucrats did not have to face the prospect of Diet proceedings, they would not consider it necessary to consult the politicians. Hence, these interactions do add an imponderable element – by virtue of its being hidden from public view – to the process whereby the LDP can exercise some control over the bureaucracy, if that is what it wants to accomplish.

Where do the opposition parties fit into this process? By and large, they tend to be excluded. Of course, government officials do read the election returns as well as everyone else who is interested; possibly, more carefully than most. One senior Socialist, a veteran of his party's "Diet Strategy Policy Committee (*Kokkai Taisaku Iinkai*)" and the House of Representatives "Management Committee (*Giun*)" stated: "During the close balance of power period, some government officials made efforts to inform us of the outlines of pending legislative proposals before they were introduced by the Cabinet" (Interview, November 1982). He went on to note that this kind of consultation was of considerably less salience than what he understood to be the fairly constant interaction between the Government and the LDP.

Each of the opposition parties has its own policy councils (*Kokkai Binran*, February 1985, pp. 180–4). Their work is

Table 3.5 Liberal Democratic Party Policy Research Council, December 1983

Position	Name	Faction	Times elected	District	Age
Chairman	Fujio Masayuki	Fukuda	8	Tochigi 2	67
Deputy Chairman	Imai Isamu	Suzuki	5	Ehime 3	64
Deputy Chairman	Karasawa Shunjirō	Nakasone	6	Nagano 4	53
Deputy Chairman	Satō Megumu	Tanaka	6	Osaka 6	60
Deputy Chairman	Shiina Moto'o	No faction	3	Iwate 2	53
Deputy Chairman	Mitsuzaka Hiroshi	Fukuda	5	Miyagi 1	56
Deputy Chairman	Yamashita Tokuo	Kōmoto	6	Saga	64
Deputy Chairman	Kawamoto Kakuzo	Tanaka	3[b]	Shiga	66
Deputy Chairman	Koga Raishirō	Tanaka	3[b]	National	68
Chairman, Cabinet	Ikeda Yukihiko	Suzuki	4	Hiroshima 2	46
Chairman, Local Administration	Aichi Kazuo	Tanaka	4	Miyagi 1	46
Chairman, Defense	Miyashita Sōhei	Fukuda	3	Nagano 3	56
Chairman, Justice	Hirai Takushi	Nakasone	3[b]	Kagawa	52
Chairman, Diplomacy	Ishikawa Yōzō	Suzuki	4	Tokyo 11	58
Chairman, Finance	Fukuya Takashi	Nakasone	4	Tokyo 8	48
Chairman, Education	Aoki Masahisa	Nakasone	5	Saitama 4	61
Chairman, Social	Imai Isamu	Suzuki	5	Ehime 3	64
Chairman, Labor	Ōtsubo Ken'ichirō	Suzuki	2[b]	Saga	58
Chairman, Agriculture and Forestry	Tamazawa Tokuichirō	Fukuda	4	Iwate 1	46
Chairman, Fisheries	Kikuchi Fukujirō	Suzuki	4	Miyagi 2	58
Chairman, Commerce and Industries	Noda Takeshi	Nakasone	5	Kumamoto 1	42

Chairman, Traffic	Kano Michihiko	Fukuda	4	Yamagata 1	42
Chairman, Communications	Kondō Tetsuo	Kōmoto	6	Yamagata 1	54
Chairman, Construction	Muraoka Kanezō	Tanaka	4	Akita 2	52
Chairman, Science and Technology	Hayashi Hiroko[a]	Fukuda	2[b]	National	50
Chairman, Environment	Santō Akiko[a]	Tanaka	2[b]	National	41

Source: *Kokkai Binran* [Diet Handbook], February 1984, pp. 176–7.

Notes: [a] = women.

[b] = Members of the House of Councillors, all others are members of the House of Representatives.

Factional line-up of 6 Tanaka, 6 Suzuki, 6 Fukuda (including the chairman), 5 Nakasone, 2 Kōmoto, and 1 no faction reflects the numerical strength of each clique within the parliamentary party. Also worth noting is the factional affiliation of each section's chairman, either because of a particular faction's interest in that issue area, or because some factions have been given short shrift by the mainstream coalition that is in power.

circumscribed by the party platforms that are debated and adopted at party conventions. It is, therefore, extremely difficult to alter significantly a party's policy stance during the course of a Diet session, particularly so because any adjustment may involve issues of basic party ideology for the Socialists and Communists. Hence, Representatives or Councillors belonging to these parties have almost no room to maneuver in responding to any Cabinet-sponsored legislative initiatives. For them, their party platform's policy pronouncements, which often are the products of intensive intra-party debates, must be honored much more explicitly than in the case of the LDP. Hence, it is frequently impossible for their members to join in meaningful discussion with their counterparts in the governing party. Instead, opposition members will expound their party's basic policies. To do otherwise would be disloyal to their party and to its external supporters who are highly organized.

By the time the Cabinet introduces a legislative bill into the Diet, or introduces a new policy, at a very minimum the following steps will have been taken:

1 Government officials within a Ministry prepare a draft. This process generally begins at the working level – "division chief (*kachō*)" or even lower. The initiative may come from within the Ministry itself or the governing party, or the Cabinet can order its preparation.
2 This draft is circulated within the Ministry for general approval.
3 Discussions begin to take place between the Ministry's officials and the relevant "study group (*bukai*)" in the LDP's Policy Research Council.
4 Within the government, the draft of the new legislation is discussed at one or several meetings of the "Council of Vice-Ministers (*Jimu-Jikan Kaigi*)" to insure that the prerogatives of all ministries or agencies have been considered.
5 Within the governing party, the draft legislation receives consideration by the full Policy Research Council.
6 Within the government, the bill is considered by a meeting of the Cabinet.
7 Within the governing party, the bill is discussed by the "Executive Board (*Sōmukai*)" in order to determine its place on the party's legislative agenda for that particular session of the Diet.
8 More or less simultaneously (within the governing party)

discussions begin between the party's leadership and its Diet Strategy Committee whose members may decide to test the sentiment in the House Management Committee, generally that of the House of Representatives first.

9 Meanwhile, the opposition parties may be informed, either directly by Ministry officials, or through the media, that the Cabinet is likely to introduce this particular bill to this session of the Diet.

10 The opposition parties discuss the stance that they will take. On occasion, the discussions may include interparty consultations in order to determine whether the opposition parties will mount a united campaign against the legislation.

11 In turn, the opposition parties' positions will be communicated by their "Diet Strategy Committee (*Kokutai*)" members to the House Management Committee, whose members determine whether the bill may or may not be controversial.

It is only after this largely pre-parliamentary process has been completed that the relevant standing (or, on occasion, special) committee of the Diet begins to play its role by holding public hearings in order formally to process the legislative bill. Once this stage of the legislative process has been actually reached, it is virtually certain that all of the participants will know in precise detail what is expected of them. Should they have doubts, their party strategists are available to inform them by invoking party discipline. The contending groups will march into the Diet arena to grapple with each other verbally, or – under compelling circumstances – physically by the Opposition's imprisoning the Speaker in his office so that he cannot convene a plenary session, or conversely, by the governing party's protecting access to the Speaker's chair so that he is able to convene a plenary session.

These kinds of scenes of near violence have become exceptional since most participants now prefer to emphasize "mutual consultations (*hanashiai*)" among the relevant actors, given the constraints imposed by near parity. These consultations do not necessarily take place in the Diet building itself. They may occur instead in much more comfortable surroundings such as a private room in a Japanese restaurant (*ryōtei*) down the hill from the Diet itself in the Akasaka district, or in Shinbashi. These venues have the distinct advantage of being removed from the prying eyes and ears of the electronic and print journalists who are eager to learn about the latest "understanding (*ryōkai*)" that might have been arrived at in order to insure a bill's passage.

Understandings arrived at in these settings may well include the governing party's willingness to indulge the opposition parties' desire to delay the bill's passage for a specified period of time, so that the opposition parties will not lose face with their external supporters. If that is part of the agreement, then the seemingly hostile confrontations in the halls of the Diet will also have been reduced to exercises in a kind of ritual.

Throughout these proceedings and consultations it is the manipulation of time that is the critical variable. The governing party, after its sometimes lengthy consultation with the Government's officialdom and its internal debates, will want to have as much of its legislative program as possible processed as smoothly and quickly as possible by the Diet. Furthermore, it has the necessary votes in most of the important committees, and most certainly in the plenary sessions, to accomplish its purpose. Conversely, the opposition parties will try to delay proceedings in the Diet, if that is what they have decided to do.

From this perspective, Mochizuki (1982) has calculated that Diet sessions are not as long as they appear to be. "Ordinary (*tsūjō*)" sessions last for 150 days, but since they are convened during the latter half of December, much of the first month is consumed by convivial gatherings that see the old year out and new year in. Furthermore, much of the Diet's schedule is tied up in considering the Government's Budget during February and March, as the new fiscal year is supposed to begin on 1 April. Sometimes, the Opposition's delaying tactics create some slippage in that schedule. In any case, only the months of April and – if the session is extended, which it can be, but only once – May and June remain for the consideration of other legislation. This means, in effect, that an ordinary session may provide no more than 50 to 80 days for the processing of all other legislative bills.

There are two other types of sessions. "Special (*Tokubetsu*)" ones must be convened within thirty days after a General Election for the House of Representatives. "Extraordinary (*Rinji*)" ones can be convened by the Cabinet or by petition of 25 percent of the members.

> The Cabinet may determine to convoke extraordinary sessions of the Diet. When a quarter or more of the total members of either House makes the demand, the Cabinet must determine on such convocation (Constitution, Chapter IV, Article 53).

> To demand the convocation of an extraordinary session a written request must be presented to the Cabinet through the

President of either House under the joint signature of at least one-fourth of the total membership of that House (Diet Law, Chapter I, Article 3).

Terms are not fixed for these special and extraordinary sessions. On occasion, the opposition parties use the determination of a session's length as a bargaining tool. This is especially the case if the legislative agenda is likely to include bills that the Cabinet wants approved, but which the Opposition plans to contest. Under these circumstances, the shorter the length of the session, the more likely that the Diet's ponderous procedures will not yield to the governing party's will. Should that occur, the session must be extended to accommodate more negotiations between the LDP and its opponents. Even if the governing party is victorious in extending the session and in approving the bill(s), the opposition parties can claim a moral victory. Or, if not that, they will at least be able to report to their supporters that they fought the good fight. Moreover, these procedural wrangles also provide opportunities for extracting some concessions from the LDP so that the final product is not completely unpalatable to the opposition parties. The more the prevailing norms of behavior are based on mutual consultation instead of the majority forcing its will, the more time can be consumed.

The opposition parties have one additional device with which to try to influence proceedings in the Diet. They can mobilize public opinion through demonstrations and through the mass media of communications (*masu-komi*). It must be added that pressure groups which *support* the LDP have also used this technique. When the Government announces that it must increase the import quota of certain foodstuffs (beef and oranges, for example) or reduce certain tariffs, large groups of farmers will parade through the streets of Tokyo – peacefully, to be sure – to remind their representatives that it was they who elected them to office in the first place.

More frequent is the Opposition's use of this strategy, especially if a Government proposal that has been adopted by the LDP touches some sensitive ideological nerves. Among these would be any amendment to the existing Constitution, or – in the recent past at least – increasing defense expenditures in the National Budget above the ceiling of 1 percent of the gross national product. By the time these lines appear in print, the latter limitation may well have been overcome. As some of my friends have put it: "That has already happened. It is only a case of the Government manipulating the statistics" (personal interviews). Nonetheless, the opposition parties do continue to mount demonstrations, most of which are extremely orderly, and to make their case to the public over the air-waves and via the newspapers, weekly magazines and monthly journals.

The Japanese people remain voracious readers. The "Big Three" newspapers – *Asahi, Mainichi* and *Yomiuri* – have a combined circulation of between 25 and 30 million every day. Furthermore, as national newspapers, their editorial policies influence opinion from the northern tip of Hokkaido to the southernmost tip of Okinawa. A concerted campaign on their part, for or against a policy change or a piece of legislation, can give the appearance of being enormously influential. It is very difficult, however, to accurately gauge their true impact, because measurement is so difficult.

I am personally convinced that the media campaign against pollution during the final years of the 1960s did influence government officials, and LDP and opposition leaders, as well as the public, to shift away from the exclusive concern with economic growth toward at least some interest in emphasizing environmental protection. On the other hand, some bureaucrats with whom I have discussed this fundamental shift in policy have greeted my comment or question with a total lack of comprehension. For them it was simply a case of their having decided that *their* interpretation of what is best for Japan now included the importance of controlling and limiting environmental devastation (Interviews, September 1974). Furthermore, these bureaucrats seemed oblivious to the political costs to the LDP incurred by the adoption of anti-pollution legislation, which antagonized several powerful interest groups that had made substantial contributions either to the LDP itself or to the re-election campaigns of some of its leaders.

One thing is clear: media journalists believe that they are influential. Indeed, many see themselves as the Government's and LDP's true "loyal Opposition." Consequently, many news articles – not to mention editorials (which tend to be extremely moralistic and are often ignored) – imply that the Cabinet consists of knaves and fools, that the Diet is riddled with corruption, and that the bureaucrats are more interested in protecting their turf than in governing. Although a grain of truth may be found in each of these criticisms, they are not the entire story by any means. Collusion between the opposition parties and the media journalists – to the extent that it exists – has been of only marginal utility in influencing the public, and, thereby, proceedings in the Diet.

Journalists do function as political participants in an entirely different fashion. Many of them, especially those in the "political department (*seiji-bu*)," acquire close links with a particular faction or a factional leader in the LDP. This kind of affiliation can begin quite naturally. A young reporter is assigned to cover a ministry. He meets the minister and finds him to have a political outlook on a range of issues (that go far beyond the jurisdiction of that ministry) with which the reporter mostly agrees. The minister finds the young man to be bright, perceptive, and personable, and invites him to join the existing coterie of journalists that meet at the minister's private residence for informal "late evening rounds (*yomawari*)".

The reporter gradually becomes a member of the inner circle. He and the minister, who may have acquired a new portfolio or a party assignment, find that they have more and more to tell each other. The minister can provide background information of extraordinary value to the journalist in fulfilling his duties, providing of course that confidences are observed. The reporter can inform the minister of moves that are being contemplated by his factional rivals or by the opposition parties, or within another ministry which affects his specific jurisdiction.

These multiple networks of communication are so pervasive that one occasionally has the sense that nothing counts for so much in Tokyo as being among those who know the latest piece of gossip, only some of which is ever publicized. On the other hand, the weekly news magazines have acquired a well-earned reputation as purveyors of innuendo and salacious rumors – the more scandalous the better – which they use to increase their competitive edge.

In all of this ceaseless activity, the reporters more often than not act as if they were members of the ruling elite. It is important for them to know as much as possible about what is going on. They do not necessarily share all that they have learned with the public, either because they decide that divulging some information is premature, or because their editors or their publishers have decided that doing so would be imprudent. For a student of Japanese politics, therefore, becoming friends with reporters is frequently infinitely more rewarding than reading what they write, especially if the information they provide is used with discretion.

A recent case classically illustrates what can transpire. Tachibana Takashi, who has become one of Japan's best-known investigative reporters, published an article in the September 1974 issue of *Bungei Shunjū* – a high-quality monthly journal – describing in copious detail former Prime Minister Tanaka's financial empire. Initially, the political reporters paid little attention to the exposé; for them, Tachibana's essay contained nothing they did not already know very well. Hence, their overlooking the import of the essay was not a case of suppressing allegations and information to protect the Prime Minister's reputation.

Tanaka, however, had accepted an invitation, tendered prior to Tachibana's article having been published, to appear before the Foreign Correspondents' Club of Japan. Understandably, the foreign journalists who had read Tachibana's piece and to whom some of the information about the Prime Minister's wheelings and dealings were newsworthy did ask questions. Instead of asserting, as he could have done quite easily, that the essay contained nothing new, Tanaka allowed himself to respond. The more he spoke, the more he aroused the curiosity of the foreign journalists, who filed their stories which inevitably raised questions about the Prime Minister's probity.

Once the foreign correspondents determined the story to be newsworthy, there was no alternative for the Japanese journalists. They, too, had to enter the thicket and, ultimately, thereby played a role in ending Tanaka's term as Prime Minister and his replacement a little over two months later by Miki Takeo, one of his arch rivals in the Liberal Democratic Party. All this took place well over a year before Lockheed Vice President Kotchian's revelations before the US Senate's Foreign Relations Committee concerning pay-offs made to some of Japan's senior officials – including Tanaka (Baerwald, 1976).

This example of the media's influence is, of course, a very special case. After all, the downfall of an incumbent Prime Minister is exceptional and highly unusual. This case cannot, therefore, serve as a yardstick for measuring other instances of journalism's impact on Japanese politics in general or the processing of bills by the Diet in particular. Nonetheless, it is useful as a reminder that the bureaucrats and governing party cannot program everything to their liking. The endless flow of information is simply too great, especially so in Tokyo. Ultimately, nothing can be kept secret for very long. This may mean that carefully orchestrated scenarios fail, but their failure reflects the undeniable fact that Japan is an open society, and to that extent fulfills one of the basic criteria which distinguish democratic from non-democratic political systems.

CHAPTER 4

Accommodation, Confrontation and the Diet

Perceptions have differed over time regarding the behavior of members of the Diet, as well as the functioning of this national assembly. Most observers agree that the members of the governing LDP and opposition parties altered their attitude towards each other when they entered into the era of "near parity (*hakuchū*)" during the latter half of the 1970s. This change has been attributed to two alternative explanations that are different, but mutually reinforcing. One is that election results do make a difference because they determine the respective strengths, measured in number of seats, between the governing and opposition parties. The other is that members of the Diet gradually recognized the need for being more accommodating towards each other than they had been when the LDP had exercised control hegemonically (during the latter half of the 1950s and throughout the 1960s) and began to behave more in accord with the norms of conduct set forth in the Diet Law and the Rules of the respective Houses (Krauss, 1984).

A more controversial perception is that this less confrontational style of behavior not only flourished during the *hakuchū* years, but has become imbedded in the behavior of the antagonists (that is, the LDP and its opponents) towards each other. Furthermore, that this pattern of behavior has continued even in the aftermath of the LDP's massive victory in the 1980 "double election" for the entire membership of the House of Representatives and half of the membership of the House of Councillors.

Another, equally controversial perception is that an explanation for the changed behavior of LDP Diet members during the *hakuchū* years can be attributed to the civil war that they were conducting with each other. In other words, the internal strife within the LDP was as important – possibly even more so – as any alternative explanation for changes in their posture towards the opposition parties. Moreover, the opposition parties, both because of the increase in the number of seats that they controlled, and because of the LDP's disunity, were encouraged to search for greater co-operation among themselves so that they might be in a position to seize power should the LDP fail. An exploration of this set of perceptions is the underlying theme for the material in the opening section of this chapter.

Why has there been this difference in perceptions? Part of the answer is that the Diet is a complex institution, as is true of any national assembly. Another part of the answer is that an observer's perceptions tend to be influenced by the functioning of the Diet during a specific period of time. My earlier work (Baerwald, 1974) was based on the 1960s, a period when the LDP could enforce its will on the Diet whenever it wanted to do so. By contrast, Mochizuki (1982) and Krauss (1984) emphasized the *hakuchū* period when the LDP could not afford to use steamroller tactics. Moreover, they gave greater weight to the interplay between the governing LDP and the opposition parties. In the first section of this chapter, I will stress the internal situation in the LDP and, to a lesser extent, the relationships among the various opposition parties towards each other and *vis-à-vis* the LDP. A basic premise of my approach is that what is transpiring inside the majority LDP – since it has been the governing party – tends to be more crucial in understanding the functioning of the Diet during a specific time frame, than the interaction between the governing and the opposition parties.

On a different level of analysis, this chapter addresses a broadly-based debate about Japanese society. Many foreigners perceive Japan as being socially harmonious, a view of their traditional culture that is preferred by many Japanese themselves. Yet, Japan also provides observers with episodes of conflict (Krauss, Rohlen and Steinhoff, 1984). The Japanese people may prefer to make decisions on the basis of consensus, but what alternative modes of resolving conflict are available? Prior to the *hakuchū* years, the LDP periodically used its overwhelming majority strength to force the legislation that it sponsored through the Diet. It could do so because it controlled a sufficient number of seats to manipulate all of the levers of power (Baerwald, 1974). Did the LDP and its Opposition revert to the presumably deeply-imbedded desire for achieving consensus once their power relationship altered during the *hakuchū* years? Or, did the LDP decide to pursue a strategy of avoidance by not introducing legislative and policy proposals that its members knew would lead to confrontations with the Opposition? After all, the opposition parties frequently had criticized the LDP for its forceful tactics (in the 1960s) as an exercise of majority rule in a tyrannical fashion. Once again, answers that might be offered tend to be controversial, but the material that follows is intended to provide some data for addressing the debate.

The Civil War in the LDP

Members of the House of Representatives convened in plenary session at the regular hour of one o'clock on 6 November 1979. Almost one calendar month had elapsed since the General Election for that House on 7 October. Yet, the formal election of the Prime Minister had not occurred. In and of itself this was unusual as a newly-elected House of Representatives normally convenes within seven to ten days – sometimes with even greater alacrity – in order to cast its vote formally installing the leader of the majority party as the new Prime Minister.

To be sure, the LDP had emerged from the election with only a razor-thin majority that consisted of 248 who had been formally endorsed as its official candidates and 9 who had been elected as Unaffiliated members and whom the party quickly invited to swell its ranks to 257. Still, 257 members constituted a one-seat margin above the absolute minimum of 256 seats (out of the total membership of 511) for it to continue to be the majority party. What could have caused the normal schedule to slip so badly, and could have accounted for such an exceptional delay?

Fundamentally, a long-simmering dispute inside the governing party had shattered its occasionally tenuous unity. As noted in Chapter 1, this division could be traced back to the LDP's origins when it was formed by the coming together of two conservative parties – the Liberals and the Democrats, each also having their own factions. That event had taken place in 1955. It was now twenty-four years later, and many divisive conflicts had rent the LDP in the intervening years. One of these disputes, however, had been a central feature of Japanese politics for the better part of a decade: the so-called "Kaku-Fuku War" between former LDP Prime Ministers Tanaka *Kakuei* and *Fukuda* Takeo.

Many of the governing party's national conventions, especially those at which a new Party President was to be elected, had not been exercises in party solidarity. At the 1972 Convention, for example, Fukuda, who had been retiring Prime Minister Satō Eisaku's staunchest supporter (outside of Satō's own factional followers) and presumed heir apparent, was challenged by Tanaka who had been Satō's key factional lieutenant and fund raiser. Fukuda presumably had the inside track because of the generally accepted custom that an outgoing Party President (and, thereby, Prime Minister) would not be succeeded by a member of his own faction. In this particular instance, however, Tanaka won by assembling a numerically larger coalition.

This unanticipated outcome, at least from Fukuda's perspective, was the starting point of an internal LDP conflict that had not ended in 1985, despite Fukuda's respected status as a senior (80 years old) party advisor and Tanaka's massive cerebral hemorrhage in February. For, even if the principals were no longer direct participants (in itself a possibly questionable premise) their factional followers have continued the grudge war.

Another episode in the LDP's civil war took place in conjunction with the 1974 House of Councillors election. LDP fortunes had declined from having won 69 seats in 1968 to only 62 seats in 1971, an outcome which if repeated would result in the loss of the LDP's majority status in that chamber. (With the reversion of Okinawa, the House of Councillors membership

Table 4.1 Liberal Democratic Party Convention, 5 July 1972: Ballots for Party President

First ballot		Second (run-off) ballot	
Tanaka Kakuei	156	Tanaka Kakuei	282
Fukuda Takeo	150	Fukuda Takeo	190
Ōhira Masayoshi	101		
Miki Takeo	69		

Source: Tomita *et al.* (1983), Tokyo: Hokuju Shuppan, p. 218.
Note:
Nearly all voting delegates to LDP national conventions are members of the Diet. In addition, each Prefectural Federation of the party has one vote. However, it is the LDP's Diet members that dominate the party conventions and it is their factional alignments that determine the outcome. If none of the candidates obtains an absolute majority on the first ballot, the top two candidates run against each other on the second ballot. Tanaka's victory was assured when the Ōhira faction decided to support him in the run-off. Furthermore, Nakasone and most of his faction had pledged their support to Tanaka prior to the opening of the convention. Fukuda's long rivalry with Nakasone in Gumma's Third District played a role in that decision which became a source of controversy among those of its voters who had hoped that one of their own would become Japan's Prime Minister. Ultimately, both did.

became 252. Half of that plus one would be 127. Winning 62 seats in successive elections would give the LDP control over 124.) Tanaka, as Prime Minister and, of course, Party President, wished to strengthen his position by leading his party to victory and continued control in the House of Councillors.

He embarked on a strategy of having some of Japan's large commercial–industrial combines, such as Hitachi and Mitsubishi, sponsor LDP candidates in the national constituency (Curtis, 1976, pp. 45–80). More of them lost than won, but for many critics (including some inside the LDP) it was an all-too-blatant use of corporate power to achieve political ends. Moreover, Tanaka also sought to gain personal advantage by candidate endorsement decisions that would benefit his own factional followers. The most controversial was in Tokushima Prefecture. Incumbent Kujime Kentaro of the Miki faction was denied the party's official endorsement, and was thereby forced to run as an Unaffiliated candidate. In his stead, Tanaka and his Party Secretary-General Hashimoto Tomisaburo (a senior member of the Tanaka faction) arranged for the endorsement of Gotōda Masaharu, a former senior official in the National Police Agency and a close ally of Tanaka's. Kujime won (196,000 votes to 153,000), but that result – while welcomed by Miki – did not engender feelings of brotherly love among the principals. No wonder, therefore, that Miki lent his full weight to the moves to oust Tanaka that same fall, in the aftermath of Tachibana's article in *Bungei Shunjū* detailing Tanaka's commercial–financial empire, aided and abetted by Tanaka's own disastrous appearance before the Foreign Correspondents' Club of Japan. The LDP's official candidates won 62 seats. The party retained control over the House of Councillors by inviting victorious Unaffiliated candidates – including Kujime – to join its ranks.

Much to nearly everyone's surprise, Miki Takeo became Tanaka's successor. LDP Vice President Shiina Etsusaburo was the king-maker. After the event, he issued a flowery explanatory statement (Tomita *et al.*, 1983, p. 225). Most observers, however, believe that Shiina's real motive for orchestrating Miki's selection was to avoid a contest between Fukuda and Ōhira Masayoshi, the leaders of the second and third largest LDP factions; such a confrontation it was feared, might lead to a split in the LDP.

Miki, by contrast, headed the fourth largest faction, and was a neutral alternative – or, at least, Shiina perceived him to be as such in the context of the dangers to party unity posed by the rivalry between Fukuda and Ōhira. Party elders took the further precautionary step of making all of the necessary preliminary arrangements by means of "mutual consultations (*hanashiai*)" in order to avoid a divisive vote. Decision-making by achieving consensus before there would be a need to vote was the preferred option. The need to rely on this traditional device, however, also was a reflection of the parlous state of LDP unity.

No one, in all likelihood, could have foreseen that Miki would still be Prime Minister when the LDP was forced to face a crisis that many Japanese consider their version of the Watergate miasma in American politics. 1976, or the 51st Year of the Showa era, forever will be linked with the "Lockheed Incident" in the annals of Japanese politics. Reduced to its barest essentials, this scandal centered around the Lockheed Corporation's payment of bribes to various business and senior government officials in order to promote the sale of its L1011 wide-body passenger planes to All Nippon Airways. (Lockheed executives asserted that the payments had been extorted, and therefore should not be considered as inducements.) After months of maneuvering – the case broke as a result of testimony given in February before a subcommittee of the US Senate's Foreign Relations Committee – the public procurators in Tokyo indicted former Prime Minister Tanaka for having accepted 500 million Yen ($1.6 million at the then prevailing exchange rate) from Lockheed's agents. Furthermore, Lockheed also had made payments to former Minister of Transportation Hashimoto Tomisaburo and Parliamentary Vice Minister of Transportation Satō Takayuki (Baerwald, 1976).

Prime Minister Miki, whom everyone referred to as "Mr Clean," favored full exposure of all the malefactors of "money politics (*kinken seiji*)." In doing so, he knew – especially after Tanaka's having been indicted – that some old political scores could be settled. Fukuda, at least initially, also was not displeased that his rival had again been caught in a web of scandal. (Very early in his political career, Tanaka had been implicated, but found innocent, in a bribery scandal at the time of the Coal Nationalization Bill during the Occupation era.) However, Fukuda, as well as other senior LDPers, gradually became increasingly concerned about the overall impact of the spreading stain of the Lockheed scandal on the party's ability to surmount the crisis. He and Ōhira joined hands (temporarily, as it turned out) and actively participated in "The Council to establish Party Solidarity (*Kyōtō Taisei Kakuritsu Kyōgikai*, or *Kyōtō-kyō*)" the goal of which was to oust Prime Minister Miki from office. It was not only that Miki seemed to be all too interested in full exposure of the scandal, but that he had supported the strengthening of anti-trust legislation which upset some of the party's most influential financial supporters in the Federation of Economic Organizations, or *Keidanren*.

An election for the House of Representatives loomed as a constitutional necessity, because the four-year term of the one that had been elected on 10 December 1972 was about to expire. The LDP entered the contest badly divided – not only between Miki's supporters and opponents, but also as a result of the New Liberal Club's defection. It emerged from the contest with a net loss of twenty-two seats (from 271 in 1972 to 249 in 1976); but, its real decline was greater because of reapportionment having added twenty new seats (271 of a total of 491 amounted to 55.1 percent, whereas 249 of 511 was only 48.7 percent). It was the party's worst performance, until then.

Mutual recriminations abounded. Miki and his partisans argued that their *Kyōtō-kyō* opponents had undermined all efforts to conduct a unified campaign. Furthermore, had Prime Minister Miki not been forceful in his efforts to unravel the Lockheed scandal, the LDP's performance would have been even worse. Fukuda, Ōhira and their allies took the position that Miki should accept responsibility for the party's disastrous performance, and resign (in time-honored Japanese fashion). In the end, the *Kyōtō-kyō* forces prevailed for the simple reason that they were numerically larger (163 to 70 among LDP Representatives). Prime Minister Miki submitted his resignation, and was succeeded by Fukuda – once again on the basis of mutual consultations among party elders. A further part of the bargain was that Ōhira would become Party Secretary-General. The LDP retained control over the House of Representatives by inviting nine Unaffiliated victors to join its ranks, thereby raising the total number of seats it controlled to 258, two above the absolute minimum of 256.

This coalition brought back some much-needed stability to internal party affairs. However, the LDP's ability to control the legislative process in the Lower House was hampered by its extremely narrow majority – or, at least so it seemed at the time. (This issue will be discussed from a different perspective in a subsequent section of this chapter.) On the other hand the Fukuda-Ōhira mainstream did lead the LDP to a marginally better performance in the July 1977 House of Councillors election by winning sixty-three seats outright and being able to count on the support of four Unaffiliated victors (Uchida and Baerwald, 1978). While by no means a stellar showing, it was sufficient to soften the tone of intra-partisan recrimination.

By the fall of 1978, party unity would be tested again. Under Prime Minister Miki's leadership, the party had adopted new regulations governing the process of electing the Party President. Rank and file party members and "party friends (*tōyū*)" would participate in a pre-convention primary election. This would be followed by a run-off between the two top contenders at the Party Convention itself. Four candidates entered the contest: incumbent Prime Minister Fukuda, Party Secretary-General Ōhira, incumbent Minister of Trade and Industry Kōmoto Toshio (who had become the leader of the Miki faction), and Nakasone Yasuhiro who had served Miki as Party Secretary-General. Fukuda was so certain of victory that he announced the convention should dispense with the run-off balloting and install the winner of the primary as Party President by acclamation.

Ōhira was victorious (see Table 4.2), in part because his friend Tanaka provided his faction's unstinting support, in part because Prime Minister Fukuda was over-confident and had spent a good deal of his time being the international statesman. He cherished this role, especially because the annual Summit Meeting of the Advanced Industrial Countries was scheduled to meet in Tokyo in 1979. Instead, once again, his hopes had fallen victim to the ongoing "Kaku-Fuku War". Furthermore, his pre-election pronouncement left him with no alternative except to support Ōhira's formal election as LDP President at the Convention, and as the LDP's candidate for Prime Minister in the Diet. It was the last

Table 4.2 The LDP's Primary Election for Party President 27 November 1976

Candidate	Votes	Points	% of points
Ōhira Masayoshi	550,891	748	49.0
Fukuda Takeo	472,503	638	41.9
Nakasone Yasuhiro	197,957	93	6.1
Kōmoto Toshio	88,917	46	3.0
Total	1,310,268	1525	100.0

Source: Tomita *et al.* (1983), pp. 228–9.

Note:

Party members and friends cast their ballots in each Prefecture which was allocated points on the basis of a mathematical formula based on the percentage of total vote that had been cast. In turn, these points were proportionally divided, but only between the two top candidates in that Prefecture. These complications aside, Ōhira was victorious in both categories.

supportive gesture that Fukuda extended to Ōhira (Interview, October 1979).

Prime Minister Ōhira inherited a party that was on the verge of disintegration. He could take few initiatives and even encountered difficulties with the Diet's approval of the National Budget Bill. The House of Representatives Budget Committee (50 members) was evenly divided between the governing and opposition parties. However, this meant that the Committee's LDP chairman could not vote except to break a tie (see discussion of Diet committees in Chapter 3). As a consequence, the 25 opposition party members voted as a bloc to disapprove the Bill, a process that the LDP could not prevent until the Bill came up for a division in plenary session where it had a majority. The Budget was approved by both Houses, but the LDP's leadership recognized that its ability to control the legislative process was severely constrained by the combined strength of the opposition parties.

Ōhira had decided to avoid a confrontation at the committee stage of deliberations because, as he had learned during his years of having been former Prime Minister Ikeda Hayato's parliamentary strategist, the plenary session was available. Nonetheless, some of his intra-party opponents were critical of what they considered to be his less than forceful style of leadership. Ōhira, however, had long been an advocate of consultations as a means of resolving conflicts with the opposition parties. He had often mentioned to me the advantages of not using "forced vote" tactics (see below) except when absolutely necessary. It was a procedural issue on which he and his immediate predecessor had disagreed for many years. Fukuda, for example, had mentioned – with considerable vehemence – that Ikeda (Ōhira's mentor) was the worst Prime Minister of the worst Cabinet of the worst Government in the world during the course of a late evening discussion in his home with a group of Japanese journalists who had invited me to join them. That had been in the summer of 1963, but I remember it vividly because it had been such a revelation. Fukuda had not altered his views in the intervening sixteen years, even though during his tenure as Prime Minister, he had been constrained by the presumed imperatives of near parity between the LDP and its opposition.

The Tokyo Summit of Advanced Industrial Nations in June 1979 temporarily focused attention on Japan's increasingly significant international role and away from domestic political conflicts. By September, however, Prime Minister Ōhira had decided that a General Election should be conducted for the House of

Representatives. He hoped that the results would increase his party's majority in that chamber, would thereby ease the constraints imposed by the LDP's close balance of power with its opposition, and would strengthen his position inside the LDP. The previous spring's unified local elections had reflected some improvement in the party's popularity, especially in the Prefectural (State) assemblies in which the LDP had increased its share of seats by 7½ percent. His intra-party rivals – primarily former Prime Ministers Fukuda and Miki – were not enthusiastic about such an outcome and tried to stunt the party's growth; or, at least, the Ōhira mainstream coalition's partisans made such allegations. If these charges were correct, the anti-mainstream was pursuing a strategy that entailed considerable risk, given the strength that the opposition parties had registered at the polls in the December 1976 General Election (Baerwald and Tomita, 1977). Ōhira's anti-mainstream rivals, however, presumably were more interested in shortening his tenure as Prime Minister than they were worried about the floundering (from their perspective) JSP and other opposition parties.

Be all of this as it may, the results of the 7 October 1979 House of Representatives election proved to be yet another cold shower for the LDP. Only 248 of its officially endorsed candidates won (one less than in 1976), even if its share of the popular votes cast increased by 2.8 percent (Baerwald, 1980a). Moreover, the decline in the party's number of seats, while minimal, had not affected each faction equally.

Table 4.3 .Strength of LDP Factions in the House of Representatives

Faction	Number elected in 1976	Number elected in 1979	Net change
Fukuda	54	47	−7
Tanaka	43	49	+6
Ōhira	38	49	+12
Nakasone	40	38	−2
Miki-Kōmoto	32	28	−4
Minor factions and no faction	53	47	−6

Source: *Kokkai Binran* [Diet Handbook], February 1977 and February 1980 editions.

Note: These numbers reflect the movement of Unaffiliated victors into the LDP after the elections, and therefore are different from the election results.

Displeasure on the part of the anti-mainstream factions (Fukuda, Miki-Kōmoto and Nakasone) with these results became the basis for their effort to unseat LDP President/Prime Minister Ōhira. The dissidents maintained that the precedent established in 1976, forcing then Prime Minister Miki to accept responsibility for the party's poor electoral performance, and to resign, also should govern in this instance.

Ōhira and his mainstream supporters responded that he had won the party's primary election one year earlier and that the Party Convention had duly installed him for the established two-year term, of which one year remained. There was, therefore, no reason for him to resign unless a majority of the LDP's Diet members, duly assembled in a "Caucus of Both Houses (*Ryōin Giin Sōkai*)", indicated by a formal vote that that was what he should do. This was the situation that precipitated the impasse (described at the beginning of the civil war in the LDP) and that is generally referred to as the "Forty-day Imbroglio (*Yonjū-nichi Kōsō*)" (Itō, 1982, pp. 509–41).

Neither the Ōhira and Tanaka loyalists, nor the Fukuda, Nakasone and Miki-Kōmoto resisters (*kōsō* is not just an imbroglio, but also implies engaging in a last-ditch resistance) would budge. Party President Ōhira and his supporters were reasonably certain that they had the numerical advantage of about 130 LDP Representatives: his own faction's 50 plus Tanaka's 47, plus the vast majority of those belonging to the minor factions or having no factional affiliation (see Table 4.3). By contrast, Fukuda's anti-mainstream coalition, which consisted of his own 52 plus Nakasone's 38 plus Miki-Kōmoto's 28 and a minority of those belonging to minor factions added up to about 120. Among the LDP Councillors, the split also favored the mainstream by a margin of at least twenty votes. Hence, Ōhira partisans tried to have the issue resolved at a formal Caucus of LDP Representatives and Councillors.

Meanwhile, Party Vice President Nishimura Ei'ichi – despite his advanced age (he was eighty-one) – tried to play the role of honest broker between the warring camps, just as his predecessor Shiina Etsusaburo had succeeded in having the party agree that Miki should become its leader in 1974. He was by no means alone in fearing that a formal Caucus vote would lead to a real rupture of the party, and – by the time-honored mode of mutual consultations (*hanashiai*) – tried to find some formula that would be acceptable and achieve consensus. One of his proposals was to separate the posts of Party President from that of Prime Minister, an alternative to their being combined that is periodically disinterred whenever all other choices have been exhausted. (Just how such an arrangement would function has not been fully explained and, since it has never been tried, it also has not been tested. Nonetheless, it is generally accepted that creating a dual leadership in a parliamentary party would challenge the creative political abilities of the holders of these offices to the utmost.) Nishimura's efforts failed, in large measure because his standing as a supra-factional negotiator was tarnished – from the anti-mainstream's perspective – since he was a known Tanaka follower.

When Ōhira, therefore, attempted to hold a Caucus of the LDP in the Diet on 2 November 1979, some three weeks after the General Election, in order to formalize his selection as the party's candidate for Prime Minister, the anti-mainstream boycotted the gathering and decided to meet separately. In effect, this meant that the party had divided itself into two separate entities, even though the deadline for the formal vote for Prime Minister was imminent. The Constitution required that the Diet be convened "within thirty days from the date of the election" (Chapter IV, Article 54, Paragraph 10), and the election had been conducted on the seventh of the previous month. Furthermore, the Constitution also commanded that the designation of the Prime Minister "shall precede all other business" (Chapter V, Article 67, Paragraph 1). The Diet was convened on the sixth, and the LDP, having been unable to agree on a single candidate, fielded two nominees: incumbent Prime Minister Ōhira and former Prime Minister Fukuda (see Table 4.4 for the outcome).

The mainstream's calculations of its support had been remarkably accurate. Particularly welcome were the few added votes that the anti-mainstream factions' dissidents provided, and those that the four members of the New Liberal Club cast. In point of fact, the NLC was the only group outside the LDP that fully participated in the run-off balloting. All of the other members belonging to the LDP's opposition behaved as if they were spectators at a spectacle in which they were not really involved. Yet, the long-governing party – against which their opponents had hurled so much invective over the years – had provided them with an opportunity to cast their ballots for one of two nominees. Had they cast their ballots for either Ōhira or Fukuda, the LDP, in all likelihood, would have split irrevocably. Apparently (much of the maneuvering has not as yet become public knowledge), neither of the LDP's candidates had done more than contemplate such an eventuality and made anything more than tentative overtures to

Table 4.4 Election of Prime Minister in the House of Representatives 6 November 1979

A. First Ballot

Candidate	*Votes*
Ōhira Masayoshi, Liberal Democratic Party	135
Fukuda Takeo, Liberal Democratic Party	125
Asukata Ichio, Japan Socialist Party	107
Takeiri Yoshikatsu, Kōmeitō	58
Miyamoto Kenji, Japan Communist Party	41
Sasaki Ryōsaku, Democratic Socialist Party	36
Den Hideo, Social Democratic Federation	2
Blank ballots	0
Invalid ballots	7
Total	511

B. Second Ballot (run-off)

Ōhira Masayoshi, LDP	*Votes*	Fukuda Takeo, LDP	*Votes*
Ōhira faction	51	Fukuda faction	49
Tanaka faction	48	Nakasone faction	34
Fukuda faction	1	Miki-Kōmoto faction	25
Nakasone faction	5	Nakagawa group	9
Miki-Kōmoto faction	3	No faction, LDP	3
No faction, LDP	23	Unaffiliated [b]	1
NLC	3		
Unaffiliated[a]	3		
Total	138	Total	121

Source: Togawa Isamu (1982), *Tanaka Kakuei to Seiken Kōsō* (Tokyo: Kōdansha), pp. 288–91, provides complete lists of which members cast their ballots for each of the candidates on the second ballot.

Notes: [a]Tanaka Kakuei and Hashimoto Tomisaburo, both of whom belonged to the Tanaka faction and Watanabe Masao, who was an Unaffiliated member of the House.

[b]Satō Takayuki, who belonged to the Nakasone faction.

Ballots cast for opposition party candidates have been left out of the second ballot because they were irrelevant to the outcome.

some of the opposition parties. In turn, the latter were willing to sit on the sidelines, where it was comfortable and where they were accustomed to being.

The opposition parties did, however, have another option. They had been engaged in discussions during much of the 1970s regarding the possibility of establishing a coalition among themselves. Considerable progress had been made between the Kōmeitō and DSP initially, and later between themselves and the JSP. This grouping would have commanded just over 200 votes, more than enough to defeat either Ōhira or Fukuda. However, such a coalition on the first ballot would not have constituted a majority, and would have been faced with the LDP's Ōhira on the run-off ballot. Under those circumstances, observers assured me, the LDP's dissidents would have relented and have cast their votes for the incumbent. Hence, or so the reasoning went, why should the opposition parties try to achieve unity of purpose – extremely difficult in any case, but especially so in deciding who among their leaders should be their candidate for Prime Minister – if the LDP's candidate ultimately would win? Nonetheless, the Opposition's behavior underlined for me the extent to which its members remained unsure of themselves as full participants in the Diet's procedures, especially if it involved the possibility of their joining a governing coalition with a portion of the LDP. Their lack of experience in being involved in anything other than being opposed to the LDP and their innate antagonism towards the governing party had a paralyzing effect.

These speculations aside, the 6 November 1979 Diet election for Prime Minister was unique. The LDP behaved as if it consisted of two separate entities. Indeed, to all intents and purposes, that is what it had become. To be sure, Prime Minister Ōhira did his utmost to recreate some semblance of unity by according a proportionate share of Cabinet and important party posts to anti-mainstream members (Baerwald, 1980a, p. 267). Nonetheless, the long-simmering Kaku-Fuku War continued to take its toll. Only the inertness of the opposition parties prevented the lengthy rule of the LDP from having come to an end.

Just how ragged the strands holding the LDP together had become again became clearly visible in the late spring of 1980. In this episode, the opposition parties finally did seem to have emerged from their slumber. As noted previously, they had been discussing various forms of co-operation with each other throughout much of the 1970s. In January 1980, the JSP, Kōmeitō and DSP entered into an agreement to take concerted action in the next triennial House of Councillors election, scheduled for that summer. Their joint declaration contained the following:

1 Expel putrid money politics; achieve clean politics.

2 Control [retail] prices; abolish inequality; promote an economic system that accords preference to the welfare of [the people's] daily lives.
3 Pursue a foreign policy that is based on relationships of reciprocity and equality with all countries regardless of their [political] system in order that Japan's security and the peace of the world can be defended.
4 For the sake of creating a political [system] suitable for a new era by working towards the realization of these goals, we will defeat the LDP's single-party rule especially by co-operating in six of the [House of Councillors] single-member districts (Togawa, 1982, p. 306).

Each of these points had deep roots in the platforms of the participating opposition parties. Point #1 reflected their long-standing criticism of former Prime Minister Tanaka's political style, and of his continuing significant role in the LDP. It also was a criticism of another less well-known LDPer very much in the news at the time – Hamada Kōichi – who had lost some $1.5 million in the casinos of Las Vegas. In and of itself, his having done so would not have been noteworthy. What gave the rumors and innuendos spice was that he had allegedly used funds that were linked to Lockheed's pay-offs. (Hamada ultimately submitted his resignation to the Speaker of the House of Representatives, sat out the 1980 General Election, ran again and won in 1983, and was rewarded by becoming Chairman of the Standing Committee on Construction.)

Point #2 reflected fundamental differences with the LDP over basic economic policies. Point #3 was, of course, a criticism of the LDP's support of the Security Pact with the United States and of Japan's having aligned itself with America's allies. It was, however, noteworthy that the agreement did not mention either abrogating the Security Pact, nor advocating a foreign policy based on "unarmed neutrality (*hibusō chūritsu*)," which was the JSP's basic plank. Point #4 was the only one that, in an operational sense, really counted. If the three parties could agree jointly to support a single candidate in six districts (see discussion of joint candidacies in Chapter 2), then they might be able to end the LDP's majority status in the House of Councillors.

All of these discussions about co-operation, coalition and joint action among the JSP, Kōmeitō and DSP encouraged them to introduce a motion of non-confidence in the Ōhira Cabinet. They reasoned that the Diet's debating of such a motion would focus public attention on their policy differences with the LDP, and thus contribute to their candidates' campaigns for the upcoming House of Councillors election. Furthermore, a motion of non-confidence had the additional advantages of using up time, of displacing LDP-sponsored legislative bills from the Diet's calendar – a motion of non-confidence takes precedence over all other Diet procedures – and, thereby, upsetting the LDP's legislative agenda.

This opposition strategy entailed risks, of course. If the LDP voted as a bloc, the motion would be defeated and the opposition parties would lose face, as they had so often in the past when they had used the same device. If, on the other hand, the LDP did not remain united (a possibility that was not unreasonable in the immediate aftermath of the "Forty-day Imbroglio"), and the motion carried, then the Prime Minister would have the option of dissolving the House of Representatives and calling for a General Election. Indeed, as rumors about the Opposition's impending move began to circulate, that is precisely what former Prime Minister Tanaka advocated. In such an event, the LDP could manipulate the date for the House of Representatives election to coincide with that for the House of Councillors.

Such a "double election" would provide the LDP with a substantial tactical advantage in that it would undermine the opposition parties' joint candidate strategy in selected House of Councillors single-member districts. Local districts for the House of Councillors are Prefecture-wide, but most House of Representatives districts are smaller. In the latter, each of the opposition parties would probably endorse their own candidate who would compete against each other and would thereby destroy the opposition parties' ability jointly to support a single candidate in selected House of Councillors districts (Togawa, 1982, pp. 307–12). Moreover, the LDP could handle the financial strain that a second campaign for the House of Representatives within less than one year would impose better than the opposition parties which, with the exception of JCP, always seem to be strapped for funds.

In the end, the presumed benefits of debating a motion of non-confidence in the Ōhira Cabinet outweighed the possible hazards, and the opposition parties introduced it during the plenary session that convened on 16 May. (See Table 4.5 for the vote in the House of Representatives.) As Tokyo's rumor mills had anticipated, 69 members of the LDP's anti-mainstream Fukuda and Miki-Kōmoto factions and the small Nakagawa Ichirō group (plus 4 who were indisposed) absented themselves from the proceedings. The Opposition motion was adopted by a 56 vote margin. It was the first time that the Diet had passed a motion of non-confidence

Table 4.5 House of Representatives Plenary Session, 16 May 1980: Opposition Motion of Non-Confidence in the Ōhira Cabinet

Voting in favor		Voting against		Deliberately absent	
JSP	103	LDP	183	Fukuda faction	34
Kōmeitō	58	Unaffiliated	4	Miki-Kōmoto faction	20
JCP	41			Nakasone faction	25
DSP	35			Nakagawa group	8
NLC	3			Sub-total	69
SDF	2			(Sick	4)
Unaffiliated	1				
Total	243	Total	187	Total	73

Source: Togawa (1982), pp. 312–13.

Note: It is worth noting that the Fukuda and Miki-Kōmoto factions did not remain united, in that 20 of the former and 12 of the latter voted with the LDP majority against the motion. Moreover, Nakasone and the vast majority of his faction had left the ranks of the dissidents and joined the mainstream in support of Prime Minister Ōhira.

against an LDP Cabinet in over a quarter of a century.

Prime Minister Ōhira immediately decided to dissolve the House of Representatives, and called for a General Election as prescribed by the Constitution (Chapter IV, Article 54, Paragraph 1). By moving up the already scheduled election for the House of Councillors from 29 to 22 June, both elections could be conducted on the same day. The LDP won massive victories in both contests, but Ōhira did not live to celebrate the triumph. In death, he was vindicated for his ceaseless efforts to provide leadership under conditions that his anti-mainstream enemies – especially Fukuda – had made as close to impossible as they could.

Nearly all of Ōhira's friends and admirers, among whom I am proud to include myself, have remained convinced that the tactics of his intra-party antagonists contributed to his not having had the strength to recover from his illness. As a defender of factionalism in the LDP (see Chapter 1), I must confess that the anti-mainstream's antics, from the "Forty-day Imbroglio" through the motion of non-confidence, brought me very close to changing my mind about its presumed functional utility. Even in politics, a distinction should be made between playing hard-ball and playing dirty.

Near Parity and its Legacy

Most of the material that has been covered under the heading "The LDP's Civil War" has emphasized the perception that relationships among the governing party's mainstream and anti-mainstream factions were more significant than the interaction between the LDP and its opponents, the JSP and the other opposition parties. The only exception was the Opposition's seizing the initiative by introducing the motion of non-confidence in the Ōhira Cabinet. This motion would have been defeated, however, had it not been for the deliberate absence during the division in the plenary session of about seventy LDP dissidents. That episode aside, did the existence of a "close balance of power" (another translation for *hakuchū*) alter the relationship between the governing and opposition parties?

Before turning to possible answers to this question, it is necessary to examine the meaning of "near parity" in somewhat greater detail. In general, the term has meant that the number of seats held respectively by the governing and opposition parties was nearly equal; or, to put it another way, that the LDP had nothing more than a razor-thin majority of one or two seats, or had not even managed to retain control over a majority of seats. In the 1976 and 1979 as well as in the post-*hakuchū* 1983 House of Representatives elections, endorsed LDP candidates only won 249, 248 and 250 seats, or seven, eight, and six short of the 256 necessary to retain their party's majority standing. Similarly, in the House of Councillors, the LDP only controlled an exact half (126) after the 1974 election and two less than that (124) after the 1977 election out of the total of 252 seats in that chamber.

These official election results did give the impression that the long-governing party had lost its ability to win a majority in the Diet. As is the case in much of Japanese politics, appearances can be deceptive. A somewhat different alignment of respective party strengths could have been observed if one's attention had shifted to include those members who were elected as Unaffiliated candidates, but who ended up sitting as members of a political party – more often than not, of the LDP. Tables 4.6 and 4.7 provide examples of the actual distribution of seats during *hakuchū*.

As these tables indicate, the real margin separating the LDP (and its allies) from the opposition parties ranged from between twelve and fifteen seats in the House of Representatives during the height of near parity, and went up to twenty-eight seats after the

Table 4.6 Actual Distribution of Seats, by Party, House of Representatives

Date	LDP and allies		Opposition parties		Margin of LDP to Opposition
January 1977	LDP	257	JSP	123	
	Unaffiliated[a]	2	Kōmeitō	55	
			DSP	29	
			JCP	19	
			NLC	17	
			Unaffiliated–NLC	9	
	Total	259	Total	252	17 seats

Notes: There were no vacancies.
[a]Unaffiliated, Hashimoto Tomisaburo (ex-LDP), Tanaka Kakuei (ex-LDP).

Date	LDP and allies		Opposition parties		Margin of LDP to Opposition
July 1978	LDP	257	JSP	123	
	Unaffiliated[b]	3	Kōmeitō	55	
			DSP	29	
			JCP	19	
			NLC	17	
			Unaffiliated–NLC	0	
			Soc. Dem. Fed.	0	
			Unaffiliated[c]	8	
	Total	260	Total	251	19 seats

Notes: There were 9 vacancies.
[b]Unaffiliated, Hashimoto Tomisaburo (ex-LDP), Hori Shigeru (ex-LDP, now Speaker), Tanaka Kakuei (ex-LDP).
[c]Unaffiliated, Miyake Shoichi (ex-JSP, now Deputy Speaker).

Date	LDP and allies		Opposition parties		Margin of LDP to Opposition
July 1979	LDP	249	JSP	116	
	Unaffiliated[d]	5	Kōmeitō	56	
			DSP	28	
			JCP	19	
			NLC	16	
			Soc. Dem. Fed.	3	
			Unaffiliated[e]	1	
	Total	254	Total	239	15 seats

Notes: There were 18 vacancies.
[d]Unaffiliated, Hashimoto Tomisaburo (ex-LDP), Nadao Hirokichi (ex-LDP, now Speaker), Nishioka Takeo (ex-LDP, ex-NLC), Tanaka Kakuei (ex-LDP), Utsunomiya Tokuma (ex-LDP, ex-Unaffiliated–NLC).
[e]Unaffiliated, Miyake Shoichi (ex-JSP, now Deputy Speaker).

continued

Table 4.6 *continued*

Date	LDP and allies		Opposition parties		Margin of LDP to Opposition
January 1980	LDP	253	JSP	107	
	Unaffiliated[f]	6	Kōmeitō	58	
			JCP	41	
			DSP	36	
			NLC	4	
			Soc. Dem. Fed.	2	
			Unaffiliated[g]	4	
	Total	259	Total	252	17 seats

Notes: There were no vacancies.
[f]Unaffiliated, Hashimoto Tomisaburo (ex-LDP), Nadao Hirokichi (ex-LDP, now Speaker), Nishioka Takeo (ex-LDP, ex-NLC), Satō Takayuki (ex-LDP), Tanaka Kakuei (ex-LDP), Watanabe Masao (Unaffiliated Conservative).
[g]Unaffiliated, Okada Haruo (ex-JSP, now Deputy Speaker).

Date	LDP and allies		Opposition parties		Margin of LDP to Opposition
February 1984	LDP	259	JSP	113	
	NLC	8	Kōmeitō	59	
	Unaffiliated[h]	3	DSP	39	
			JCP	27	
			Soc. Dem. Fed.	3	
			Unaffiliated[i]	2	
	Total	270	Total	242	28 seats

Notes: There were no vacancies.
[h]Unaffiliated, Fukunaga Kenji (ex-LDP, now Speaker), Satō Takayuki (ex-LDP), Tanaka Kakuei (ex-LDP).
[i]Unaffiliated, Katsumata Sei'ichi (ex-JSP, now Deputy Speaker), Tsuji Kazuhiko (ex-JSP).

Source: *Kokkai Binran* [Diet Handbook], for relevant year and month.

1983 general election when Prime Minister Nakasone decided to invite the New Liberal Club to join the LDP in its first coalition cabinet. In the House of Councillors, the margins were between six and eight seats. While not as overwhelming as the LDP's majorities had been in the two decades 1955–75 (see Chapter 2), these disparities between the LDP and the opposition parties should have provided the governing party with more room for maneuver than the initial election returns, taken by themselves, would have led one to anticipate. Furthermore, if the NLC's seats were added to those of the LDP even before their 1983 coalition

Table 4.7 Actual Distribution of Seats, by Party, House of Councillors

Date	LDP and allies		Opposition parties		Margin of LDP to Opposition
July 1974	LDP	127	JSP	62	
	Unaffiliated[a]	3	Kōmeitō	24	
			JCP	20	
			DSP	10	
			2nd Chamber Club	4	
			Unaffiliated[b]	2	
	Total	130	Total	122	8 seats

Notes: There were no vacancies.
[a]Unaffiliated, Kōno Kenzō (ex-LDP, now Speaker), Kujime Kentarō (ex-LDP), Maeda Kazuo (ex-LDP, now Deputy Speaker).
[b]Unaffiliated, Fukuma Tomoyuki, Shimomura Yutaka, aka "Columbia Top."

Date	LDP and allies		Opposition parties		Margin of LDP to Opposition
February 1977	LDP	127	JSP	61	
	Unaffiliated[c]	2	Kōmeitō	24	
			JCP	20	
			DSP	10	
			2nd Chamber Club	4	
			NLC	1	
			Unaffiliated[d]	1	
	Total	129	Total	121	8 seats

Notes: There were 2 vacancies.
[c]Unaffiliated, Kōno Kenzō (ex-LDP, now Speaker), Matsuoka Katsuyoshi (pro-LDP).
[d]Unaffiliated, Nozue Chinpei (Unaffiliated–NLC)

Date	LDP and allies		Opposition parties		Margin of LDP to Opposition
August 1979	LDP	125	JSP	53	
	Unaffiliated[e]	3	Kōmeitō	28	
			JCP	16	
			DSP	11	
			2nd Chamber Club	5	
			NLC	5	
			Soc. Dem. Fed.	3	
			Unaffiliated[f]	1	
	Total	128	Total	122	6 seats

Notes: There were 2 vacancies.
[e]Unaffiliated, Kōno Kenzō (ex-LDP), Maejima Eizaburō, aka Yashiro Eita (later joined LDP), Yasui Ken (ex-LDP, now Speaker).
[f]Unaffiliated, Kase Kan (ex-JSP, now Deputy Speaker).

Source: *Kokkai Binran* [Diet Handbook], for relevant year and month.

(on most public policy issues, the members of the two parties agree with each other), then the gap would have been even larger. It is therefore reasonable to conclude that *hakuchū* was something of an illusion.

Near parity was enough of a reality, however, for the LDP to be forced to share some control over the Diet's internal governance with the opposition parties: the deputy presiding officers in both chambers, some (less significant) committee chairmanships and the loss of majority status on some committees (see Chapter 3). The LDP could no longer – as it had for so many years – simply have controlled the Diet by itself (Baerwald, 1974). It did have to allow the allotment of some quotient of power (minimal, I believe) to its Opposition. This circumstance was sufficiently different, especially in the House of Representatives, from that which had prevailed in the years of LDP single-party rule, that it could have influenced the functioning of the Diet.

Hakuchū can also be perceived from a different perspective: the LDP's declining percentage of the aggregate popular vote. In each of the elections from the onset of near parity in the Diet (those for the House of Representatives in 1976, 1979, 1980, and 1983 as well as those for the House of Councillors in 1974, 1977, 1980, and 1983), the LDP received less than 50 percent of the votes cast. If percentage of the popular vote were taken as the sole variable, then the LDP should have lost its majority status in both chambers in each of these four elections for the respective Houses. This should have been the case even in the 1980 "double election" when it won overwhelming majorities of seats: 284 plus 9 Unaffiliated totalling 293 LDP and allies to 218 Opposition – or a margin of 75 seats in the House of Representatives; and 135 plus 1 Unaffiliated to give 136 LDP to 116 Opposition – or a margin of 20 seats in the House of Councillors. Such expectations would have presumed that the apportioning of seats in the Diet should reflect nothing more than the distribution of aggregate vote totals obtained by each of the parties. Obviously, that was not the case.

Tables 4.8 and 4.9 also indicate that the voters' relatively adverse verdicts – to the LDP – were offset by the governing party's ability to transmute its proportion of the popular vote into a larger share of seats won (see Chapter 2). This factor was particularly noteworthy in the 1976 and 1980 House of Representatives elections, and in all of the House of Councillors elections in the local constituencies. Thus, both the LDP and its Opposition were well aware that the governing party's majorities *in the Diet* did not accurately reflect its standing with the Japanese voters, and

Table 4.8 1976, 1979, 1980 and 1983 House of Representatives Elections: LDP's percentage of Popular Vote and percentage of Seats Won

Election	Popular vote %	% of seats won
1976	41.8	48.7
1979	44.6	48.5
1980	47.9	55.6
1983	45.8	48.9

Source: *Juristo* (Spring 1985), *Senkyo* [Elections], pp. 267, 269.
Note:
These results reflect popular votes cast for officially endorsed LDP candidates only.

Table 4.9 1974, 1977, 1980 and 1983 House of Councillors Elections: LDP's percentage of Popular Vote and percentage of Seats Won

	National Constituency		Local Constituency	
Election	Popular vote %	% of seats won	Popular vote %	% of seats won
1974	44.3	35.2	39.5	56.6
1977	35.8	36.0	39.5	59.3
1980	42.7	42.0	43.2	63.2
1983	35.3	38.0	43.2	64.5

Source: *Juristo* (Spring 1985), *Senkyo* [Elections], p. 272.
Note:
These results reflect popular votes cast for officially endorsed LDP candidates only.

rested on quicksand. Members of the Diet were influenced in their behavior by these electoral outcomes. After all, their first priority has been to insure their re-election in order to continue to be participants in what has been, among its other functions, a representative assembly.

In the fall of 1982, I had the opportunity of discussing the *hakuchū* years with members of the Diet drawn from a wide spectrum of parties (Interviews, 1982). They tended to agree that near parity had occasioned few overt changes in the functioning of this national assembly. Instead, they emphasized the impact of specific events such as the LDP's having had to accept the Budget Committee's disapproval of the 1979 Budget (by virtue of having been outvoted) – an unprecedented development since the LDP had come into power – and relying on their majority in plenary session to overturn the committee's decision. Clearly, the close balance of voting power between the governing and opposition parties had influenced these proceedings.

Some of the LDPers also discussed, at considerable length, their party's internal disunity on occasions such as the "Forty-day Imbroglio" or the division at the time of the Opposition non-confidence motion in the spring of 1980. Many of the Liberal Democrats also linked their comments with the feelings of frustration that they felt when negotiating with opposition party members, especially in the Committee on House Management. Agreement on procedural questions had been easier to achieve when an understanding with the JSP was all that really mattered – the other opposition parties, in the earlier period, had been too weak to make much of a difference. Nowadays, it was not only that power centers among the opposition parties had proliferated, but that the JSP itself was so badly divided internally that one never could be sure whether an agreement on a procedural issue would be honored.

Members of the opposition parties, by contrast, placed much greater emphasis on the LDP's not having used "forced vote (*kyōkō saiketsu*)" tactics. The LDP had relied on this device to counteract Opposition efforts to delay proceedings during the years when the governing party had controlled massive majorities. In its essentials, a "forced vote" involved enforcing abrupt changes of an agreed-upon agenda, or a committee chairman calling for a vote even while an Opposition member was asking a question – or in general bending the Diet's elaborate rules of procedure, which had been designed to protect the minority's right to participate in a meaningful fashion, to the majority's will (Baerwald, 1974, pp. 103–20). Members of both the opposition and governing parties agreed that dispensing with the "forced vote" had lowered the level of tension which had been so much a part of Diet proceedings in the latter half of the 1950s and throughout the 1960s.

There was disagreement, however, whether the onset of *hakuchū* had been the principal cause for the LDP's having eliminated the "forced vote" tactic from its arsenal. Togawa (Interview, 1982), a life-long Diet-watcher, pointed out that House of Councillors President (Speaker) Kōno Kenzō had pledged himself not to employ it as early as 1972, several years before the LDP and the Opposition became relatively evenly balanced. Others, however, emphasized that Kōno had made the pledge in order to obtain the support of the opposition parties, and that, in general, it was only the LDP's having had narrow majorities that made its leaders abjure from using *kyokō saiketsu* to force its will on its Opposition.

Krauss, in his illuminating essay (1984) on the institutionalization of conflict management in the Diet, adduces evidence that certain members of the Diet, especially those who were in positions of authority (such as the Speaker, or a committee chairman) consciously sought to lessen confrontations in the Diet. In his discussions of Maeo Shigesaburō and Hori Shigeru, both of whom successively served as Speaker of the House of Representatives during *hakuchū*, he noted their efforts to enhance the presiding officer's authority in supervising proceedings in their chamber. Both, however, were exceptional. Maeo had been leader of a major faction in the LDP, and at one time had been a serious contender for Party President (and Prime Minister). Hori, while not quite of the same standing, also was one of the most senior and widely-respected Liberal Democrats. As has been noted in Chapter 3, the role of the presiding officer in both Houses of the Diet has not necessarily remained what Maeo (and, to a somewhat lesser extent Hori), as well as Kōno had intended it to become.

This brings me back to the question: What, if anything, has been the legacy of the lower levels of tension between the governing and opposition parties during the *hakuchū* years? Under Prime Minister Suzuki Zenkō (July 1980–November 1982), the Diet's proceedings remained relatively calm (Uji, 1985), despite the LDP's having had once more a "stable majority" (that is, control over all levers of power), presumably allowing the governing party to ram its legislative program down the throats of the opposition parties if they were recalcitrant, and, thereby, to risk the re-occurrence of scenes of near violence. Furthermore, this relative calm continued under Prime Minister Nakasone Yasuhiro (1982–), during his first year in office (that is, before the December 1983 election which brought an end to the LDP's massive majority in the House of Representatives). Had the experience under conditions of "near parity" been sufficient to induce the members of the Diet fully to accept the norms of conduct that the "Diet Law" and the "Rules" of the respective Houses commanded?

My discussions with members of the Diet (in the fall of 1982 and subsequently) have led me to accept answers that place greater emphasis on broader situational factors than on the members necessarily having internalized norms of behavior based on parliamentary rules. First, Prime Minister Suzuki may have been the beneficiary of having a "stable majority" in the Diet, but that good fortune did not mean that his LDP colleagues had forgotten their ruinous fratricidal conflict, or that their "civil war" had ended. Furthermore, his style of leadership was to search for areas of agreement within his party as well as between it and the Opposition. So much was this the case that, towards the end of his tenure, observers attributed to him the motto: "Doing Nothing is Best" (Baerwald and Hashimoto, 1983).

Secondly, Prime Minister Nakasone – even though he has exhibited a very different style, including the mastery of rhetorical flourishes and the use of symbolic acts – has had to face fundamentally different challenges from those that confronted his predecessor. Whereas Suzuki was the leader of the LDP's second largest faction which had always been part of the "conservative main current (*hoshu honryū*)" (an amorphous, but nonetheless consequential concept that involves one's lineage within the LDP), Nakasone was head of the fourth largest faction and had been viewed as a maverick by many of his party colleagues. He had depended heavily on the support of former Prime Minister Tanaka and his "troops (*gundan*)" in having won the LDP's primary election in the fall of 1982, which had paved the way for his becoming Prime Minister, whereas "mutual consultations" among party elders had led to Suzuki's having become Party President and Prime Minister in July 1980. Furthermore, Nakasone was Japan's Chief Executive when the Tokyo District Court found former Prime Minister Tanaka guilty in the Lockheed bribery scandal (a verdict that has been under appeal). Wounds of the "Kaku-Fuku War" again became festering sores, undermining the LDP's fragile unity. Moreover, the LDP's performance in the December 1983 General Election returned it to near parity with its Opposition, an outcome that some of Nakasone's critics seized upon, for him to accept responsibility and to resign.

The actual results of the election have been obscured by Nakasone's initiative to invite the NLC into the Cabinet – the first coalition during the LDP's thirty years in power. In itself this was a controversial move inasmuch as it underlined the party's weakness in the House of Representatives. Nakasone's high approval ratings (close to 60 percent) in many public opinion surveys, and his cordial personal relationships with foreign leaders have not enabled him to do much better than Suzuki in obtaining the Diet's approval of controversial pieces of legislation such as those based on the recommendations of the Second Special

Commission on Administrative Reform. In any case, Nakasone has not been willing to risk serious confrontations with the Opposition. He has been as careful and prudent as any of his more cautious predecessors on highly sensitive issues such as dramatic increases in Japan's defense budget, or amending the Constitution.

Thirdly, the opposition parties have had to face their own difficulties. Their success in the Diet's approval of their motion of non-confidence in the Ōhira Cabinet merely presaged their disastrous performance in the 1980 "double election." Furthermore, they were forced to accept an unpalatable implication of the voter's verdict: all of their open discussion of various combinations of alliances among themselves apparently had frightened their fellow citizens, for it had not only been an outpouring of sympathy votes for the LDP and its fallen leader that had influenced the election's outcome (Baerwald, 1980b). The defection of the NLC from their ranks into the arms of the LDP (with the creation of the LDP–NLC coalition Cabinet) also altered the relationship of the other opposition parties – towards each other and *vis-à-vis* the governing party. No longer have the middle-of-the-road Kōmeitō and DSP engaged in intensive discussions about an anti-LDP alliance as much as they have explored their prospects for becoming potential partners in an LDP-led coalition. That eventuality, however near or far its actualization may be, also has altered the larger political environment within which the Diet functions. After all, the possibility of finally becoming a Minister in the Cabinet (even if it were dominated by the LDP) apparently has blunted the eagerness of some of the centrist opposition leaders to engage in trench warfare against the governing party. In any case, the kind of broadly based anti-LDP coalition that seemed viable at the beginning of the 1980s has lost much of its luster and thereby has provided the LDP with more possibilities to play coalition politics should it want or need to do so.

Concluding Comments

As is true of any national assembly in non-authoritarian governments, the Diet has not functioned in a political vacuum. Its members have had to be sensitive to the shifting attitudes and priorities of Japan's voters. Vagaries of the electoral system, uneven distribution of political (especially election) funds, as well as skillfully or clumsily conducted campaigns may have distorted the image of the public's aspirations that is reflected in the Diet's mirror. This asymmetry, however, has been less significant than that its members have represented a broader cross-section of the people's attitudes than any other Japanese public or private institution.

When viewed from abroad, it has been all too easy to assume that Japanese politics has revolved around: (1) the national bureaucrats, who have tended to remain convinced that they know what is best for Japan, and who have had the competence to control and to regulate much of the legislative agenda; (2) big business associations (such as the "Federation of Economic Organizations (*Keidanren*))", that have assiduously promoted the interests of the banking–commercial–industrial sector which has played so consequential a role in Japan's international economic success; and (3) the LDP, that has managed most of what has transpired in the Diet. The foregoing triad – to which the large communications media enterprises should be added in any case – may well be Japan's "Establishment," but over the last decade roughly half of Japan's voters consistently have supported candidates belonging to the opposition parties, which came very close to winning at least half the seats in both Houses. Some foreigners, and Japanese as well, may have wished to ignore these election outcomes, but those who have been responsible for managing the Diet have not been afforded this luxury.

Moreover, as I have emphasized throughout this chapter, the long-governing LDP teetered on the brink of having its "civil war" end in a formal dissolution of the party. These internal disputes have tended to be obscured by the discipline that the party's leadership has imposed during formal votes in committee or plenary meetings – with the obvious exception of the division on the motion of non-confidence in May 1980 – but that has not made them any less palpable to participants and observers alike. On the other hand, members of the LDP have exhibited remarkable powers of resilience in averting an irreparable party split, far more so than their antagonists in the socialist parties. Hence, an observer must be cautious – always – in not mistaking "surface (*omote*)" manifestations for what has been transpiring at the "sub-surface (*ura*)" level. I would submit, nevertheless, that the "Forty-day Imbroglio" and the anti-mainstream's behavior during the vote on the motion of non-confidence in the Ōhira Cabinet were not staged productions of theatre. The latter episode also reflected a greater desire on the part of the Opposition for confrontation against the LDP rather than any search for accommodation, which presumably had governed Diet proceedings during the years of "near parity." Furthermore, the slogans that the opposition parties had jointly fashioned as a major element of their anti-LDP campaign were not couched in language that could be expected to lead to agreements with the governing party on certain fundamental issues such as Japan's domestic economic policy or its security relationship with the United States.

In general, however, the Diet has functioned more smoothly during and after *hakuchū* than it had in the years of the LDP's dominance. While the LDP had been the hegemonic master of the Diet (1955–75) by virtue of its overwhelming majorities and its control over all of the levers of power, it could and did manage to force the assembly to approve most of its legislative and policy agenda, providing that the party remained more rather than less united. On occasion, the Opposition's dilatory tactics and recalcitrance required the LDP's to use "forced votes (*kyōkō saiketsu*)" which resulted in scenes of near violence and made observers (including me) wonder whether conducting politics within a parliamentary framework had much of a future in Japan.

These earlier concerns have diminished since the onset of "near parity" and the much more accommodationist pattern of behavior (with some exceptions, of course) that members of the Diet have exhibited over the last decade. However, a "forced vote" had the advantage of breaking a procedural log-jam between the governing and opposition parties. "Mutual consultations (*hanashiai*)" – while more peaceful and presumably more in accord with the Japanese cultural bias favoring a consensual style of decision-making – have had the disadvantage of the Diet's procedures having slowed to the level of "cow-walking (*gyūho senjutsu*)," which the opposition parties had employed to obstruct the LDP's *kyōkō saiketsu* leviathan.

Most members of the Diet have become so cautious much of the time, that the Cabinet – in which the Constitution vests executive power – has been loath to submit legislative proposals that may be controversial. (Of course, that had happened even before the onset of "near parity", as for example, when both the Japanese and American governments agreed in 1969 not to submit to either national legislature a prolongation for a specified number of years of the Treaty of Mutual Co-operation and Security. Instead the automatic extension formula, which did not require legislative approval, was used.) Mutual consultations between the governing and opposition parties have slowed the legislative process. One possible consequence is that the Japanese government (specifically, the national bureaucracy) may attempt to circumvent the National

Assembly altogether on legislative proposals that could lead to confrontations. If that option were exercised frequently, the Diet's authority could be threatened as much as earlier scenes of near-violence had undermined public confidence in its efficacy.

During an interview (1985) with a senior Cabinet minister, I asked what generalization above all others I should include in this book. He responded: "No other institution is as inefficient as the Diet. The Opposition knows that we [LDP] will not use *kyōkō saiketsu*, and that everything will be handled by means of mutual consultations. In effect, it is the opposition parties that have controlled the Diet's agenda." Not everyone (in the LDP) might have put it quite so forcefully, but avoidance of confrontation obviously has engendered feelings of frustration. Yet, the voters of Japan have shown their preferences. By limiting the LDP's majority, they have chosen to circumscribe its ability to enact controversial new legislation and to embark on discordant policy ventures. The members of the Diet can do no more than to reflect the people's verdict at the polls.

CHAPTER 5

Japanese Politics and the Diet

Certain salient features of Japanese politics have been covered in the preceding chapters. Three decades of single-party rule by the Liberal Democratic Party was attributed to division and weakness among its opposition parties and the LDP's factions that have provided the party with enough flexibility to adapt and adjust itself to Japan's rapidly changing socio-economic environment. The governing party also has been able to maximize its ability to win seats in both chambers of the National Assembly by organizing its strength within the framework of the rules governing elections. One of its advantages has been that, despite its being a confederation of factions, it has been able to control the endorsement of candidates better than the opposition parties whose joint candidate strategy has not fully solved the dilemma that they have faced in endorsing their own candidates, by virtue of being separate entities.

In assessing the Diet's capacity to behave autonomously, notice was taken of external – principally bureaucratic – controls, especially in the drafting of legislative bills. Furthermore, the governing party's continuing ability to control most of the levers of power over the Diet's internal machinery, when linked to the norms of tight party discipline, have resulted in vitiating the autonomous behavior of this institution's members. In turn, this has meant that most of the crucial decisions have not been the consequence of interaction between the governing and opposition parties, even when their numerical strengths have been nearly equal, but have been dominated by struggles within the governing party itself.

In this concluding chapter, the major issues that have been discussed will be reconsidered by raising specific questions. First, has the National Assembly (Diet) lived up to its constitutional mandate of being "the highest organ of state power, and . . . the sole law-making organ of the State" (1947 Constitution, Chapter

IV, Article 41)? Secondly, what has been the relationship between national elections and the Diet's functioning – by virtue of both of its chambers being popularly elected – as a representative assembly? Related thereto, is the question of whether "near parity" between the governing and opposition parties will continue and, if so, what its implications might be for the future role of the National Assembly. Fourth, and finally, are there specific aspects of Japan's culture and history that must be considered in assessing the societal framework within which the political process has evolved in that country? Has Japan's cultural heritage been so unique that comparisons with other political systems are extremely difficult, if not impossible to make? Answers to each of these questions will have to be speculative and only should be considered as guideposts to the future.

Is the National Assembly (Diet) Supreme?

In one crucial respect, Japan's National Assembly has lived up to its constitutional mandate. In the last forty years, the Diet has been *the* final, formal arbiter of official legislation, whether it be a domestic law or an international treaty. Its supremacy has not been challenged by any other political institution in Japan.

In and of itself, the National Assembly's having achieved this position of eminence has reflected a major shift in the formal allocation of power. Under the Meiji Constitution (1890–1946), the Emperor had been "head of the Empire, combining in himself the rights of sovereignty" (1890 Constitution, Chapter I, Article IV). A constitutional revolution had taken place when the new basic law came into force in 1947.

Furthermore, that this political upheaval originally had owed as much to the foreign Occupation authorities as it had to somewhat recalcitrant Japanese government officials has become less relevant with each passing year. The 1947 Constitution has remained pristine despite more than a little discussion about possible amendments having taken place. No one, as yet, has introduced any formal revision, nor – obviously – has any been approved. Even if certain amendments were adopted, it is extremely doubtful that any of them would affect the Diet's formal supremacy inasmuch as two-thirds of its members would have to play a central role in initiating that process (1947 Constitution, Chapter IX, Article 96). The likelihood of that many Representatives and Councillors agreeing, voluntarily, to give up their constitutional prerogatives or of lowering any aspect of their current status would be a form of mass suicide that is simply beyond the realm of rational calculation.

Constitutional provisions do not by themselves guarantee that they will be observed. Political principles often differ widely from the conduct of practical affairs. Japan's National Assembly has neither existed nor survived in a political vacuum, nor has it been some kind of *deus ex machina* making "democracy" work or a mystical embodiment of the General Will. It has been and is a human institution which has served as the focal point for contention among a variety of political forces that, by competing with each other, have sought to gain control over it. Principal among the antagonists have been the political parties and their leaders versus the government's bureaucracy and its senior officials. They have not been alone, however. Various interests such as the Federation of Economic Organizations, the major trade union federations, the farmers' co-operative or the myriad of other groups reflecting special or particularistic concerns, as well as the media of communication (*masukomi*), have sought to influence what transpires in and around the Diet. The politicians and the bureaucrats constitute the core.

In the very end, however, it is the members of the National Assembly who decide what will become the law of the land or national policy. Since all of the members belong to political parties – the handful of those who are unaffiliated are not "independent" – it follows that party leaders are among the principal decision-makers. In the case of the LDP and to a somewhat lesser extent in the JSP, the chiefs of the factions often play as important a role as the formally designated party leaders in determining the decisions that the Diet makes.

Executive power is vested in the Cabinet. Its ministers are drawn from the members of the Diet (although there have been three exceptions over the last three decades). Formally, it is they who determine most of what transpires in the National Assembly, but they must share some of their power with the vast array of committees and boards in the LDP. Furthermore, since four-fifths of them belong to their party's factions, they must also be mindful of their chief's views.

As in all parliamentary systems derived from the Westminster model of British politics, it is the Prime Minister who is the "first among equals" in the Cabinet. However, nearly all postwar Japanese Prime Ministers – Yoshida Shigeru may be the sole exception, but his period in office was unusual, especially those years when the Occupation still held sway – have been far more constrained by factional alignments within the governing party than their counterparts in the United Kingdom.

A Prime Minister's power tends to be circumscribed by the numerical strength of his own faction and the degree of cohesion within the factional coalition that supports him. Current Prime Minister Nakasone has exemplified these limitations. He is the leader of the fourth largest faction and is therefore dependent on the continued support of the Tanaka faction which remains the largest despite its leader's illness. This circumstance inevitably limits his capacity to be a forceful leader, regardless of his successful efforts to project a contrary image, cast in the mold of Prime Minister Thatcher.

Formally, however, a Prime Minister of Japan sits at the apex of two political pyramids over which he simultaneously presides. He is the President of the governing party (or, is the head of the major party within the coalition that controls the Cabinet), and he and his Cabinet ministers are the executives of the ministries and agencies that in their totality constitute the formal government of Japan.

These two bureaucracies (the LDP has become as bureaucratized as any government agency) coexist within a symbiotic relationship that is alternately mutually supportive and/or ridden by conflict. Most of the interactions between these two groups that have been and are so central to Japanese politics – government officials in a ministry or agency and their counterparts in the relevant section of the LDP's Policy Research Council – have remained hidden behind an impenetrable bamboo thicket. From the perspective of the study and, conceivably, understanding of Japanese politics, it is regrettable that these crucial interactions have not been more open to public scrutiny. For it has meant that all generalizations, based on the assumption that these consultations are significant, must remain at the level of hypotheses which are substantiated by hardly any empirical evidence. Participants have let it be known that their discussions are meaningful. That is all that we can state until the authorities permit the veil of secrecy to be lifted.

There is agreement on one basic element in this complex process, however. It is the government officials – that is, the bureaucrats – who draft most of the legislative bills and policy pronouncements that the Diet considers. To be sure, some members' bills are introduced, but they have been so few in number and so relatively meaningless within the overall framework of the legislative process, that they have been a relatively minor component of the National Assembly's work-load. The Diet, in this respect as well, has operated within a system that is much more in consonance with the British model than with that based on Presidential–Congressional relations in the United States.

These comparisons aside, has the overwhelming influence of Japan's government officials meant that they not only propose, but – by virtue of their close ties with the governing party – also dispose of all legislation? Or, to put the question in its most extreme form, is the National Assembly irrelevant to the legislative process? Not necessarily, and for one crucial reason. Government officials cannot ignore the balance of political forces in the National Assembly. Even if it were to be assumed that the governing LDP has been nothing more than an eager and willing partner of the government's bureaucracy (in itself, a questionable premise), then what about the LDP's Opposition? Can their policy orientations simply be dismissed because they are the views of a minority? There have been occasions, especially during the decades 1955–75, when the LDP enjoyed hegemonic power, that the Diet served as little more than a rubber stamp for approving legislation that the government officials and LDP leaders had prepared. However, that kind of imbalance of political power between the governing and opposition parties has not prevailed over the last decade at the very least, and – unless the public's voting patterns change dramatically – is not likely to be repeated.

Hence, government officials, as influential and powerful as they have continued to be, must calculate the possible fate of their draft legislation not only by assessing the reaction by the LDP and its constantly shifting coalition of factions. They must also take into consideration the views of the opposition parties. For, the LDP's parliamentarians have not been willing, since the onset of near parity, to ride roughshod over the Opposition. A bill that is known to be anathema to the minority parties will not be introduced. Neither the bureaucrats nor the LDP can publicly ignore the representatives of that half of Japan's voters that do not support the governing party's candidates.

These relatively recent changes in the power equation inside the Diet have had their political consequences, as will be indicated later in greater detail. For the moment, it is only necessary to note one major change in bureaucratic behavior. No longer can government officials act as if all that is necessary is to gain the LDP's approval, a process that was not without its pitfalls and was by no means automatic. They must also ask themselves whether the LDP not only approves, but if it is willing to grapple with the opposition parties without endangering other – possibly more pressing – pieces of legislation.

After all, it is within the chambers of the Diet that the fate of a legislative bill will be determined, and this process perforce involves both the governing and opposition parties. It is this aspect of the lengthy procedures involving the approval of legislation that has gained for the National Assembly the greater degree of influence that it now enjoys in comparison with the past. It is not just constitutional provisions that have breathed life into the National Assembly. It is also the changing balance of political forces represented within its halls that has helped the Diet to acquire some of the most salient functions that the 1947 Constitution had commanded.

Elections: Is the Mirror Cracking?

Japan's political parties have responded with varying degrees of success to the constraints and opportunities of the electoral systems for the two Houses of the National Assembly. Over the last three decades, the governing Liberal Democratic Party has managed to win majorities in both the House of Representatives and House of Councillors. It has done so with decreasing success as the years have slipped by and, since December 1983, has found it necessary to invite the New Liberal Club to be its coalition partner in the Cabinet, primarily to retain a sufficient majority of seats so that control over most of the standing committees would be possible.

In and of itself, the addition of the NLC to the Cabinet did not require a major shift in government policy because this splinter group did not espouse attitudes or policies that were basically at variance with those of the LDP. Nonetheless, the need that was felt by the leaders of the governing party to invite an external partner into the Cabinet so as to buttress its numerical majority among the Representatives provided concrete evidence of some weakness in the LDP's capacity to win national elections.

This slow decline of public support had begun almost as soon as the LDP came into being in 1955, but had become a serious problem by the middle of the 1970s. Over the last decade, with the 1980 "double election" as a major exception, the LDP has not been able to win a majority of seats – counting its officially endorsed candidates only – in the House of Representatives. Instead, it has had to invite successful Unaffiliated conservative candidates into its ranks in order to retain its majority standing.

Furthermore, the LDP's decreasing margins of victory have been achieved even though the party has been helped by the malapportionment of seats in relation to population, and by the inability of the opposition parties to translate their shares of the popular vote (slightly above or below 50 percent of the total) into electing their candidates. The lack of reapportionment has benefitted the LDP because rural districts, in which the party has strong support, have been over-represented, whereas metropolitan and urban districts, in which the opposition parties tend to be stronger, have been under-represented.

LDP candidates also have won seats that they might have lost had it not been for the difficulties that the opposition parties have encountered by having too many of their candidates compete against each other, thereby going down together in defeat. Especially consequential in this respect has been the Japan Communist Party's electoral strategy of endorsing its own candidates in nearly all of the constituencies. By the same token, the LDP also has had its share of losses that were the consequence of either errors in its endorsement of too many candidates in a given district, or the difficulties that all parties face in accurately predicting what percentage of voters will go to the polls. Nonetheless, the biases of the electoral rules have helped the LDP win some marginal seats without which it could not have retained its majorities in the National Assembly.

This gradual shift of public preferences that has favored the opposition parties has not been as serious in its implications for the stable equilibrium of Japanese politics as it might have been at the beginning of the 1970s. At that time, the differences over a wide range of domestic and foreign policy issues separating the LDP from its multi-party Opposition was relatively wide and deep. In the intervening years, both the Democratic Socialist Party and the Kōmeitō have moved towards the moderate center. In so doing, their disagreements with the LDP have become less salient. Moreover, the Japan Socialist Party has tried, under the leadership of Chairman Ishibashi Masashi, to extricate itself from its earlier commitment to class warfare based on its particular brand of Marxist dogma. Only the Japan Communist Party remains, therefore, as the self-righteous guardian of a basic alternative to the LDP; but the Communists too have softened the harsh and militant images that they had previously projected.

This comparatively benign image of Japanese politics could change dramatically and suddenly. Highly volatile shifts in the public's mood have been a fairly frequent feature. Serious economic dislocations occasioned by a world trade war, to mention only one contingency, easily could shatter the tenuous consensus within the governing party, not to mention the commitment by all parties to operate their politics within the existing governmental framework. Public pronouncements by the leaders of all political parties, including the LDP, of their continued devotion to parliamentarianism could vanish into thin air. A placid surface may hide tensions that could erupt with little warning. Moreover, politics everywhere tend to be unpredictable."

These dreary but necessary speculations to the contrary, what alternative courses for the future evolution of Japanese politics might be considered as being within the realm of the possible? Any answer cannot avoid being tentative and subject to almost endless qualification, given the unpredictability of politics in general and Japanese politics in particular. Nonetheless, on the premise that past is prologue and that the development of past trends continues to be evolutionary, what prospects are more rather than less likely?

Assuming, for the moment, that a fairly broadly-based consensus is not sundered, and assuming that there are no dramatic shifts in the party preferences of Japan's electorate, then it would follow that the LDP would continue to be the dominant party. It might not, however, be able to form a Cabinet by itself because of its inability to win a majority of seats in the National Assembly, especially in the House of Representatives which has the final voice in electing the Prime Minister. Two major alternatives would then be available to the long-governing party. It could broaden the base of its support in the Diet by inviting one or more of the opposition parties to participate in the formation of a coalition Cabinet; or, it could try to govern by forming temporary voting coalitions with the opposition parties that might support a specific piece of legislation. Both have problems.

A coalition Cabinet with the LDP as the major partner, but which also includes either the DSP or Kōmeitō, or both, would face certain difficulties. First, not all LDPers are necessarily willing to accept having representatives of any opposition party in the Cabinet, and might be sufficiently opposed that they would be willing to split their party. In that event, the new coalition could lose as many supporters through defections from the LDP as it might gain by the inclusion of its new partners. Secondly, the apportioning of Cabinet portfolios would become even more complex than it has been already when only the balancing of factional strengths within the LDP has had to be considered by those who have made these delicate decisions. After all, each ministerial post that would have to be accorded to the minority parties within the coalition would reduce the number available to reward loyal LDPers, thereby exacerbating factional strife. (One relatively painless solution would be to increase the size of the Cabinet by having each minister responsible for only one agency, instead of two as has often been the case.) Thirdly, the consensus formation process within the Cabinet could become more complex because of including a larger mix of political viewpoints.

A "selective coalition (*bubun rengo*)" LDP strategy also poses difficulties, even though the late Prime Minister Ōhira had managed it to good effect during his brief tenure. First, it requires bargaining with one or more of the opposition parties for their possible support of each legislative bill. Secondly, this process easily could be so time-consuming that the National Assembly's already-clogged legislative machinery could come very close to a standstill. Thirdly, if its use is necessitated by the LDP's having lost its majority, then the Cabinet's longevity might be very brief since the opposition parties would have sufficient votes to approve a motion of non-confidence at any time. On the other hand, this alternative has the obvious advantage, from the LDP's perspective, that the Cabinet would remain its exclusive domain.

A third scenario would be for the parties that have been in opposition for the last thirty years to form a coalition Cabinet by themselves. This alternative suffers from even greater obstacles than those that have been considered. First, the DSP's and Kōmeitō's long and deep hostility towards the JCP would have to be overcome. While anything in politics is always possible, the likelihood that this enmity could be resolved into even chilly co-operation must be considered as unlikely. Secondly, if the previous assertion holds, then the shift in the number of seats that would be required for a JSP-Kōmeitō-DSP coalition has its inherent difficulties. This group of parties won 211 seats in the 1983 General Election. They would therefore need to win an additional 45 seats, at a minimum, in order to gain a majority (256) in the House of Representatives. Such a dramatic shift in electoral outcomes is only conceivable if one assumes that a fundamental realignment of voting behavior is within the realm of the probable. However, the prior trend of incremental, rather than dramatic, shifts among Japanese voters in their preferences would argue against such an outcome in the near future.

A fourth – and final – scenario would be for the LDP to make the kind of dramatic comeback in the number of seats that it achieved in the 1980 "double election." A repetition of that result is not improbable. LDP candidates finished as "runners-up (*jiten*)" in almost half of the constituencies (61 out of 130) in the 1983 election. Many of these near-victors undoubtedly have been assiduously cultivating their potential supporters so that at least a third of them might be victorious in the next election. However, there were at least an equal number of LDPers whose margin of victory was extremely narrow and who are therefore vulnerable. Furthermore, given the vagaries of the multiple-member districts, the potential (new) LDP victors might do nothing more than replace an incumbent party colleague. Nonetheless, the LDP has not remained in power for three decades without having learned how to manipulate available electoral support into victories at the polls.

(None of these scenarios has factored in the consequences of reapportionment. At the moment, the Diet has not agreed to any changes in the existing system. Until one is actually approved, it is futile to speculate about its possible consequences.)

Of the four scenarios that were outlined, a larger coalition in which the LDP remains dominant but that also includes the DSP and/or Kōmeitō, or a minority LDP Cabinet that forges temporary alliances with the moderate opposition parties for the approval of specific legislative bills, are more probable than the other two alternatives. Selective coalitions with the moderates would be the least troublesome for the LDP, but would necessitate its being involved in endless negotiations with its temporary partners. By contrast, more broadly-based coalition Cabinets would be difficult for certain LDPers to accept, but would have the advantage of providing the Cabinet with relatively stable support in the National Assembly.

Either of these alternatives would alter the legislative process from the way it has operated over the three decades of LDP dominance. The long-governing party could not, as it has been able to in the past, rely solely on its members (and since 1983, those belonging to the NLC) to approve legislative bills. Some quotient of power would have to be accorded to what have been elements of its Opposition. Government officials could not negotiate just with members of relevant sections of the LDP's Policy Research Council, but would also be forced to do so with at least some of the opposition parties to a much greater extent than has been the case heretofore in order to gain their understanding. Moreover, the utilization of "forced vote (*kyōkō saiketsu*)" tactics – a largely discarded device in any case – no longer would be tolerated.

Each of these changes, while significant in the development of the National Assembly's influence, would not necessarily alter the power balance between this supreme organ of state power and the government's bureaucracy. For that to eventuate, even more fundamental changes might be necessary, as will be indicated in the final sections of this chapter.

Bureaucrats and Politicians: Is the Balance of their Power Shifting?

Participants in and analysts of Japanese politics have agreed that it is the government officials – the bureaucrats – who are the brains of the policy-making process. The bureaucrats have immense advantages: they have been trained at the best universities and their elite is still dominated by University of Tokyo Law Faculty graduates; they have the technical skills that are required to translate a policy proposal into a legislative bill; most important of all, they have the expert knowledge – because of their daily, often nightly, need – to deal with that particular aspect of public policy which is their responsibility. Moreover, it is they who have that special prestige which has been based for centuries on the old Chinese–Confucian tradition that accorded government officials – the mandarins – the highest status. It was exemplified by the Meiji-era slogan "officials are to be revered, the people (and, by implication at least, their representatives) are to be despised (*kanson minpi*)."

It is no wonder, therefore, that the struggle for influence and power between them and their challengers has been won, fairly consistently, by the bureaucrats. Politicians, after all, have many competing concerns on their energy and time, not the least being those that involve their next election. Furthermore, members of the National Assembly are as dependent as is everyone else – including the journalists and interested academicians – on the bureaucrats for the expert knowledge without which meaningful discussion about a policy problem has become increasingly difficult.

This set of circumstances is not unique to the realm of Japanese politics. It has become a hardy perennial in capitals as diverse as Washington, DC where many Presidents and Congressmen have battled the career civil service, or London where the mystique of Whitehall has been challenged – not always effectively – by Westminster, or Beijing which has seen its share of conflicts between those who are "red" (party ideologues) and those who are "expert" (government officials). Politicians may come and go, but the bureaucrats go on forever, and that too would seem to give the latter an enormous advantage against the former in the endless struggle.

Elected Japanese politicians can and do make some special claims for being superior, and these should not be dismissed. First, they have been elected. They can therefore assert, with more than a little validity, that they represent the wishes of their constituents, or the people. They go on to aver that bureaucrats obtain their positions of authority by virtue of passing examinations of one sort or another that are frequently difficult, and by proving their worth within the confines of a particular agency or ministry.

Moreover, the officials' much-advertised expert knowledge may not be as significant as initial impressions might lead one to expect. An official's career advancement tends to be based on having held a series of responsible positions in a variety of sections or bureaux, not ever staying with any long enough to acquire exceptional expertise. Furthermore, their legal skills may enable them to draft legislation or to provide administrative guidance (within the framework of existing statutes), but they may not know very much more than the politicians about the latest advances in science and technology.

Some Japanese politicians also have argued that by virtue of their lengthy tenure in the Diet and their membership in a "policy tribe," they have as much of a grasp of a specific area of public policy as their rivals. Furthermore they have complained that the bureaucrats often tend to view a policy dispute through the narrow prism of their ministry's prerogative – or "turf" in the vernacular – than competing considerations. Consequently, the bureaucrats who have often behaved as if they were the true defenders of Japan's "national interest," as opposed to the partisan or parochial interests of the politicians, on closer examination are seen by the politicians as being far more concerned with protecting their ministry or agency than with the much more broadly-based aspirations of the Japanese public. On these, the politicians in the National Assembly maintain that they speak far more authoritatively than even the council of administrative vice-ministers, the most senior policy-making group of career government officials.

The debate between Japanese politicians and bureaucrats, that has been outlined, in recent years has included a new factor: the shifting alignment and respective strengths of the political parties in the Diet. As the ranks of the opposition parties have swelled, the bureaucrats have responded by developing some lines of communication (or "pipes" as they have been called in Japan) with opposition members. These budding relationships may not have become as close as they have been all along with the governing LDP, but their having come into existence at all has had the effect of raising new issues for discussion.

Participants and observers have tended to assume that most bureaucrats and LDP politicians have shared an identity of interests on basic issues of public policy. They therefore have gone on to argue that the kind of general agreement and ease of communication which have prevailed between these groups cannot be expected to continue if Cabinet ministers were to come from the ranks of the DSP or Kōmeitō, let alone the JSP. Since this problem – if that is what it might become – has not arisen as yet (the NLC's inclusion can not be considered as an indicator), no evidence is available on which to base even a tentative conclusion. However, what can be said is that the government officials have managed to cope with the complexities of LDP factionalism, and that they can be expected to manage their relationships with erstwhile oppositionists with equal skill.

Nonetheless, the obverse flow of influence may become even more of a problem than it has been heretofore. It is, after all, one thing for bureaucrats to adjust the targeting of their influence to a different coalition of party leaders. It is quite another for politicians to enforce their influence over the bureaucrats. For example, Prime Minister Nakasone has had his difficulties in obtaining the compliance of some government officials in having them accept his market opening measures to increase the flow of foreign imports into Japan. If even he, as leader of the LDP which presumably has been so closely tied to the bureaucracy, has encountered obstacles to gaining the bureaucracy's compliance, it is at least reasonable to imagine that any policy initiatives of a broadly-based coalition Cabinet might easily encounter even more stubborn resistance. Admittedly, such a prospect is hypothetical; but, whereas the policy process in Japan may allow the politicians to make proposals, it is still the bureaucrats who carry them out – if that is what they want to do.

Politicians do have the capacity to be the masters of the bureaucrats in one crucial arena. While the Diet is in session, government officials must be prepared to answer questions at committee meetings or plenary sessions. They must also accompany their minister to assist him with expert advice during the course of the "interpellations." These question periods can, in theory, cast light on a controversial aspect of public policy or a problematic provision in a proposed bill. The potential is there, but it is frequently not realized primarily because the bureaucrats stage-manage most of the proceedings. It is they who have prepared the questions and it is they who provide the answers either by having briefed the minister or by answering the questions themselves. Only rarely have these carefully prepared, staged productions broken down, and observers have had the uneasy feeling that the bureaucrats had a hand in making them happen.

Despite the foregoing limitations, there have been occasions when members of the Diet influenced the policy process by exercising their function of overseeing or scrutinizing proposals that the bureaucrats have generated. Politicians can block the initiatives of government officials, but they cannot compel compliance if only because the bureaucrats have tended – with some noteworthy exceptions – not to respect the politicians. In part, their attitude is a reflection of the Confucian heritage alluded to earlier. It has been compounded by what the bureaucrats have perceived as the indebtedness (frequently financial) of the politicians to their supporters such as that of the Liberal Democrats to major corporate or banking enterprises or of the Socialists to the large trade unions. Improprieties, such as the Lockheed scandal, merely serve to confirm the bureaucrats' suspicions that all politicians tend to be either corrupt or corruptible. By contrast, government officials have jealously guarded their well-deserved reputation for probity.

Over the last one hundred years, the hard wall of bureaucratic power in Japanese politics has become so impenetrable that even the foreign occupiers after the end of the Second World War could not challenge it effectively. Officials in General MacArthur's Headquarters made some efforts in this direction, but they ultimately failed because they too became dependent on Japanese government officials. If an army of occupation with close to dictatorial powers could not undermine the all-pervasive influence of the Japanese bureaucracy, then it is hardly surprising that domestic political leaders have not met with great success whenever they have tried to mount an assault against those who walk the corridors of power in Kasumigaseki, Tokyo's ministry row.

Nonetheless, there have been some indications in recent years that the politicians have been gaining somewhat greater influence. "Administrative reform," much favored by Prime Minister Nakasone, can be perceived as little more than reducing the growth of government expenditures. It can, however, also be perceived as an effort to reduce the power of the bureaucrats by means of reducing their ranks. As yet there has been little evidence that the recommendations of the Second Commission on Administrative Reform will be fully implemented. Nor is there any guarantee that the achievement of greater efficiency in government will reduce bureaucratic controls.

Another development that has been under way since the immediate postwar years may be even more significant in the long run. It is that a large number of ex-bureaucrats have entered the world of electoral politics, especially as Diet members belonging to the LDP. All too often, the bureaucracy's function as one of the principal incubators for politicians has been perceived as exemplifying the close links that have been established between the LDP and the government. Many LDPers with whom I have discussed this issue view their own background as ex-bureaucrats very differently. They assert that their experience as government officials has taught them how to control the bureaucrats, or at least not to be controlled by their erstwhile colleagues who have remained in the government. In any case, the generalization that the LDP is nothing more than the willing agent of government officials because so many leaders in the governing party are ex-bureaucrats remains a hypothesis which has not been proven.

When all is said and done, however, there is very little prospect that the bureaucrats' dominant influence will lessen in the near future. Government officials, as they have in the past, will continue to draft the vast majority of legislative bills. In doing so, they will consult the party (or parties) that control the Cabinet and they will assess the respective strengths of the governing and opposition parties to determine which of their legislative proposals have the prospect of being approved by the National Assembly. Nonetheless, it is the government officials who will control most of the process.

Politicians, on the other hand, may acquire greater influence as the progenitors of policy proposals as contrasted with formal legislation. The LDP, for example, has established its own policy "think tank," and the establishment of the National Institute for Research Advancement (NIRA), as well as the proliferation of smaller research institutes, to study non-traditional public policy problems may provide alternative hot-houses for generating new ideas. Furthermore, recent Prime Ministers, beginning with Tanaka Kakuei in 1972, have established their own groups of policy advisors whose views may challenge existing government policy. In the end, however, it is the bureaucrats who will decide whether any of these alternative proposals will become official government policy.

Americans might find themselves stifled by this level of bureaucratic guidance. Most Japanese – but by no means all of them – have been much more accepting, especially because they have prospered. There has been, therefore, little reason for them to doubt that the government officials know what is best for Japan, even when some of the controls have proven to be irksome. Moreover, that this bureaucratic dominance has reduced the politicians to being marginal participants in the governmental process might be frustrating to the members of the National Assembly, but not to the degree that they are unwilling to acquiesce.

Culture and Politics: Is Japan "Unique"?

In this final section, I intend to speculate about two features of Japanese culture that have influenced the conduct of politics in that society. The first is the importance of groups as the building blocks of social interaction. The second revolves around certain features of the Japanese language. Implicit in any commentary is the question of whether Japanese politics is unique. Many Japanese prefer to believe that they are. I am not certain, nor am I convinced that the question has much meaning because each country's politics are, to varying degrees, different. That does not necessarily make them so different that they are *sui generis*.

The group basis of Japanese society is discussed in almost any book about that country. This feature, which is deeply imbedded in Japanese culture, is also politically significant. In an official setting – such as plenary or committee meetings of the National Assembly, or a party caucus – it is groups of individuals, rather than the individuals who are its members, that are the actors.

Extensive prior consultations, that the Japanese refer to as "binding the roots (for planting) (*nemawashi*)," or preparing the soil in English, will have taken place among the individuals who belong to a group. Once consensus has been achieved however, public deviation frequently results in expulsion. As always, there are exceptions. During the "Forty-day Imbroglio" in the fall of 1979 and the vote of non-confidence in the Ōhira Cabinet in May 1980, the behavior of the anti-mainstream factions violated the presumed primacy of party unity. In both instances, it was the party's sub-groups – the factions – that were more important than the larger group (party) to which they belonged. Only the requirements imposed by the party's desire to remain in power prevented the dissident factions from being expelled.

Of course, it has become well known that factional strife within Japanese political parties periodically prevents their acting in a unified manner. All that this really signifies is that group identity with one's faction has been stronger than with the party to which the faction belongs, especially in the LDP but also in all Japanese political parties. As a consequence, the relationship among factions can be more influential than the interaction between parties. In general, this feature of Japanese politics has been less salient on matters of public policy or legislation – both of which tend to be dominated by the bureaucrats – than in leadership struggles and patronage. A specific example from Japan's recent political history will illustrate the point.

Just prior to the LDP Convention in the fall 1984, Party Vice President Nikaido Susumu challenged incumbent Nakasone Yasuhiro for the Party Presidency. Various factional chiefs lent their support to each of the contestants. When, during a visit to Japan some six months after the event, I asked for explanations, most of my respondents answered along the following lines.

Former Prime Minister Suzuki Zenkō was angry because his role as kingmaker had never been fully acknowledged by Nakasone. Furthermore, Nakasone had publicly criticized Suzuki's stewardship and had refused to accept Suzuki's nominee (Miyazawa Kiichi) for Party Secretary-General and had selected another member of the Suzuki faction (Tanaka Rokusuke) instead. Former Prime Minister Fukuda Takeo had had a long-time rivalry with Nakasone in Gunma's Third Electoral District. Moreover, all Prime Ministers since Satō had only had one term as Party President–Prime Minister. Why should Nakasone be allowed to have two? Kōmoto Yoshio, then leader of the smallest LDP faction, had been Nakasone's principal rival in the fall 1982 party primary election. He had long been an enemy of former Prime Minister Tanaka Kakuei whose faction had staunchly supported Nakasone in his bid to succeed Suzuki. Hence, from Kōmoto's perspective, anyone except Nakasone would be better. As to Nikaido himself: he was a senior member of Tanaka's faction who believed that factional unity would be threatened unless it put forth its own candidate. (The Tanaka faction, by far the largest in the LDP, had not even had a nominee for Party President since Tanaka's downfall in December 1974. If that were so, what were the advantages to be gained by continuing to be a member of the faction?) Furthermore, Nikaido had good ties with the DSP and Kōmeitō, either or both of which might be ready to join in a coalition Cabinet, should the leadership struggle lead to a split in the LDP. For former Prime

Minister Tanaka – regardless of whether he had or had not endorsed Nikaido's willingness to fish in troubled waters – the end result would be the same. Nakasone would be even more dependent, given his diminishing support by the other major faction leaders, on Tanaka's continued support. If, on the other hand, Nikaido was successful, a Tanaka lieutenant would have become Japan's Prime Minister.

This set of explanations concerning the motives of the factions and their chiefs is significant, both for what it does and does not include. In each instance, the settling of personal scores or of gaining ambitions was crucial. There was barely a hint of any factor even remotely linked to an issue of public policy. However, one that was mentioned was that Suzuki considered Nakasone as being "too hawkish" (that is, too willing to increase the defense budget). However, it was accorded far less significance than those involving the personal motives of the factions and their leaders. In the end, of course, the revolt proved to be abortive, and Nakasone was re-elected unopposed.

What does all of this have to do with the group basis of Japanese politics? First, it is not necessarily political parties that should be the principal units of analysis. Parties are important, but they can be overwhelmed by their constituent sub-groups. Secondly, these factions tend to be made up of retainers who are loyal to their respective leaders. Unless, therefore, one gains some familiarity with the names of some of the principals and how they relate to each other, some of the most dynamic aspects of Japanese politics will be overlooked. Unfortunately, it is easier to learn about institutional arrangements or policy disputes based on ideological differences. Their significance, and that of a myriad of other factors, is not being denied. My only point is that they are not as salient in Japanese politics as they tend to be in other societies.

Language is the second factor about which I will speculate. Spoken Japanese can be direct, precise and full of nuance. It can also be ambiguous, imprecise and so obscure that it becomes incomprehensible to the most attentive listener. These bold assertions sustain the belief held by many Japanese that no foreigner can understand them or their politics. I partially agree, but many more foreigners have become conversant in Japanese than was true in the past. Furthermore, it is not only foreigners who have had difficulties. Many Japanese who were alive in August 1945 and heard the Emperor's famous broadcast, in which he announced the end of hostilities, have mentioned that they hardly understood a word.

Various societies have used language as a device to separate the rulers from the ruled. Japan has not been among them over the last one hundred years. Its system of education has been highly developed and the literacy rate probably is the highest in the world. In addition, nowhere is the latest technological innovation of information transmittal more enthusiastically embraced than in Japan. What, then, is the problem?

It is that Japanese consists of many different languages, not in the sense of dialects, but in including many levels of complexity. English is not without similar features as evidenced by such terms as "bureaucratese" or "legalese" which involves the use of obfuscating jargon that hinders rather than promotes communication. In Japanese, these difficulties can be duplicated by the simple device of increasing the number of words derived from Chinese, and by the use of complex verbs and even more complicated verb endings. In years past, when I regularly listened to formal discussions in the Diet, it was only the member's party affiliation that helped me guess whether he was speaking for or against a motion.

These difficulties also become noticeable on such occasions as when the Prime Minister or another member of the Cabinet delivers his policy address at the beginning of a legislative session. These speeches tend to be the products of intensive and lengthy negotiations among government officials who will have left their imprint on the language. It is as if the ministers were reading a committee report, that has tried to incorporate conflicting views. In many respects, that is precisely what they are doing.

Language, like politics, does not exist in a vacuum. It is the product of human inventiveness and imagination. Hence, if language has layers of complexity, it is because those who have created and use it desired that outcome, not because it inheres in the language itself. As is well known, Japanese society is replete with distinctions that are based on status. (I will leave for others the tangled web of possible correlations between status and class.) Styles of language provide an effective device for expressing these status distinctions. If the Japanese people had not wanted to create a society in which status was significant, then they would not have had to invent a language that expresses it verbally.

At least one of the distinctions based on status has left its imprint on Japanese politics. As noted, language within an "in group" of close friends is simple and direct. However, that kind of free and easy conversation tends to be considerably more constrained between individuals belonging to different groups that may not wish to communicate with each other. One method to avoid this dilemma is to restrict oneself to expounding the views of the group to which one belongs and to pay little or no attention to those expressed by other groups. That is what frequently happens during public discussions between governing and opposition party representatives in the National Assembly. As a consequence an issue of public policy is not debated so much as that the various parties expound their respective positions. In turn, all of this has meant that much of the talk in the public forums of the National Assembly tends to be ritualistic. It has also meant that the participants use a carefully prepared script so that the Diet becomes the stage for the presentation of well-rehearsed dramatic productions.

Any expectation that open committee meetings or plenary sessions of the National Assembly might become something other than exercises in ritual would have to take into consideration the societal constraints within which the Diet functions. Ritual predominates, and has enormous value. It legitimizes such crucial decisions as the formal election of Japan's Prime Minister, as well as legislative bills and public policy. In the final analysis, it is the performance of these functions that is the Diet's real achievement.

CHAPTER 6

Epilogue
August 1986*

"In politics, one inch ahead is darkness (*Seiji no sekai wa issun saki wa yami*)." This aphorism was one of the favorite expressions of the late Kawashima Shōjirō, LDP Vice President during most of the years of the Satō Eisaku cabinets in the latter half of the 1960s and early 1970s. Kawashima was particularly fond of repeating this saying whenever even he could not find a ready explanation for some of the ministerial appointments that Satō made to his many cabinets.

Incumbent Prime Minister Nakasone Yasuhiro has provided his own set of surprises which also illustrate the element of unpredictability in Japanese politics. By far the most significant of these was the generally unanticipated outcome of the 6 July 1986 elections for the entire membership of the House of Representatives and half the members of the House of Councillors. While the LDP had been expected to do better than its dismal performance in December 1983 (see Chapter 2), in all of the pre-election surveys that the major newspapers and the Government-sponsored television and radio network NHK (Nippon Hōsō Kyōkai) had conducted, none had foreseen the dimensions of the governing party's victory in the House of Representatives: 304 seats out of a total of 512. Even without adding former Prime Minister Tanaka Kakuei and former Parliamentary Vice Minister of Transportation Satō Takayuki – both of whom, while formally having been elected as "Unaffiliated (*mushozoku*)," would be members of the governing party except for their involvement in the Lockheed bribery scandals – to the list of this conservative party's victors, the LDP

* Nearly all of the material in this chapter was collected by me during two brief research trips (February and July 1986) to Tokyo. I am deeply indebted to Sam Jameson, *Los Angeles* Tokyo Bureau Chief, for his hospitality and to Mr Masuko Hideo, Director of UCLA's Tokyo Liaison Office, for his assistance in arranging my schedule and for sending me all available newspaper reports concerning the formation of the new Nakasone Cabinet.

had returned to the kind of electoral performance that was considered routine in the 1960s.

One basic question that needs to be considered therefore is whether the LDP has been able to overcome the condition of "near parity between the governing and opposition parties (*yo-yatō hakuchū*)." Has Japan's electorate become imbued with a renewed commitment to conservatism, or were the results of the 6 July electoral contest exceptional in the same sense as that of the 22 June 1980 "double election"? These and related questions will be discussed in this chapter.

Before turning to these issues, however, it is necessary to provide a brief overview of the political events leading up to the "Elections for the House of Representatives and House of Councillors on the same day (*Shūsan Ryōin Dōjitsu Senkyo*)." For some, as yet unexplained, reason the June 1980 election always was referred to as a "double," whereas the July 1986 was dubbed as the "same day" election. One possibility that was mentioned was that the difference in appellation would provide a shorthand way of distinguishing between the two. Another was that the Japanese public had turned more nationalistic in the intervening six years, and that it would be more appropriate to use a Japanese expression – "*dōjitsu* (same day)" – than one derived from English.

Rumors had begun to float through the by-ways of Tokyo as early as the summer of 1985 that Prime Minister Nakasone personally favoured conducting elections for the two Houses simultaneously. The six-year term of half the members of the House of Councillors – those who had been elected in June 1980 – was to expire in any case. Hence, the only unknown was whether an election for the much more powerful House of Representatives could be arranged to coincide. For that contingency, all that would be necessary would be for the Prime Minister to dissolve that chamber in a timely fashion. Constitutionally, the Representatives' term would not expire until December 1987, but a new election after an interval of two-and-a-half years would not be out of the ordinary.

By February 1986, it had become apparent to Japanese political commentators (Interviews, February 17 to 25) that Nakasone had arranged the Spring's schedule so as to set the stage for a "same day election." On 29 April, Emperor Hirohito's birthday would provide the occasion for celebrating his sixtieth anniversary on the throne. From 4 to 6 May, leaders of the seven industrialized nations having market economies would assemble in Tokyo for their annual Economic Summit. During the middle of May, Great Britain's

Prince and Princess of Wales would be Japan's state guests. Each of these events could be expected to, and did, provide numerous photo opportunities and clips for the day's television news. Moreover, each occasion would reflect favorably on the Prime Minister: the first as the leader of the Emperor's loyal subjects, the second as one of the recognized leaders of the advanced world, and the third as host to British royalty's most glamorous couple. Nakasone, far more than any of his predecessors, had recognized the importance of television as a medium of communication. Furthermore, Japanese analysts of demographic trends pointed out that over half of Japan's electorate belonged to the generation for whom television was the major source of news.

Despite these – at the time still scheduled – high profile events, no one was willing to predict with complete assurance that the Prime Minister could arrange for the conduct of a "same day election." All of the opposition parties' leaders repeated their disapproval as frequently as possible; they remembered their respective party's losses in the 1980 "double election." More important, the LDP's three "new leaders" – Foreign Minister Abe Shintarō, Finance Minister Takeshita Noboru, and LDP Executive Board Chairman Miyazawa Kiichi – all expressed their opposition. They reasoned, it was widely reported, that the LDP would gain seats and that the incumbent Party President/Prime Minister (that is, Nakasone) would therefore be in a position to justify extending his years in office beyond the two two-year terms stipulated by Party rules.

Their cause was aided by initially hostile Japanese Press reactions to the Tokyo Summit. Nakasone, it was asserted, had not served Japan's national interests for two principal reasons. First, he had signed the Joint Communiqué singling out Libya (by name) as an instigator of international terrorism. (Japan's foreign policy has tried to avoid antagonizing any Arab country since the OPEC Oil embargo of 1973.) Second, his pleas to US President Reagan for help in overcoming the rapid upward valuation of the yen (that was causing serious dislocation among Japan's medium and small enterprises) allegedly fell on deaf-ears. So vociferous was the Press's criticism that nearly everyone freely predicted that it would be impossible for the Prime Minister to conduct a "same-day election."

Moreover, an additional hurdle had to be overcome. The Supreme Court had declared the existing apportionment of electoral districts in the House of Representatives as contrary to the Constitution because of the substantial disparity – in certain instances, in excess of five to one – of the weight of one vote in some rural as opposed to urban districts (see Chapter 2). One reapportionment plan under which six districts would lose one and six would gain one seat had failed in the closing days of the Fall 1985 legislative session.

Could a new plan be fashioned and receive the National Assembly's approval before the regular session would end on 23 May? Furthermore, House of Representatives Speaker Sakata Michita announced that even if the reapportionment legislation were to be approved, a thirty-day period would have to ensue in order for the candidates and voters in the affected districts to become familiar with the new apportionment. This stipulation appeared to render the holding of a "same-day election" virtually impossible inasmuch as the House of Councillors election was scheduled for 22 June. By now, it was the middle of May.

Some unusually speedy – for the Diet, at least – legislative maneuvering brought forth a compromise reapportionment bill under which seven districts would lose one and eight would gain one seat. LDP Secretary General Kanemaru Shin announced that the Prime Minister was not giving consideration to a "same-day election" in order to gain the approval of Nakasone's rivals inside the LDP and to smother the vociferous criticism of the opposition parties. In the end, most of the latter boycotted – to emphasize their disapproval – the Representatives' and Councillors' sessions (22 and 23 May) at which the reapportionment bill was approved.

That, by itself, did not solve the problem posed by the thirty-day familiarization period. To do so, Prime Minister Nakasone convened the Diet in a Special Session for one day only (2 June) for the sole purpose of formally dissolving the House of Representatives without which an election for that chamber could not take place. He also announced that the election for both Houses would be held on 6 July. The House of Councillors election officially began on 18 June, leaving a few days in excess of two weeks for the campaign. In the case of the House of Representatives, the familiarization period permitted exactly two weeks for the official campaign. To all intents and purposes, the shortened period of the official campaign, which normally lasts between thirty and forty days, was pure "form (*tatemae*)," rather than "substance (*honne*)" since the vast majority of candidates had been campaigning for several months.

It has been impossible to determine how much of the posturing by all concerned – the Prime Minister's coyness about his intentions, his LDP rivals' rhetoric that was presumably intended to derail the possibility of holding a "same day election," the opposition parties' cries of having been misled by Nakasone's alleged prevarications – was anything more or less than political theatre. Nearly everyone had been collecting campaign chests, printing campaign posters, making trips to their constituencies at every opportunity – in short, acting as if they were candidates who anticipated an election – all Spring. The LDP's "new leaders" finally did close ranks behind their Party President, although Miyazawa held out as long as possible. In contrast, the opposition parties' leaders relied heavily in their campaigning on vilifying Nakasone as a liar. In the aftermath of the LDP's massive victory, it was generally conceded that the Prime Minister had been adroit and that his opponents, inside and outside the LDP, had made a serious tactical error in making Nakasone's alleged lack of veracity *the* issue in the campaign.

The 6 July 1986 "Same Day Election"

Television and newspaper analysts initially emphasized the enormous increase in the number of seats that the LDP had won: from 250 (out of 511 in 1983) to 300 (out of 512, not counting the 4 Unaffiliated victors who joined the Party, in 1986), and the losses suffered by the JSP (112 to 85) and DSP (38 to 26). Nakasone, in his initial televised press conference (7 July, 4 p.m.) after the vote count had been concluded for all except a handful of seats, stated it had been a triumph beyond the scope of any single individual. "It was the voice of the people and of the gods that had spoken." He had accomplished his cherished dream of bringing the LDP not only back to the number of seats (284) that it had had when he became Party President/Prime Minister in November 1982, but actually had added to its strength. Moreover, he had expunged the LDP's "defeat" that it had suffered in the December 1983 election. (Actually, the Party had retained its majority standing in the House of Representatives, but had done so only with the induction of Unaffiliated victors into its ranks.) It was a personal triumph for Nakasone, and one that he should not be denied.

Once the initial shock of the dimensions of the LDP's victory had begun to dissipate, analysts began to discuss what factors had lifted the governing party to its new plateau. Among the variables that were considered, the following tended to be among the most significant: (a) voter turnout; (b) the weather on election day; (c) percentage of the popular vote cast for each of the political

Table 6.1 House of Representatives Elections: Popular Vote in 1980, 1983 and 1986

	Eligible Voters	Voters	%
June 1980	80,925,034	60,342,329	74.57
December 1983	84,252,605	57,239,830	67.94
July 1986	86,426,845	60,448,668	71.40
Net Change 1980–1986	+5,501,811	+106,339	−3.17
Net Change 1983–1986	+2,174,240	+3,208,838	+3.46

Source: *Yomiuri Shimbun* (Morning Edition) 7 August, 1986, p. 7.

parties; (d) comparison of popular vote cast for parties and the number of candidates who were elected; (e) the "Runner-up (*Jiten*)" syndrome; (f) the "Going Down Together (*Tomodaore*)" factor; (g) opposition parties joint candidacy strategy. Some of these variables tended to be more salient in determining the outcome in one or the other of the two Houses. Hence, whenever appropriate, the discussion will deal with the two elections separately, even though they took place on the same day.

(a) *Voter turnout*. 71.4 percent of the eligible voters cast their ballots in the House of Representatives election, 3.5 percent higher than in the December 1983 election, but 3.2 percent lower than in the "double election" of June 1980. (Tables 6.1 and 6.2.) It is generally agreed that the LDP gains from a higher popular vote, in part because its candidates attract more of the floating voters who have relatively weak identifications with any political party, in part because the major opposition parties have relatively stable percentages of core supporters. Moreover, to the degree that a simultaneous election for both chambers heightens public interest and brings out a higher percentage of voters, the two cases (1980 and 1986) would support the conclusion that it is the LDP which benefits.

Participation in the House of Councillors elections – each voter cast one ballot in the National (Proportional Representation), and one ballot in the Local (Prefecture-wide) constituencies – was marginally lower: 66.4 percent in the former and 67.0 percent in the latter (see Tables 6.3 and 6.4). There is, as yet, no agreement regarding the reasons for this disparity. Some analysts emphasized lower public interest in the House of Councillors. Others pointed to the requirement that the voters write the name of a party in the

National Constituency election, and that a significant segment of the public simply does not like any political party even if it is willing to vote for its candidates. A third hypothesis is that the voters are confused by the separate contests for the House of Councillors and make errors in filling out the ballots which, therefore, must be disallowed. In any case, it is within the realm of the possible that the system for electing Members of the House of Councillors will undergo careful scrutiny before the next triennial election for that chamber in 1989.

(b) *The weather*. Early July falls within the rainy season, and forecasts predicted that Sunday 6 July would be wet. A light rain did fall on most of Japan, but only in the morning. By about noon, the skies had cleared. It was an almost perfect combination to encourage a higher turnout of voters. The weather was not good enough to justify a family outing beginning in the morning, but not bad enough to keep potential laggards at home. Truly, the gods – especially those having an influence over the weather – did smile on the LDP. Of course, there were some substantial disparities of voter participation. Once again, the urban sophisticates of Tokyo Metropolis and Kanagawa Prefecture (Yokohama) won the prize for having the lowest percentage of voters (61.1 and 62.1 percent) going to the polls. By contrast, the voters of relatively rural Tottori and Shimane prefectures registered the highest (86.9 and 85.9 percent) turn-out.

(c) *Percentage of popular vote cast for each political party*. The LDP's endorsed candidates came very close to winning 50 percent of the votes in the House of Representatives election (see Table 6.2.). In doing so, the Party increased its share of the popular vote by 3.6 percent over its 1983 performances, but only 1.5 percent over its showing in the "double election" of 1980. Almost all of the voters who cast their ballots in 1986, but had not done so in 1983, therefore, can be said to have supported LDP candidates! It is no wonder that the LDP considers voter turnout an extremely important variable in its electoral fortunes. By contrast all of the opposition parties lost, mostly marginal, shares of popular support, with the sole exception of the JSP which registered a 2.3 percent drop in comparison with the 1983 election. In addition, the percentage of voters that cast their ballots for minor party and Unaffiliated candidates (some of whom, of course, were unendorsed Liberal Democrats) increased by over 2 percent and 1 percent in comparison with the 1980 and 1983 election results.

Similar shifts were registered in the House of Councillors election, although the results differed to some degree between the

Table 6.2 1980, 1983, 1986 House of Representatives Election Results: Popular Vote (%) and Seats Won

	Popular Vote (%)					Seats Won									
	June 1980	Dec. 1983	July 1986	Net Change 1980–86	Net Change 1983–86	June 1980 A	June 1980 B	Dec. 1983 A	Dec. 1983 B	July 1986 A	July 1986 B	Net Change 1980–86 A	Net Change 1980–86 B	Net Change 1983–86 A	Net Change 1983–86 B
LDP	47.9	45.8	49.4	+1.5	+3.6	284	289	250	259	300	304	+16	+15	+50	+45
JSP	19.3	19.5	17.2	−2.1	−2.3	107	107	112	113	85	86	−22	−21	−27	−27
Kōmeitō	9.0	10.1	9.4	+0.4	−0.7	33	34	58	59	56	57	+23	+23	−2	−2
DSP	6.6	7.3	6.4	−0.2	−0.9	32	33	38	39	26	26	−6	−7	−12	−13
JCP	9.8	9.3	8.8	−1.0	−0.5	29	29	26	27	26	27	−3	−2	0	0
NLC	3.0	2.7	1.8	−1.2	−0.9	12	12	8	8	6	6	−6	−6	−2	−2
Soc. Dem. Fed.	0.7	0.7	0.8	+0.1	+0.1	3	3	3	3	4	4	+1	+1	+1	+1
Unaffiliated & Minor Parties	3.7	5.0	6.0	+2.3	+1.0	11	4	16	3	9	2[a]	−2	−2	−7	−1
Total						511	511	511	511	512	512				

Source: *Asahi Shinbun* (Morning Edition), 8 July, 1986, pp. 1 and 7.
Notes: Columns A reflect totals of officially endorsed candidates.
Columns B reflect totals after Unaffiliated joined parties.
[a] Tanaka Kakuei, Sato Takayuki (both will vote with LDP).

Table 6.3 6 July, 1986 House of Councillors Election Popular Vote, % of Popular Vote by Party

	Nationwide Constituency	%	Net Change '80–'86	Net Change '83–'86	Local Constituencies	%	Net Change '80–'86	Net Change '83–'86
LDP	22,132,573	38.6	−3.9	+3.3	26,110,458	45.1	+1.6	+1.9
NLC	1,367,291	2.4	–	−0.3	–	–	–	–
JSP	9,869,088	17.2	+4.1	+0.9	12,464,216	21.5	−1.1	−2.8
Kōmeitō	7,438,501	13.0	+1.1	−2.7	2,549,037	4.4	−0.6	−3.4
JCP	5,430,838	9.5	+2.2	+0.6	6,617,742	11.4	−0.3	+0.9
DSP	3,940,325	6.9	+0.9	−1.5	2,643,370	4.6	−0.6	−1.1
2nd Chamber (Niin) Club	1,455,532	2.5	–	+0.1	–	–	–	–
Salaryman New Party	1,759,484	3.1	–	−1.2	–	–	–	–
Tax Party	1,803,051	3.1	–	–	–	–	–	–
Welfare	570,995	1.0	–	–	–	–	–	–
Minor Parties	1,595,064	2.8	–	–	1,193,276	2.1	–	–
Unaffiliated	–	–	–	–	6,032,683	10.4	–	+6.6
Total	57,362,742				57,938,226			

Sources: Asahi Shinbun 8 July, 1986 (Morning Edition), p. 2; Sankei Shinbun 8 July, 1986 (Morning Edition), p. 7; Table 2.14.

National (Proportional Representation) and the Local (Prefecture-wide) constituencies. In the former, the LDP's gain was 3.3 percent (over 1983), but only 1.9 percent in the latter. By contrast, the JSP actually gained almost 1 percent in its share (in comparison with 1983) in the National, but lost 2.8 percent in the Local constituencies. (For details, see Table 6.3 which also includes comparisons with the parties' 1980 performance.)

(d) *Comparison of the parties' popular vote and seats won.* With an increased share of 3.6 percent of the popular vote, the LDP won an additional fifty seats, or 20 percent more than it had obtained in 1983! (See righthand columns in Table 6.2). By contrast, the JSP, with a loss of 2.3 percent of the popular vote, lost twenty-seven seats, or nearly 24 percent less than it had obtained in 1983. In the same vein, a decline of 0.9 percent of the popular vote for the DSP turned into a loss of thirteen seats, or 33 percent less than it had won in 1983. Of the opposition parties, only the Kōmeitō and the JCP were able to retain roughly the same number of seats while registering minor reductions in their respective share of the popular vote.

Somewhat comparable results were to be seen in the House of Councillors. For example, in the National Constituency, the LDP won 22 seats, or 44 percent of the 50 seats in this category with 38.6 percent of the popular vote. This disparity in percentages is to be explained primarily by the number of votes that were cast for minor party candidates. In the Local constituencies, however, the LDP won fifty, or 65.8 percent, of the 76 seats with just 45.1 percent of the popular vote! This enormous disparity can be explained only by the LDP's victories in the single-member (23 out of 26) and two-member (19 out of 30) districts. In the latter two categories of the Prefecture-wide constituencies, the opposition parties have not been able to discover a formula that will permit them to challenge the LDP's juggernaut. (For a more extended discussion of this generalization, see Chapter 2.)

(e) *The "runner-up (jiten)" syndrome.* One of the difficulties that party strategists must confront in the House of Representatives multi-member districts and the House of Councillors two-, three- and four-member constituencies, is how many candidates to endorse. If there are too few, seats that might have been won are lost. If there are too many, seats are lost that might have been won. (Please see discussion of this point in Chapter 2.) A yardstick to measure the success or failure of party strategists is provided by the number of "runners-up (*jiten*)", that is, the first-place losers.

On this score, LDP Secretary-General Kanemaru Shin oversaw

Table 6.4 House of Councillors 6 July, 1986 Election: Total Seats by Party

Type of Constituency	No., Total Seats	Political Party Affiliation of Winners LDP	NLC	JSP	Kōmeitō	DSP	JCP	Unaffiliated[*]
National (Proportional Representation)	50	22	1	9	7	3	5	3
4-Member	8	4	–	1	1	–	2	–
3-Member	12	4	–	2	2	1	1	2
3-Member	30	19	–	8	–	1	1	1
1-Member	26	23	–	–	–	–	–	3
Sub-total	126	72	1	20	10	5	9	9
% of Seats		57%	1%	16%	8%	4%	7%	7%
Carryover[a]	125	68	1	21	14	7	7	7 (1 Vacancy)
New Line-up	251	142[b]	2	41	25[b]	12	16	13[b] (1 Vacancy)
% Total Seats		57%	1%	16%	10%	5%	6%	5%

Source: Vernacular Newspaper Reports, 8 July, 1986.
Notes: [*]Includes minor parties.
[a] Carryover = Councillors not up for election in 1986 because their term of office does not expire until 1989.
[b] These totals reflect the movement of candidates elected as "Unaffiliated" into their respective parties: 2 into the LDP and 1 into the Kōmeitō.

an endorsement policy that was extraordinarily effective, especially when contrasted with the Party's performance in the previous House of Representatives election. In 1983, the LDP had 61 runners-up, whereas in 1986 it only had 17. Furthermore, 41 of the 1983 "losers" were candidates in 1986 and an astonishing 38 (92.7 percent) of them were among the victors. Among the opposition parties, in sharp contrast, the JSP went from 19 runners-up in 1983 to 41 in 1986, the Kōmeitō from 1 to 5, the DSP from 11 to 19, with only the JCP registering a slightly better performance, from 19 to 16 – obviously not counting those candidates, especially the JCP's, who came in further down the list. (*Yomiuri Shinbun*, 8 July, 1986, morning edition, p. 6.) A more astringent endorsement policy by the LDP in comparison with 1983 rather than a large swing in the popular vote provided another element in explaining the governing party's enormous success.

(f) *The "going down together (tomodaore)" factor*. This element also is linked to the respective parties' endorsement policy. (Please see section on *tomodaore* in Chapter 2.) The LDP made almost no errors. To be sure, in Ibaraki 3, first place winner Nakamura could have shared some of his 25.5 percent of the total vote with fellow LDPers Akagi (12.6 percent), a winner, and Mori (10.4 percent), a loser, in order to defeat the JSP's Takeuchi who won with 12.7 percent of the votes cast. In Aichi 5, two Unaffiliated conservatives, one supported by the Tanaka faction (a loser with 14.9 percent), the other by Suzuki (also a loser with 14.8 percent), could have defeated the JSP candidate (16.1 percent) if only one had run and been able to obtain a share of his fellow conservative's vote. In this particular instance, it was rivalry among the LDP's factions that brought about the defeat of both.

By contrast, the opposition parties repeatedly helped each

Table 6.5 Joint Opposition Party Candidates 6 July, 1986 Election

	Victors	Losers
House of Representatives		
Kōmeitō supported by JSP and Soc. Dem. Fed.	0	1
JSP supported by Kōmeitō	3	0
Kōmeitō supported by JSP	1	0
JSP supported by Soc. Dem. Fed.	9	9
Soc. Dem. Fed. supported by Kōmeitō, DSP, NLC	1	0
Kōmeitō supported by DSP and Soc. Dem. Fed.	3	2
DSP supported by Kōmeitō and Soc. Dem. Fed.	4	2
Kōmeitō supported by DSP	10	0
DSP supported by Kōmeitō	6	1
Unaffiliated supported by DSP, NLC, Soc. Dem. Fed.	0	1
DSP supported by Soc. Dem. Fed.	4	4
Soc. Dem. Fed. supported by DSP	1	0
Sub-total	42	20
House of Councillors		
Unaffiliated supported by JSP, Kōmeitō, DSP	1	0
Minor Party supported by JSP, Kōmeitō, JCP, Soc. Mass.	0	1
JSP supported by Soc. Dem. Fed.	2	3
Unaffiliated supported by JSP, Soc. Dem. Fed.	0	2
DSP supported by Kōmeitō, Soc. Dem. Fed.	1	0
Kōmeitō supported by DSP	0	1
DSP supported by Kōmeitō	0	1
DSP supported by Soc. Dem. Fed.	0	2
Unaffiliated supported by DSP, Soc. Dem. Fed.	0	1
Sub-total	4	11
Total for Both Houses	46	31

Source: Yomiuri Shinbun, 8 July, 1986 (Morning Edition), p. 6.

other's candidates lose. There were nine seats that the JSP lost because JCP candidates also ran in the same districts. (Aomori 1 and 2, Iwate 1, Miyagi 1, Yamagata 1, Saitama 4, Aichi 2, Hiroshima 2, Ehime 2.) There were three instances in which the JSP ran two endorsed candidates, when one of them might have emerged victorious (Hokkaido 5, Niigata 2, Kumamoto 2). In Akita 1 the JCP candidate could have won if the JSP had not run its own, in Tokyo 6 a Democratic Socialist lost because of a JSP candidate's interference, and in Tottori a Kōmeitō candidate would have been victorious had it not been that yet another JSP candidate picked up some of the anti-LDP vote. In short, fifteen opposition party candidates went down in defeat together. While their potential successes would not have undermined the LDP's victory, they could have reduced its scope.

(g) *Opposition parties' joint candidate strategy*. Most of the opposition parties have recognized, for at least the last fifteen years, that their only hope of winning more seats is jointly to back their respective candidates. They pursued this strategy in 62 cases in the House of Representatives (42 victors, 20 losers) and for 15 candidates in the House of Councillors (4 victors, 11 losers). Most successful were the Kōmeitō candidates backed by the DSP and vice versa as well as those Socialist standard bearers who also had the support of Social Democratic Federation, a splinter group that had broken away from the JSP in the late 1970s. As had been true in previous national elections, there was only one instance in which the JCP participated in jointly backing a particular candidate. That was in Okinawa which has political traditions which are not entirely congruent with those prevailing in the rest of Japan. This particular candidate lost, but the opposition party losses reflected in the previous section ("going down together") indicate that unless the JCP is either willing (or is allowed) to participate more fully, the effectiveness of joint candidacies will continue to be limited.

Concluding comments. The LDP's extraordinarily impressive victory was a triumph of strategy. Its leadership pursued an almost perfect endorsement policy and relied, with great effectiveness, on the benefits that could be derived from conducting an election for both chambers on the same day. Doing so heightened public interest which, in turn, generated a higher rate of voter participation, an element that is undeniably beneficial to the governing party. In sharp contrast, the opposition parties mounted a lackluster campaign. There was hardly any discussion of policy or program, except for Prime Minister Nakasone's presumed prevarications in his maneuvers to make it possible to have a "same day election." That strategy backfired in the face of the LDP's emphasis on its ability to be the governing party and to continue with the large tasks of administrative and educational reforms and coping with the problems created by the rapid upward valuation of the Yen. Moreover, within the LDP, the simultaneous election provided many additional opportunities for factional rivalries, especially among the "new leaders." More often than not, these intra-party conflicts were more powerful in motivating supporters of individual candidates to vote than the LDP's contest with its external opposition.

LDP Factions and the 6 July 1986 Election

Liberal Democratic Party candidates – especially those running in the House of Representatives multi-member districts and the House of Councillors Local multi-member constituencies – have long recognized that they are involved in two distinct contests simultaneously. One involves them in campaigning against opposition party candidates. From the perspective of whether the LDP will continue to be the majority – and, therefore, governing – party, these inter-party national electoral outcomes are crucial. A second contest involves them in campaigns against their own party's candidates who, however, belong to one of the other of the LDP's factions. From the perspective of who will have a dominant voice in the governing party – as measured by appointments to senior positions in the Party or to ministerial posts in the Cabinet – these intra-party contests tend to be more significant, particularly for the faction leaders.

Table 6.6 provides an overview of how each of the factions fared in the July 1986 election. Former Prime Minister Tanaka's group made the largest gains. Among the Representatives, it has become numerically larger (87) than the JSP (86), the major opposition party. If its members in the House of Councillors (54) are added, this faction is now – with a total of 141 members – the largest that has been in existence in the thirty-one year history of the LDP, accounting for over 31 percent of the Party's entire membership in the National Assembly. Its enormous size may prove to be a liability, however, unless "new leader" Takeshita Noboru can provide the same kind of charisma that former Prime Minister Tanaka had displayed even after becoming entangled in the Lockheed scandal (but not subsequent to the stroke that he

Table 6.6 LDP Factions 8 July, 1986

	Before Election			After 6 July, 1986 Election						Net Change		
	HR	HC	Total	HR	HC Loc.	HC Nat'l	Carry-over	HC Total	Grand Total	HR	HC	Total
Tanaka	65	55	120	86	20	8	26	54	140	+21	−1	+20
Suzuki	51	29	80	59	7	5	16	28	87	+8	−1	+7
Abe (ex-Fukuda)	46	25	71	56	10	2	14	26	82	+10	+1	+11
Nakasone	47	10	57	59	7	2	7	16	75	+12	+6	+18
Kōmoto	27	7	34	28	2	0	4	6	34	+1	−1	0
No Faction	14	12	26	16	6	5	2	13	29	+2	+1	+3
Total	250	138	388	304	52	22	69	143	447	+54	+5	+59

Source: Asahi Shinbun 8 July, 1986, (Morning Edition), p. 2.
Notes: HR = House of Representatives
HC = House of Councillors
Carryover = Councillors not up for election in 1986 because their term of office does not expire until 1989.

suffered in February 1985). As was noted, however, not everybody in the faction seems, as yet, to be ready to pledge fealty to Takeshita.

Prime Minister Nakasone's faction made the second largest gains. It overtook the factions of both former Prime Ministers Suzuki and Fukuda in the House of Representatives. Not only the LDP's major victory, but also the growth of his faction insures Nakasone a major voice in Party affairs even after his tenure as Party President/Prime Minister has ended.

Both the Suzuki and Fukuda factions made gains, although the latter made a marginally greater improvement in its strength. Nonetheless, "new leaders" Abe Shintarō (who has officially become head of v.hat had been the Fukuda faction) was generally conceded to have outshone "new leader" Miyazawa Kiichi (Suzuki faction) by campaigning more actively. Furthermore, Miyazawa wounded himself by his prolonged opposition to Nakasone on holding a simultaneous election for both chambers. Had the outcome been a setback for the LDP, Miyazawa would have emerged as the strongest contender to succeed to the premiership. In view of the LDP's landslide victory, his prospects have darkened considerably. Also ominous, for the Suzuki faction, was its small number (5) of new victors.

The same problem continued to beset the Kōmoto faction, the smallest of the current five major groups. Its gain of one seat in the House of Representatives was offset by a loss in the House of Councillors, so that it ended up with the same number (34) as it had had. In many respects, this group no longer has the numerical strength to participate on an equal footing with the others in inter-factional bargaining. It is, after all, only one fourth the size of Tanaka's and less than half the size of Nakasone's factions.

Charting the rise and fall of LDP factions is an analytic imperative that must be undertaken far more systematically than has been the case in western studies of Japanese party politics. This Epilogue is not the place for this much-needed exercise. Suffice it, for the moment, to state that by having emphasized the electoral rivalry between the LDP and its opposition parties, too much of the English language literature has neglected the frequently more significant element of growth and decay among LDP factions. At a minimum, more systematic studies need to be undertaken on such basic issues as candidate recruitment and endorsement. It may have been mere coincidence that the Tanaka faction was so successful in this election and that LDP Secretary General Kanemaru happened to be a senior member of this faction. Somehow, I doubt it, but evidence is simply lacking. What is available is the influence of factional strengths and weaknesses on the formation of the new Nakasone Cabinet.

The Third Nakasone Cabinet, 22 July 1986

Massive majorities in both Houses of the National Assembly formally elected Nakasone as Prime Minister on 22 July. He and his fellow party leaders already had made one crucial personnel decision in the two weeks that had elapsed since the "same day election." Incumbent House of Representatives Speaker Sakata Michita had not been among the Prime Minister's closest allies. Immediately after the election, Nakasone had publicly mentioned Party Vice-President Nikaido Susumu as his preferred candidate to become Speaker. Nikaido let it be known that he would decline the honor for at least two reasons. First, as the presiding officer he could no longer be even a potential contender for LDP President/Prime Minister, a custom that has not been broken. Second, he would no longer be able to identify himself too closely with the Tanaka faction of which he was the senior leader. Given Tanaka's slow recovery from his stroke, presumptive successor Takeshita would – in all likelihood – be installed as the faction's new chief. Nikaido, as well as other Tanaka loyalists, were not yet prepared for that eventuality.

Consequently, Nakasone turned to Hara Kenzaburo, the most senior (80 years old) member of his own faction to become Speaker. Socialist Tagaya Shinnen, who had previously served as his Party's Secretary General, became Deputy Speaker. Both decisions were almost by acclamation. They reflected the legacy of "near parity (hakuchū)" far more than the election's outcome that readily could have justified the LDP's reserving both posts for itself. Moreover, the NLC had decided – after nearly splitting on the issue – to continue in its role as the LDP's coalition partner, thereby swelling the governing party's ranks by six. One specific consequence was that NLC Secretary General Yamaguchi Toshio was appointed as Chairman of the Standing Committee on Foreign Affairs in the House of Representatives. In addition, two Socialists and one Kōmeitō member became chairmen of three relatively unimportant Special Committees (Price Problems, Northern Territories and Okinawa, Traffic Safety). On the other hand, in the House of Councillors, the opposition parties were accorded the chairmanships of six Standing Committees and three of the eight

Special Committees. These appointments suggested that the LDP's leadership considered it prudent to share some minimal levers of power with the opposition parties in the internal governance of the National Assembly.

Prime Minister Nakasone, once he had been formally elected by the Diet on 22 July, quickly implemented the personnel decisions that he and his closest advisors had been pondering. By far the most important were the placement of his three potential successors. Finance Minister Takeshita (of the Tanaka faction) became LDP Secretary General, Foreign Minister Abe (of the now Abe faction) became LDP Executive Board Chairman and Executive Board Chairman Miyazawa became Finance Minister. Former Foreign Minister Itō Masayoshi (Suzuki faction), who had briefly served as interim Prime Minister in the immediate aftermath of former Prime Minister Ohira's sudden death in June 1980, was selected to become Chairman of the LDP Policy Research Council. As a consequence, each of the four major factions was represented at the apex of the Party's hierarchy.

Balancing factions also played its traditional role in the allocation of ministerial portfolios in the new Cabinet (see Table 6.7). The "Thursday Club," i.e. the Tanaka faction, was rewarded with 8 of the 21 seats (38 percent). They included former LDP Secretary General Kanemaru as Deputy Prime Minister as a reward for his role in fashioning the LDP's electoral triumph, as well as the ministries of Justice – a sensitive assignment so long as former Prime Minister Tanaka's appeal against his conviction in the Lockheed bribery case continues – and of International Trade and Industry – very possibly the most difficult assignment in view of the continuing foreign criticism of Japan's trade policies. In addition, Minister of State Gotōda was retained as Chief Cabinet Secretary, a powerful position which combines the roles of coordinator and spokesman of the Cabinet.

Nakasone reserved four portfolios for his own factional followers. By far the most significant of these was that of Foreign Minister Kuranari, whose appointment was interpreted as reflecting the Prime Minister's desire to keep the major elements of Japan's international relations under his own control. Both the Abe (ex-Fukuda) and Suzuki factions could obtain no more than three portfolios. As noted, Suzuki faction chief heir apparent Miyazawa became Minister of Finance, generally considered to be the second most prestigious and powerful position, only below that of Prime Minister, in the Cabinet. In addition, Defense Agency Director General Kurihara returned to the post he had held in an earlier

Table 6.7 The Third Nakasone Cabinet 22 July, 1986

Post, Ministry Agency	Name	Age	District	Faction
Prime Minister	Nakasone Yasuhiro	68	Gunma 3	Nakasone
Deputy Prime Minister	Kanemaru Shin	71	Yamaguchi	Tanaka
Justice	Endō Kaname[a]	70	Miyagi	Tanaka
Foreign	Kuranari Tadashi	67	Nagasaki 1	Nakasone
Finance	Miyazawa Kiichi	66	Hiroshima 3	Suzuki
Education	Fujio Masayuki	69	Tochigi 2	Abe (Fukuda)
Health & Welfare	Saitō Jūrō[a]	46	Mie	Tanaka
Agriculture, Forestry & Fisheries	Katō Mutsuki	60	Okayama 2	Abe (Fukuda)
International Trade & Industry	Tamura Hajime	62	Mie 2	Tanaka
Transportation	Hashimoto Ryūtarō	48	Okayama 2	Tanaka
Posts & Telecommunications	Karasawa Shunjirō	56	Nagano 4	Nakasone
Labor	Hirai Takushi[a]	54	Kagawa	Nakasone
Construction	Amano Kōsei	79	Fukushima 1	Nakasone
Local Autonomy (Home Affairs)	Hanashi Nobuyuki	57	Ibaraki 1	Suzuki
Chief Cabinet Secretary	Gotōda Masaharu	71	Tokushima	Tanaka
Management and Co-ordination Agency	Tamaki Kazuo	63	Wakayama 2	No Faction
Defense Agency	Kurihara Yūkō	66	Shizuoka 2	Suzuki
Economic Planning Agency	Kondō Tetsuo	56	Yamagata 1	Kōmoto
Science & Technology Agency	Mitsubayashi Yatarō	67	Saitama 4	Abe (Fukuda)
Environment Agency	Inamura Toshiyuki	50	Tochigi 2	Tanaka
Land, Hokkaido & Okinawa Development Agencies	Watanuki Tamisuke	59	Toyama 2	Tanaka
	Senior LDP Officers			
President	Nakasone Yasuhiro	68	Gunma 3	Nakasone
Vice-President	Vacant	–	–	–
Secretary General	Takeshita Noboru	62	Shimane	Tanaka
Chairman, Executive Board	Abe Shintarō	62	Yamaguchi 1	Abe (Fukuda)
Chairman, Policy Research Council	Itō Masayoshi	73	Fukushima 2	Suzuki

Source: Mainichi Shinbun, 23 July 1986 (Morning Edition), p. 1.
Notes: [a] Members of House of Councillors; all others are members of House of Representatives. Summary of factional distribution: Tanaka 8 plus LDP Secretary General; Nakasone 5 plus LDP President; Abe (Fukuda) 3 plus Chairman LDP Executive Board; Suzuki 3 plus Chairman LDP Policy Research Council; Kōmoto 1, No Faction 1.

Nakasone Cabinet. The Abe faction, by having had its leader become Executive Board Chairman, had to accept relatively less significant portfolios, although both the ministries of Education and of Agriculture, Forestry and Fisheries play major roles in the daily life of the Japanese people. Economic Planning Agency

Director General Kondō, as the sole Kōmoto faction representative, reflected the continuing decline of former Prime Minister Miki's group.

None of the appointees know the length of his expected tenure. Conceivably, it could end with the LDP's Convention in late October 1986 when the Party could decide to elect a new President on the expiration of Nakasone's second two-year term. In the interim, however, Party rules prohibiting a third term could be amended, assurances to the contrary notwithstanding. Alternatively, the incumbent's term could be extended without violating any legalistic constraints and could readily be justified by the impressive victory at the polls and the many reforms that Nakasone has begun, but which require much additional work for their full implementation. Party politics in Japan has not come to an end as a consequence of the LDP's, once again, having established itself as the hegemonic governing party. Nor has that triumph finished off the Party's factions. As to Prime Minister Nakasone's future and who his successor might be, ". . . one inch ahead . . .".

BIBLIOGRAPHY

Arima, M. (1984), *Kenpo Kokkai Nami Takashi* [The Health Insurance Diet: Making Big Waves] (Tokyo: Marima).

Baerwald, H. H. (1959), *The Purge of Japanese Leaders under the Occupation* (Berkeley and Los Angeles: University of California Press).

Baerwald, H. H. (1970), 'Nikkan Kokkai: The Japan–Korea Treaty Diet,' in L. Pye (ed.), *Cases in Comparative Politics: Asia* (Boston: Little, Brown).

Baerwald, H. H. (1974), *Japan's Parliament, An Introduction* (New York: Cambridge University Press).

Baerwald, H. H. (1976), 'Lockheed and Japanese Politics,' *Asian Survey*, September, pp. 817–29.

Baerwald, H. H. (1979), 'Committees in the Japanese Diet,' J. D. Lees and M. Shaw (eds), *Committees in Legislatures*, (Durham, NC: Duke University Press), pp. 327–60.

Baerwald, H. H. (1980a), 'Japan's 35th House of Representatives Election: the LDP Toys with a Return to 1954,' *Asian Survey*, March, pp. 257–68.

Baerwald, H. H. (1980b), 'Japan's Double Elections,' *Asian Survey*, December, pp. 1169–84.

Baerwald, H. H. (1984), 'Japan's December 1983 House of Representatives Election: The Return of Coalition Politics,' *Asian Survey*, March, pp. 265–78.

Baerwald, H. H. and Hashimoto, A. (1983), 'Japan in 1982: Doing Nothing is Best?,' *Asian Survey*, January, pp. 53–61.

Baerwald, H. H. and Tomita, N. (1977), 'Japan's 34th General Election: Cautious Change amidst Incremental Instability,' *Asian Survey*, March, pp. 221–36.

Belloni, F. P. and Beller, D. C. (1978), *Faction Politics: Political Parties and Factionalism in Comparative Perspective* (Santa Barbara, Calif. and Oxford: ABC–Clio).

Benjamin, R. and Ori, K. (1981), *Tradition and Change in Postindustrial Japan: The Role of the Political Parties* (New York: Praeger).

Bisson, T. A. (1954), *Zaibatsu Dissolution in Japan* (Berkeley and Los Angeles: University of California Press).

Blaker, M. K. (ed.) (1976), *Japan at the Polls: The House of Councillors Election of 1974* (Washington, DC: American Enterprise Institute).

Blaker, M. K. (1979), 'The Conservatives in Crisis,' in H. Passin (ed.), *A Season of Voting* (Washington DC: American Enterprise Institute), pp. 1–9.

Cole, A. B., Totten, G. O. and Uyehara, C. H. (1966), *Socialist Parties in Postwar Japan* (New Haven, Conn.: Yale University Press).

Curtis, G. L. (1976), 'The 1974 Election Campaign: The Political Process,' in M. K. Blaker (ed.), *Japan at the Polls* (Washington, DC: American Enterprise Institute), pp. 45–80.

Curtis, G. L. (1979), 'The Opposition,' in H. Passin (ed.), *A Season of Voting* (Washington, DC: American Enterprise Institute), pp. 43–80.

Dore, R. P. (1959), *Land Reform in Japan* (London: Oxford University Press).

Fukui, H. (1970), *Party in Power: The Japanese Liberal Democrats and Policy-making* (Berkeley and Los Angeles: University of California Press).

Fukui, H. (1978), 'Japan: Factionalism in a Dominant Party System,' in F. P. Belloni and D.C. Beller (eds), *Faction Politics: Political Parties and Factionalism in Comparative Perspective* (Santa Barbara and Oxford: ABC–Clio), pp. 43–72.

Government Section, GHQ, SCAP (1949), *The Political Reorientation of Japan*, 2 vols (Washington, DC: Government Printing Office).

Hadley, E. M. (1970), *Antitrust in Japan* (Princeton, NJ: Princeton University Press).

Halloran, R. (1969), *Japan: Images and Realities* (New York: Alfred A. Knopf).

House of Councillors (1969), *The National Diet of Japan* (Tokyo: House of Councillors). 'The Constitution of Japan,' pp. 3–24; 'The Diet Law,' pp. 25–66; 'Rules of the House of Councillors,' pp. 67–116; 'Rules of the House of Representatives,' pp. 116–64.

Ike, N. (1972), *Japanese Politics: Patron–Client Democracy*, 2nd edn (New York: Alfred A. Knopf).

Interviews (1982). I formally interviewed eight members of the LDP, one of the JSP, one of the Kōmeitō, one of the DSP, one who was Unaffiliated, three officials in the House of Representatives Secretariat, several senior officials in LDP Headquarters, ten newsmen and political critics, and met about fifty Representatives and Councillors.

Itō, M. (1982), *Jimintō Sengokushi* [The Civil War in the LDP] (Tokyo: Asahi Sonorama).

Jiyū Minshutō [LDP] (1982), *Sōgō Seisaku Kenkyūjo* [The LDP Institute for Policy Research] (Tokyo: Liberal Democratic Party).

Juristo [Jurist], (1984a), *Nihon no Seitō* [Japan's Political Parties], no. 35.

Juristo, (1984b), *Nihon no Rippō* [Japan's Legislation], no. 805.

Juristo, (1985), *Senkyo* [Elections], no. 38.

Kakizawa, K. (1978a), *Kanryōtachi to Nihonmaru* [Bureaucrats and the (Ship) Japan] (Tokyo: Gakuyō Shobō).

Kakizawa, K. (1978b), *Nagata-chō* (Tokyo: Gakuyō Shobō).

Kawai, K. (1960), *Japan's American Interlude* (Chicago: University of Chicago Press).

Kokkai Binran [Diet Handbook] (Tokyo: Nihon Seikei Shinbunsha), yearly or twice yearly.

Krauss, E. S. (1984), 'Conflict in the Diet: Toward Conflict Management in Parliamentary Politics,' in E. S. Krauss, T. P. Rohlen and P. G. Steinhoff (eds), *Conflict in Japan* (Honolulu: University of Hawaii Press), pp. 243–93.

Langdon, F. (1967), *Politics in Japan* (Boston and Toronto: Little, Brown).

Langer, P. F. (1972), *Communism in Japan: A Case of Political Naturalization* (Stanford, Calif.: Hoover Institution Press).

Liberal Democratic Party (1984), *The National Constituency System Revision of the House of Councillors* (Tokyo: LDP International Bureau).

Marriott, J. A. R. and Robertson, C. G. (1937), *The Evolution of Prussia*, new edn (Oxford: Oxford University Press).

Mochizuki, M. (1982), 'Managing and Influencing the Japanese Legislative Process,' PhD dissertation, Harvard University.

Mori, K. (1982), *Kokkai Giin no Hisho* [Diet Members' Administrative Assistants] (Tokyo: Chōbunsha).

Murakawa, I. (1978), *Nihon Hoshutō Shōshi* [A Brief History of the Japanese Conservative Party] (Tokyo: Kyōikusha).

Murakawa, I. (1979), *Seisaku Kettei Katei* [The Process of Policy Decision-making] (Tokyo: Kyōikusha).

Naka, K. *et al.* (1982), *Kokkai Giin ni okeru Keireki patān no Renzoku to Henka* [Continuity and Change in Career Patterns of Diet Members] (Kyoto: Kyoto University).

Nisihira, S. (1979), 'Historical Statistics,' in H. Passin (ed.), *A Season of Voting* (Washington, DC: American Enterprise Institute), pp. 81–114.

Odawara, A. (1984), 'The Union of the LDP and the Bureaucracy,' *Japan Echo*, vol. 11, no. 4, pp. 68–75.

OECD, Interviews (1974–5). In preparation of the Background Report for *Social Sciences Policy: Japan*, I interviewed about fifty senior officials of the Japanese government. These interviews influenced my perceptions of Japan's government bureaucrats.

OECD (1977), *Social Sciences Policy: Japan* (Paris: OECD).

Ōhira, M. (1979), Private Interview, 24 October.

Passin, H. (ed.) (1979), *A Season of Voting: The Japanese Elections of 1976 and 1977* (Washington, DC: American Enterprise Institute).

Pempel, T. J. (1982), *Policy and Politics in Japan: Creative Conservatism* (Philadelphia: Temple University Press).

PHP Kenkyūjo (1984), *The Data File 1984* (Tokyo).

Quigley, H. S. (1932), *Japanese Government and Politics* (New York and London: Century).

Richardson, B. M. and Flanagan, S. C. (1984), *Politics in Japan* (Boston and Toronto: Little, Brown).

Satō, S. and Matsuzaki, T. (1985), 'Jimintō Kokkai Un'ei no Tettei Kenkyū [A Complete Study of the LDP's Diet Management],' (Tokyo: Chūō Kōron), pp. 394–415.

Scalapino, R. A. (1967), *The Japanese Communist Movement, 1920–1966* (Berkeley and Los Angeles: University of California Press).

Scalapino, R. A. and Masumi, J. (1962), *Parties and Politics in*

Contemporary Japan (Berkeley and Los Angeles: University of California Press).

Seiji Kōhō Senta [Political Information Center] (1984 and 1985), *Seiji Handobukku* [Political Handbook] (Tokyo).

Shiratori, R. (1972), *Seron – Senkyo – Seiji* [Public Opinion – Elections – Politics] (Tokyo: Nihon Keizai Shinbunsha).

Shiratori, R. (1980), *Nihon no Seitō Chizu '80–'90* [Japan's Political Map '80–'90] (Tokyo: Gakuyō Shobō].

Shūkan Yomiuri [Yomiuri Weekly] (1985), 'Kore ga Zoku da [These are the (policy) Clans],' 23 June, pp. 132–42.

Stockwin, J. A. A. (1982), *Japan: Divided Politics in a Growth Economy*, 2nd edn (London and New York: Norton).

Tachibana, T. (1974), 'Tanaka Kakuei Kenkyu: Sono Kin'myaku to Jin'myaku' [Research on Tanaka Kakuei: His Money Connections and Personal Contacts], *Bungei Shunjū*, September.

Thayer, N. B. (1969), *How the Conservatives Rule Japan* (Princeton: Princeton University Press).

Togawa, I. (1982), *Tanaka Kakuei to Seiken Kōsō* [Tanaka Kakuei and Political Confrontations] (Tokyo: Kōdansha).

Tomita, N. *et al.* (eds) (1983), *Nihon Seiji no Hensen* [Japanese Political Change] (Tokyo: Hokuju Shuppan).

Tsuji, K. (1984), *Public Administration in Japan* (Tokyo: University of Tokyo Press).

The Tsuneta Yano Memorial Society (1955, and yearly thereafter), *Nippon, a Charted Survey of Japan* (Tokyo: The Kokusei-sha Corporation).

Tsurutani, T. (1977), *Political Change in Japan* (New York: David McKay).

Uchida, K. (1976), *Sengo Nihon no Hoshu Seiji* [Conservative Politics in Postwar Japan] (Tokyo: Iwanami Shoten).

Uchida, K. (1983), *Habatsu* [Factions] (Tokyo: Kōdansha).

Uchida, K. *et al.* (1981), *Nihon Seijo no Jitsuryokusha-tachi: Sengo* [Japan's Political Influentials: Postwar] (Tokyo: Yūhikaku).

Uchida, M. and Baerwald, H. H. (1978), 'The House of Councillors Election in Japan: The LDP Hangs in There,' *Asian Survey*, March, pp. 301–8.

Uji, T. (1985), *Suzuki Seiken 863-nichi* [The 863 Days of Suzuki in Power] (Tokyo: Gyōsei Mondai Kenkyūjo).

Valeo, F. R. and Morrison, C. E. (1983), *The Japanese Diet and the U.S. Congress* (Boulder, Colo.: Westview Press).

Watanabe, T. (1964a), *Habatsu: Nihon Hoshutō no Bunseki* [Factions: An Analysis of Japan's Conservative Party] (Tokyo: Kōbundō).

Watanabe, T. (1964b), *Seiji no Jōshiki* [The Common Sense of Politics] (Tokyo: Kōdansha).

White, J. W. (1970), *The Sōkagakkai and Mass Society* (Stanford: Stanford University Press).

Yoshimura, K. (1985), *Ikeda Seiken 1575 Nichi* [The 1575 Days of Ikeda in Power] (Tokyo: Gyōsei Mondai Kenkyūjo) [Administrative Problems Research Institute].

INDEX